Read for the Heart

Whole Books for WholeHearted Families

Read for the Heart

Sarah Clarkson

apologia WholeHeart™
FAITH-BUILDING TOOLS FOR THE FAMILY

Read for the Heart:
Whole Books for WholeHearted Families

Published by Apologia/WholeHeart,
an imprint of ApologiaPress,
a division of Apologia Educational Ministries, Inc.
1106 Meridian Plaza, Suite 220
Anderson, IN 46016
www.apologia.com

Cover Design: Mike Cox
Book Design: Joel Smythe, TheGraphicsLab.com

Printed by Courier, Inc., Westford, MA
Second Printing: April 2011

Unless otherwise indicated, Scripture quotations are from
The Holy Bible, New International Version (NIV)
© 1973, 1978, 1984 by International Bible Society,
used by permission of Zondervan Publishing House

Printed in the United States of America

Contents

Foreword

"[Living books are those that] capture the issues of life in such a way that they challenge the intellect, they inspire the emotions, and they arouse something noble in the heart of the reader."

~C. S. Lewis

Read for the Heart is different from other books about books in large part because of the fresh perspective of its author, a young lady raised by parents who surrounded her with great books and invested in her life experiences. Sarah Clarkson is a wonderful example of what can happen when you raise a child on whole, living books. Her parents, Clay and Sally Clarkson, are artists; Sarah is one of their masterpieces.

I've known Sarah since she was a young child. Yet one of my most special memories of her was when she read aloud a chapter of this book at her graduation ceremony just a few years ago. Not only does she love to read, but she beautifully conveys this passion through her writing. And I am thrilled that she is now sharing her love for and knowledge of books with you and your family.

The foundations of learning are laid for every child from the beginning of life—even from the womb—through the rhythm of voices and music. Recently a new mother asked me, "What do I do with this baby?" My reply was simple: "Experience life. And read, read, read!" You can read anything aloud to little ones. They simply want to hear the cadence of your loving voice. A baby is born with a desire to learn, but it is up to you, as the parent, to decide what, when, and how your child learns.

Reading with our children and providing them with a variety of life experiences fosters a love of reading and creates within them the desire and healthful habit of reading for enjoyment. William Butler Yeats wrote, "Education is not the filling of a bucket, but the lighting of a fire." Reading aloud to our children lights the fire in their souls, inspiring them to be more, to do more, to learn more. For this reason, I advocate that reading aloud should continue long after children have learned to read for themselves.

Within these pages, Sarah tells several stories about her family's culture of reading aloud and the way it shaped her memories and aspirations. Reading aloud as a family imparts wisdom and character, informs the intellect, and creates a "museum of memories," as Edith Schaeffer put it. In fact, reading aloud to your children can be more important than ever as they become teens and young adults because of the deep discussions that often ensue.

This then raises the question of what a family should choose to read aloud. Thousands of new books aimed at children and teens are published every year, but due to issues of content or quality, most are simply not worth considering. So what should you read to your children? Stories with important character implications; books that are slightly above the child's reading level (if you have several children, aim your reading toward the eldest child); and, finally, books you want to read!

Of course, any worthwhile reading program must begin with God's Word, the Ultimate Living Book, followed by the best books mankind has to offer. God designed us to learn through story, and He is the original Story Giver. Indeed, the Bible encompasses many genres of literature, including biography, history, poetry, adventure, romance, and mystery. Humanity's finest literary works likewise reflect God's great truths and teach us that we are all part of a much larger story.

Sarah Clarkson's *Read for the Heart* is a powerful tool in your hands. The decisions you make regarding what your family will read (or not read) will either feed or diminish your soul and those of your children. The books your children read now are destined to shape their futures. Therefore, I urge you, don't just read through this book—pray through it! Ask the Holy Spirit to show you which books to read and in what order, then obey Him.

Every family that undertakes this challenge will follow a reading journey of their own. Allow the Lord to shape yours. Feed your spirit, soul, and intellect with wonderful books, just as you would feed your body with healthy food, and share the habit with your children. Perhaps one day they will follow Sarah's inspirational example and share their journey with the rest of the world.

Tina Farewell
Co-founder, Lifetime Books and Gifts
Co-founder, Bringing Dads Home
www.BobandTinaFarewell.com

Acknowledgments

Everyone owes himself not only to God, but the whole church;
everyone is borne by invisible prayers and sacrifices, has been
nourished by countless gifts of love, is continually strengthened
and preserved by the affection of others.

~ Hans Urs von Balthasar

To my parents: Not only did you have the imaginative foresight to raise me on great books, but you also had the passion to make great stories of your own lives. I am the most blessed girl alive to have parents who were so zealous in their determination to give their kids strong minds and steadfast souls. This book is my tribute to your investment. I am who I am because of your hundreds of hours of read-aloud, because of the home you filled with art and music, because of the candlelit dinners and enthusiastic discussions afterward. Thank you, Dad, for a thousand discussions that sharpened my thought; for constantly supplying me with books, articles, and new ideas; for loving my poetry; and for walking with me through every writing idea and story concept I've had. Thank you, Mom, for loving great books, for teaching me to communicate ideas through the life-changing vehicle of story, for loving Goudge with me, and for being my kindred spirit in a world of imagination and beauty. A kid thanking her parents for a matchless childhood is like a human thanking God for existence—there just aren't words to encompass my gratitude. I guess I'll just have to a live a great story as my way of saying thanks.

To my editor Zan Tyler: I am so grateful that you saw the potential in this book and in my ability to write it. Thank you for drawing excellence out of me and for challenging me to think deeply, to write precisely, and to communicate the ideas of this book clearly. Your investment of time, encouraging critique, and vast patience as I stumbled through the maze of the editing process has deeply shaped me. You've equipped me well for my writing journey.

To my editor Mary Jo Tate: Your patience in fine-tuning this manuscript, your skill as a reader and thinker, and your gracious reworking of my mistakes has been exactly what I needed as a new author. I so appreciate your intricate work in bringing the best out of this book and helping me to express myself in clear, accurate words. Working with you has been an education and a gift.

To my book friends:

Lynn Custer, I have loved inspecting your library since I was seven years old. You know more about children's books than anyone I know, and I want to be your protégé. Thank you for loving books, and me, so much.

Phyllis Stanley, what a deep delight to have a friend and mentor who cherishes children's literature in the same way I do. Thank you for your love and interest in the world of my reading and writing, for many teatime discussions, and for our unforgettable English literary adventure.

Dr. Joe Wheeler, I met you when I was standing on the cusp of the literary world. Thank you for taking me under your wing and guiding me into a wide and varied study of the great stories of literature. You have introduced me to some of my best beloved authors and have been a voice of encouragement to me in all my literary dreams. If I ever end up a professor of literature, it will be because of you. I hope I follow in your footsteps by being a keeper of story.

And to my siblings—Joel, Nathan, and Joy—co-conspirators, fellow adventurers, pilgrims in the land of imagination: Life, reading, and the pretending that came out of it would have been downright boring without you. I will never forget our reading afternoons, our Barnes and Noble Tuesdays, and the many hours of imagination we have invested in our friendships and lives. I treasure you.

1
Reading to Live

To learn to read is to light a fire;
every syllable that is spelled out is a spark.

~ Victor Hugo

In a blue corner of my house, where the light slants down from the mountains, hangs a glossy painting of a little boy curled deep into a wide, white window seat. In his lap is an immense picture book staring up at him in a rainbow of pictures and dancing words. With the red of a fiery winter sunset streaming over the snow outside, he bends over the page, eyes bright, face flushed with the thrill of his story.

I love that picture. It embraces the essence of reading— its hushed power and its subtle, soul-shaping delight. In every line and hue, I see evidence of the way a great story wakens a child's heart. The boy's face reflects the stirring of deep thought, the sturdy joy of newly imagined worlds, the thrill of a soul widened by beauty. The heightened color of the sunset hints at the way the story is reshaping his eyes to better perceive the mystery of the world and his own unfolding tale.

Thus it is with great delight and a certain fitness of place that I begin the writing of this book on books from my own window seat. Cold and gray, a winter's dusk is settling in around me. Just like the child in my picture, I hold in my hands a sort of picture book, and it is to this tale that I invite you as my reader.

From the earliest days of my childhood, I have lived in a world shaped by the books I read. From bedtime stories with my parents to long, solitary reading hours, books have been my daily companions. They have spurred my imagination in childhood, inspired my dreams in adulthood, and filled my soul with vivid pictures of life fully and courageously lived. Before I was born, my parents decided that one of the primary gifts they would give to their little girl would be a childhood, and thus a life, shaped by great stories. Their investment of time, money, words, and wisdom is a gift that I now want to pass on by encouraging you to do the same for your children.

Experts have written many excellent books on the merits of great literature and useful guides to selecting worthy books. I am not an expert or a critic. My perspective comes from the other side—from a young heart, mind, and soul shaped by storybooks. Although this book is a handbook, with lists and tips galore to guide you into the world of children's literature, I also consider it to be a story and an invitation not just to a reading list, but to a reading life.

As I have considered the many wonderful reasons to read, a steady progression of scenes from my childhood has come to my mind, each one a poignant portrait of a reading life. One by one, these scenes remind me of the reasons I read: for a wakened heart, a strong mind, and a steadfast soul.

This book will help you discover how great stories can form the lives of your children—how books can be powerful companions and teachers that will spur your children's hearts and minds to life. I begin by sharing some picture-book glimpses of a reading life to illumine the stories that most deeply shaped my inner world and crafted the book-loving woman I have become.

Scene One: A Wakened Heart

A winter's eve has come. Dusk is tapping at the windows as a fire snaps and sings from the hearth. Shadows spring dramatically around the ceiling as I nestle into the toastiest corner of the couch, a mist of hot-chocolate steam encircling my face. My siblings and parents settle in around me, my mom lighting a candle as my dad flips his way to the bookmark in our latest family read-aloud.

We are a rapt audience, catching the cadence of my dad's words with their rumble and lilt, noticing how he imbues each character with its own distinctive voice. We sigh when he stops. "Just one more page, please?" But no, the hour is late. We are alive with excitement, exclaiming over the outrageous characters, voicing our breathless suspense at what will happen next. A glad energy threads between us, and a new zest for life lightens our eyes as we are wakened to wonder.

When the bustle dies down and I reach the quiet of my room, I sit on my bed in a thoughtful silence. I am startled by the excitement in my heart, kept wide awake by the energy of the story as it sets me to wondering about the world and my place within it. I am filled with desire—to be as brave, beautiful, and strong as the heroes and heroines in that tale. With a few good words, the story has invested an ordinary night and an ordinary me with a sense of boundless possibility. An astonishing joy that is half thrill and half yearning fills my heart as I drift off to sleep.

Those reading evenings with my family were the beginning of my passion for books. I was captivated by the power of words to kindle my heart and to spark discussion, dreams, and excitement in every person in my family. I was won by the way books liven the heart with a sense of possibility, communicate excitement, and ignite wonder. Stories invite me to leave cold apathy and self-centered boredom and to enter instead a world of heroic and wondrous adventure.

This is the first reason I read. A good book, like any great piece of art, is an agent of awakening. Vivid tales of adventure, courage, and beautiful imaginary lands prompt us to hunger after such things for ourselves. The tale of a princess pricks a little girl's heart with the desire to be one. The story of a courageous explorer shows a little boy the height of bravery to which he can rise.

Every child needs to be introduced to God's reality in such a way that it is irresistibly attractive. A good story can bring that first thrill of beauty, the dawning recognition that the world is wondrous. In an electronic and concrete age that separates us from nature, face-to-face friendship, and traditional forms of childhood creativity, we need to teach children to revel in beauty of all sorts. The inherent wonder and possibility of life will waken their hearts with a desire to know the God who made them.

The first thing that a young heart needs is an education in all that is good. The classic children's stories are a persuasive picture of beauty and goodness. They create an inner world that is a secret home for children's souls, showing them through thrilling stories and stouthearted characters exactly what it means to be noble, good, and even holy.

My parents knew that stories have a unique power to embody virtue—to make it a living, attractive thing to a child. So they began with the great story of Scripture, filling my mind with the hero tales of the Bible. To this, they added the innocent beauty of classic children's books, never underestimating the power of a good story to affirm and further illuminate the truths they were teaching me from Scripture. I was formed in my earliest childhood by an imagination filled with stories, Biblical and classic, that set my appetite for all that was righteous, true, and lovely.

Great literature also gently guides children through the second and harder wakening to an awareness of what is wrong. Insightful stories gradually confront children with the power of sin as it enters the tale of their lives and the stories they love. Characters like brave Lucy from The Chronicles of Narnia or David Balfour from *Kidnapped* who value what is beautiful and defend what is right will teach children to understand evil as something to resist and help them perceive the choice that must be made between right and wrong.

As Vigen Guroian argues in *Tending the Heart of Virtue*,[1] great children's stories exhibit an inherent morality. To read them is to enter a moral world and to subscribe to the assumptions of good and evil ruling the tale. Strong, beautiful stories present a picture of goodness so compelling that a child cannot help but desire to become part of the virtue so vibrantly portrayed.

And so, in this first scene, I remember that I read for a heart awake. I read to keep my heart aware of joy and ready to choose it, to stay alert to the real miracle of my own world and the story I live within it. I read to be shaped by the clear, moral values of the storybook world; I read to cultivate a love of all that is right.

The great stories—first of Scripture and then of classic literature—crafted the inner world of my heart from which, even in adulthood, I make my decisions and form my values. I turn to this world again and again to be convinced of a beauty that is still to be desired, a greatness still to be hoped for despite the ruinous days of life here in the shadows.

Scene Two: A Strong Mind

I was fourteen, stretched out on my floor, ringed in by a frayed rope of papers and pencils as I worked at my assignment of listening to Shakespeare's *A Midsummer Night's Dream* on tape. I was fidgety. The sheer number of words made me feel I was under a raging waterfall of old English phrases, in rhyme no less, managing to catch just a drop or two of meaning. But I kept at it day by day, often rewinding the tape when a word was unclear; and slowly, my mind began to untangle the intricate web of words. As I began to catch the sparkling wit, epic speeches, and subtle philosophy pervading every line of a Shakespeare play, I felt a sort of euphoria.

With that breakthrough, I entered a year of intellectual expansion that affected every area of my study. As I continued to read Shakespeare, I began to progress in algebra, my creative writing flourished, and my enjoyment of worldview classes soared. Though I couldn't articulate it at the time, my brain's capacity to comprehend ideas was broadening in direct proportion to the expansion of my vocabulary. My thinking was progressing simply by virtue of the words to which I was exposed.

That constant expansion of thought is the second reason I read. I read for a strong mind. I love books for their ability to train my thoughts, strengthen my comprehension, and deepen my perception of truth.

Reading is the golden key to educational success. It is impossible to be a successful student apart from a mastery of the written word. Researchers are finding that children's vocabulary—the amount of exposure they have had to a wide variety of words—is possibly the greatest determining factor in their success in all subjects in school. [2]

A healthy vocabulary is the vital key to comprehending new ideas. Psychologist Keith Stanovich found that children who were surrounded by words from an early age were able to advance in every area of education, not just reading. On the other hand, children who lacked exposure to words lost ground in every area of study and mental development.[3] Many researchers agree that a child's exposure to the spoken word and books read out loud are the best predictor for their success in school.[4] A "literacy-rich" home environment of available books and constant discussion literally enriches children's brains, enabling them to progress in reading and thus in all areas of learning.

On a more spiritual level, the habit of reading influences the ability to think deeply about life-altering ideas of faith and belief. Madeleine L'Engle, author of *A Wrinkle in Time,* once wrote that the decreasing vocabulary of modern culture would result in an inability to think greatly about God:

> The more limited our language is, the more limited we are; the more limited the literature we give to our children, the more limited their capacity to respond, and therefore, in their turn, to create. The more our vocabulary is controlled, the less we will be able to think for ourselves. We do think in

words, and the fewer words we know, the more restricted our thoughts. As our vocabulary expands, so does our power to think.[5]

When we limit our ability to articulate truth about God, we limit our awareness of His presence and power in our lives. An inadequate vocabulary sometimes equals an inadequate comprehension of spiritual reality. God formed our brains to be molded by words. He, the living Word who spoke existence into being, created us to be a people of words, both written and spoken. He gave us both Truth and great literature with His gift of the Bible. He designed us to be able to express and record every idea through our words. A young intellect nourished by a feast of words can tackle any concept—whether mathematical, scientific, spiritual, or imaginative—with confidence.

Scene Three: A Steadfast Soul

I was sixteen, stretched out over the rumpled quilts of my bed. Though my room was dim with the brooding blue of a coming storm, I leaned close to the book in my hands, eager to catch the shadowed words. My eyes were alight with an excitement as sharp as the lightning searing the sky, for I had come to a splitting of the ways. I was standing on the very cusp of adulthood, but I was confused, unsure of who I wanted to be and what I would believe about God. Restless with hunger for adventure, I was frightened by the vastness of the future, writhing in the grasp of a thousand unanswered questions.

Into that storm of spirit came a story.

It was J. R. R. Tolkien's masterpiece, *The Lord of the Rings*. I had picked it up because I needed a good long book to distract me from my own thoughts, but in it I stumbled upon a story that met me right in the depths of my questions. My yearning for adventure, my hunger for meaning, and my anger at the discovery of how painful life could be were all present in the lives and hearts of this story's characters. Here was the sort of drama for which I longed.

In the usual fashion of young souls, I was searching for a cause big enough to encompass the hunger in my heart. The world around me often seemed deeply lacking in the possibility I desired and the goodness I was trying to believe God had. I was newly aware of pain and suffering and I wanted redemption, yet the lives of many Christians I knew evidenced anything but hope. I knew the Bible and sensed its truth, but I was grappling with doubt, searching for answers to all my questions.

The characters and drama of *The Lord of the Rings* vividly portrayed my spiritual struggles and expressed my deepest desires for heroism and redemption. The humble little hobbit Frodo and his epic journey to overcome evil taught me that endurance, faithfulness to a task, and trustworthiness are what make a person great. In the battles and sorrow described in the book, I found an acknowledgment of the struggle inherent in living and yet a promise of a stronger joy that gave me hope. The warrior king Aragorn exemplified heroism and courage, while the noble elves taught me to value the slow, daily cultivation of ritual, beauty, and tradition. The whole story was lived out by a brave fellowship of companions who had decided to love what was right and give their lives to pursuing it.

It was in reading that book that I first understood that life— my life—is a story. The entire history of the world is an epic written by God and told throughout the colorful drama of each advancing generation. We are the heroes and heroines, the villains and knaves that people the pages of this one true tale. Our actions and our decisions contribute as much to light or darkness as any prince or princess in a fairy tale.

The Lord of the Rings woke me to this startling reality, and thus forms the third great reason that I read: for a steadfast soul. Great literature has a unique power to reveal the epic spiritual nature of all human life. In a great paradox, imagined stories sharpen our value for what is real. Imaginary heroes and heroines teach us what nobility and courage look like in the workaday world. Far from being escapist, great literature actually helps us to perceive how serious life and faith are. *The Lord of the Rings* affirmed the desires of my heart, helping me to understand that I was born to seek meaning, holiness, and deep relationships.

Especially in the teenage years, it is vital that kids be immersed in epic stories. Most teenagers stumble into a phase of restless desire that includes a yearning for adventure and a hunger for meaning. Life can seem limited and dull; but when restless teens are given great, redemptive stories, I firmly believe the books become a means of channeling

23

and pouring that energy into a love for what is worthy and true. Great literature validates the longing for heroism that resides in a passionate young heart—affirming it, while also modeling what heroism looks like in daily life. A really great story can teach a young soul that the heights of bravery, adventure, and beauty are reached only by the choices of faithfulness, humility, and creativity that mark everyday life.

Classic literature is a treasury of drama that vividly portrays the qualities necessary to live an epic life. By reading such writers as Tolkien, C. S. Lewis, and George MacDonald, I learned what is required for heroism and what it means to live in a noble, disciplined, valiant way.

Yet even as I embraced the thrill of living with courage, I realized my inability to be as heroic as I wanted. As a teenager struggling with the idea of suffering, when I encountered the smoke of Mordor and the oppression of tyrants, I became aware of the brokenness of my fallen world and my sinful self. I began to recognize my need for redemption, my desperate longing for a Storyteller to make my own tale turn out right. Great literature turned my heart back to the Redeemer and His one true story.

I can vividly remember the day I sat on my bed wishing that reality were more like Middle-earth, but even as that thought crossed my mind, I began to consider whether spiritual reality might be just as great. If Tolkien could envision a world of such grand proportions, then God's reality—even if I couldn't see it—must be infinitely better. From the imagined world of a storybook, I was turned back to my Bible to study and search and find an epic far greater than any I or any other human being could imagine. The truth I finally saw in Scripture captivated my soul forever.

It wasn't that the Bible itself wasn't enough or that my parents' discipleship was lacking. It was simply that in the midst of my struggle and doubt, *The Lord of the Rings* helped to rekindle my spiritual imagination, spurring me to overcome my doubts and renew my quest for a living faith. Nothing less than an epic story could satisfy the desires of my heart. *The Lord of the Rings* simply helped me to rediscover the true epic of God's redeeming love.

When you give children great stories full of heroism, rich imagery, and sacrifice, side by side with biblical truth, you fill their minds with images that bring spiritual reality to life in their hearts. Great stories flesh out biblical faith, helping children to see themselves as part of the true kingdom story.

So I read for a steadfast soul. From a child whose heart was wakened by beauty, I have progressed to a soul more aware of all that I can and should be. Now I have encountered evil, pain, and suffering as well as goodness. But the stories I have read teach me to fight for all that is good, to grasp meaning and nobility, and to wait for the Redeemer who will end my tale in triumph.

Reading to Live

I am nestled in a high-walled booth at a nearby café as I write this. The day is cold; gray has taken the outside sky and sent me scurrying for the crackle and crisp of the coffee-shop hearth with my three siblings. For the past hour, we have had one of our exhilarating family discussions (otherwise known as arguments) over the nature of art. Sitting in a coffee shop, sipping cappuccinos, and talking about art, music, and literature is one of our favorite things to do.

In a comfortable lull, I have turned to my trusty laptop to write for a few minutes. Low conversation thrums around me, joined by the rhythm of clinking cups and the light throb of violins on the radio. One of my brothers reads a quote from a book; the other parries with a quip of his own. We laugh. I look down and, with a strange and sudden reverence, feel that I am witness to a beautiful drama. In that thought, I discover just what it is I want to say.

Reading has taught me how to live.

The books I have read have shaped me to see, to engage, to love. Reading has taught me not just to think, but also to look up from the pages of my book at a world that is itself a story. Books have trained me to be active, alert, and ready to enter life as I find it. At this moment I may not be reading, but I'm writing. Watching. Laughing. In short, living. That is really the point of all this reading.

To sum it all up, I read to live. Every book I've read and every story that has made itself a part of my imagination has taught me something about what it means to live life well. I'm passionate about reading because I'm passionate about life. Great stories influence the way I live in the here and now.

Reading should always thrust us back into the drama of the real world. A healthy love of books gives birth to a renewed enthusiasm for daily living and for the people who shape its stories. A story-formed imagination is naturally driven to real-world action. The great point of excellent stories is to wake us up to beauty, dress down our pride, and teach us how to live with courage, compassion, and creativity.

Life is an epic, true story. The heart of my message is that reading prepared me to live as nobly as any hero or heroine in a storybook and that it will do the same for your children. While reading can never replace the influence of your own words and life on your children, stories can be powerful allies in the huge task of forming them into people of wakened hearts, strong minds, and steadfast souls.

In selecting the books that fill the following chapters, I have read thousands of stories, begged for the best advice from my literary friends and other experts, and compiled what I hope is a soul-worthy feast. My parents gave me the gracious gift of a reading life. I now want to pass that gift of story on to you. I hope each story you encounter will add to the treasury of knowledge, faith, virtue, and beauty that you are creating in your children's hearts. May these books form and inspire your days as they have mine.

Welcome to the reading life.

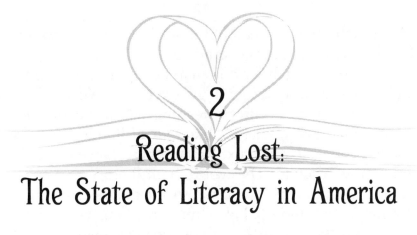

2
Reading Lost:
The State of Literacy in America

You don't have to burn books to destroy a culture.
Just get people to stop reading them.

~ Ray Bradbury

Professor Digory Kirke in the Narnia books is fond of asking, "What *do* they teach them at these schools?" I find myself with quite the same sentiment.

As a book lover, I find it hard to imagine a childhood and basic education where books are a peripheral presence instead of the driving force of learning. Until recently, no one else could either. But the world is rapidly changing. As technology, electronic media, and a globalized culture increasingly invade modern society, the old-fashioned love of good stories and long books is fading. Children are growing up reliant on electronics and textbooks to educate and entertain them instead of the stories that were so central to the formation of past generations.

I began the research for this chapter supposing it would be a quick, statistical endnote. I discovered, however, that the statistics traced the decline of reading, so I feel compelled to take you on a brisk, businesslike tour of literacy in modern society to provide a context for the importance of books in the life of your child. The world, both literary and cultural, is changing and, along with it, our interaction with the life-forming power of ideas. I also think this tour will make you, as it did me, keenly aware of how actively reading must be pursued in an age marked by distraction.

Several years ago I attended a conference in Cambridge, England, and heard a talk given by Dana Gioia, then chairman of the National Endowment for the Arts (NEA). Through him, I discovered a report on one of the largest surveys ever conducted on American literacy. I knew from some of the discussion at the conference that reading was losing ground in our time, but I was unprepared for the full scope of the stunning report.

Reading at Risk, a 2004 report on a survey by the National Endowment for the Arts (NEA), found literary reading to be declining among all ages and socio-economic groups in America. (Literary reading was defined as reading a novel, play, short story, or poetry during leisure time in the past year.) The age group with the steepest rate of decline was the youngest group surveyed, adults between the ages of 18 and 24.

Other statistics included:

- Less than half of the adult population now reads literature.

- There has been a ten percent decline in adult literary reading in the last twenty years. The ten-percentage point decline in literary reading represents a loss of twenty million potential readers.

- Only slightly more than one-third of adult American males now read literature. Reading among women is also declining, but at a slower rate.

- Over the past twenty years, young adults (18–34) have declined from being those most likely to read literature to those least likely (with the exception of those age 65 and above). The rate of decline for the youngest adults (18–24) is fifty-five percent greater than that of the total adult population.

- Literary reading strongly correlates to other forms of active civic participation. Literary readers are more likely than non-literary readers to perform volunteer and charity work, visit art museums, attend performing arts events, and attend sporting events.[6]

Dana Gioia said this in his summary of the report:

For the first time in modern history, less than half the adult population now reads literature. Anyone who loves literature or values the cultural, intellectual and political importance of an active and engaged literacy in American society will respond to this report with grave concern. . . . Literature reading is fading as a meaningful activity, especially among younger people. If one believes that active and engaged readers lead richer intellectual lives than non-readers and that a well-read citizenry is essential to a vibrant democracy, the decline of literary reading calls for serious action.[7]

This situation calls for serious action because researchers are finding that reading is linked with income, job success, and health, and it seems to directly affect a person's involvement in politics, charity, and the arts. A further NEA report in 2007 on reading in general (as opposed to exclusively literary reading) combined numerous smaller studies to look more deeply into the decline of reading. Titled *To Read or Not to Read: A Question of National Consequence*, the report presented three basic conclusions from the research:

- Americans are spending less time reading.

- Reading comprehension skills are eroding.

- These declines have serious civic, social, cultural, and economic implications.[8]

Other statistics and findings include:

- Less than one third of 13-year-olds are daily readers.

- 15- to 24-year-olds spend only 7–10 minutes a day on voluntary reading—about 60 percent less time than the average American.

- By contrast, 15- to 24-year-olds spend two to two and a half hours per day watching TV. This activity consumes the most leisure time for men and women of all ages.

- American families are spending less on books than at almost any other time in the last two decades. The number of books in a home is a significant predictor of academic achievement.

- Little more than one third of high school seniors now read proficiently.

- Employers now rank reading and writing as top deficiencies in new hires; 38 percent of employers find high school graduates "deficient" in reading comprehension, while 63 percent rate this basic skill as "very important."

- Reading for pleasure correlates strongly with academic achievement. Voluntary readers are better readers and writers than infrequent readers.[9]

Again, Dana Gioia sums up the findings:

> *To Read or Not to Read* confirms—without serious qualification—the central importance of reading for a prosperous, free society. The data here demonstrate that reading is an irreplaceable activity in developing

productive and active adults as well as healthy communities. Whatever the benefits of newer electronic media, they provide no measurable substitute for the intellectual and personal development initiated and sustained by frequent reading.[10]

Many factors contribute to our society's failure to read, but the above quote identifies the foremost: electronic media. The NEA reports show a direct drop in reading levels concurrent with greater use of electronic media. The use of technology has replaced reading as one of the common activities of our culture. For the first time in history, children are abandoning the traditional entertainments of childhood (drawing, pretending, playing outside, reading) for the indoor, virtual world of electronics.

Electronic media pervade our work, education, and entertainment. Many adults spend hours each day in front of the computer for business. Children increasingly receive large doses of their education through computer programs, games, and online classes. Sixty percent of teenagers spend an average of twenty hours per week in front of the television or computers, though a third spend closer to forty hours per week.[11] The average American watches more than five hours of TV each day.[12]

While some people try to pass off all this as progress, it's really not that simple. While we have certainly expanded our knowledge in some areas through electronic media, we have probably stunted our brains in others, especially in the area of reading. The act of reading has a profound effect on our brains; it fundamentally shapes the way we process all information. Reading is more than a pastime or even just an intellectual tradition. Our entire interaction with ideas is affected by the medium in which they are presented.

Consider TV, for example. As early as the 1960s, researcher Herbert Krugman found that while watching TV, the left side of the brain enters a state of passivity.[13] Mindless entertainment, right? Actually, no. Continuing research is finding that while watching TV, the right side of the brain remains active, retaining vivid imprints of the images and sounds presented on the screen. That switch from left to right brain also causes the body to be flooded with endorphins, the body's natural opiates, stimulating a natural craving for the instigating activity.[14] This is alarming when you understand that the left side of the brain controls reason, logic, and thought, while the right side houses emotion, creativity, and intuition.

Imagine what this means for an impressionable child. While watching TV, the emotionally tender part of a child's brain is entirely receptive to the images and ideas presented on screen, while the discerning, rational part of his mind is shut off. The child is indiscriminately receptive to whatever image or idea is presented, inhibited not only in his discernment of the truth or error of the idea but also in the basic skill of rational comprehension.

Contrast this with what happens when a child reads a single line of text on a page. Cognitive psychologist Sebastian

Wren describes the actual physical activity of the brain as we read:

> Right now, as you read this passage of text, your occipital cortex is very active, processing all of the visual information you are encountering—the words, the letters, and the features of the letters. The frontal lobe of your neocortex is engaged in processing the meaning of the text you're reading—the meanings of the words, the sentences, and the big picture, and it is working to relate what you are reading with what you already know. Surprisingly, your temporal lobe (particularly on the left side of your brain if you're right handed) is also active right now, processing all of the "sounds" associated with reading—even though you're reading silently to yourself, the areas of the brain that process speech sounds are active just like they would be if you were listening to somebody speak. . . . While it is impossible at this point to describe what is happening at the cellular level in the brain, at the gross level, what seems to be happening is that the brain is analyzing text at three major levels—the visual features of the words and letters, the phonological representation of those words, and the meanings of the words and sentences.[15]

Not only are numerous parts of the brain involved in the act of reading, but the mind is also actively questioning the new information, deciding its meaning, and choosing where it will place it within the files of its previous knowledge. Reading shapes the way the brain encounters new concepts, creating a space for contemplation and discernment that electronic media never provide. Reading requires diverse areas of the brain—each controlling a different part of sight, speech, or sound—to work together to extract meaning from a page of text. Every aspect of this description suggests that reading is an intense mental activity. It produces the exact opposite of TV's passivity, resulting in a brain trained to interact with ideas and a mind able to comprehend, choosing what it will accept or reject as true.

Reading teaches a child to grapple with every idea he receives—questioning it and considering its merits. TV (or any other electronic presentation) trains a child to passively accept whatever is shown. When the average child spends nearly four hours a day on TV, DVDs, and videos,[16] this passive reception becomes his primary mode of interaction with ideas. This is shocking.

Ideas drive our beliefs about the most basic elements of faith, morality, and worldview. To be passive in the realm of ideas is to be passive about the forces that fundamentally shape culture and life. Yet this is precisely what electronic media train children to do. Technology replaces the quieter force of literature with a constant, entertaining distraction that teaches children to be influenced by whatever idea flashes most colorfully across their screen. Children become passive recipients of spiritual values and moral beliefs—both good and bad—leaving them with little concern for the ideological forces that shape the world in which they live.

The NEA report *Reading at Risk* clearly outlines this effect in its finding that while over half of literary readers invested significant time in politics, charity work, or the arts, only 17 percent of nonreaders did. These pursuits are all idea-driven activities requiring a certain level of insight, motivation, and comprehension from their participants. These activities shape societies. But people who have never understood the power of ideas or entered stories where ideas drive the lives of characters often have less understanding or passion for such causes.

While nurturing great readers and active thinkers has always been important, it is critical now. Our culture needs parents and teachers to pour their energy into revitalizing a love for reading. But that will require a lot of dedication, which leads to the second major cause for a lack of reading in our time: the deterioration of personal relationships. Reading is also in decline because it has ceased to be passed on in a personal way from generation to generation.

Reading is a skill; a love for stories and ideas is a taught value. Most children aren't born with a natural affinity for white pages crammed with little rows of black print. If they are to love the great literature of ages past, and if they are to grow up immersed in story and truth, it must be through the dedication of their parents. I am who I am today mostly because of the daily, determined efforts of my parents to enrich my life.

Without parents and mentors to challenge and inspire them, most children have little reason to rise above their current reality. In our mobile and increasingly isolationist society, we don't have the close relationships of extended family and local community to invite kids in for cookies and lemonade and supply them with a stock of story at the same time.

It may sound a bit dramatic, but if present trends continue, we will have an alarmingly illiterate society. People may be able to read, but their brains and hearts will be so formed by media, technology, and entertainment that their souls will be barren and hungry for lack of true insight and beauty. The decline of reading really could affect the future of our society.

Children will not grow up to be readers with rich souls unless they are encouraged day after day by the people who are committed to the keeping of their hearts. The art of deep thought must be revived as one family at a time commits to the work of imparting the delight and importance of reading to the next generation.

There is hope. Another NEA report from earlier this year, titled *Reading on the Rise*, found that reading levels among adults have made an abrupt turn in the last few years and are on the rise for the first time in twenty years. Most promising is the fact that the reading participation of 18- to 24-year-olds has risen as well. It is wonderfully possible to reverse the loss of story. With work and enthusiasm, we can bring reading back into its soul-shaping place in our society.

Reading certainly won't solve every cultural problem. I don't advocate it as a miracle cure. But great stories do undergird belief in meaning, morality, and heroism. They walk with us through our days, giving us an overarching vision for life as well as the vim needed to make our small part of the world full of meaning. It is, after all, that sort of living that ends up influencing whole cultures. Books will strengthen your children with beauty and bravery, teaching them to be agents of hope to a culture that has lost any concept of a happy ending.

Certainly this is a formidable challenge, but it is also a delight. We have the opportunity to reopen the floodgates of life and beauty, of deep thought and courageous ideals. I challenge you to inspire your children to read and to think. Run toward great stories and take as many people with you as you can. Give your children books and read them yourself. Flood your home with their presence so that every soul in your sphere of influence has no choice but to drink in the truth, goodness, and beauty of life.

3
Life by Books: How to Begin

Read in order to live.
~ Gustave Flaubert

So let the journey begin!

But how?

After my highly idealistic reasons for reading, you might be tempted to assume that all the children in my family sat in neat rows on the couch, books clutched diligently in small hands as profound spiritual insights enlightened us. That is not even remotely accurate. Any ideal must always be lived out amidst the rush and tangle of the everyday. The truth is that we were a normal gang of squirming, noisy children who didn't have any more talent than the average kid at keeping our muscles still for more than ten minutes. Our home was just what every good family home is—topsy-turvy, often messy, and filled with noise, action, and relentless living.

The deciding factor in my siblings' and my becoming dedicated readers was that books were woven into the very fabric of our home. So much reading got done in the midst of school, work, chores, and play because books were an integral part of the way we lived. Reading was a driving force in our education *and* our entertainment.

Remember, this is all about a reading *life*. The making of great readers should never be some sort of elite activity or academic process. Reading should be part of the natural rhythm of living; it brings a surprising amount of laughter, comfort, and cadence to ordinary days. It is a discipline of learning, but also a pleasant means of framing life with beauty and story. So please, don't feel any pressure. Below is a smorgasbord of ideas to help you get you started on your way to a lifestyle of reading. These will provide you a peek into the window of a house run by (and running over with) books. So take a look and then . . . begin!

Rhythms of Reading

"I have a treat for you," my mom whispered one day to a very eager six-year-old me. "Mommy's going to let you read for a whole hour instead of taking a nap because you're such a big girl now."

With those words, my mom instigated my lifelong habit of reading. She was brilliant. By presenting reading as an alternative to naptime, she made it a privilege. By making it a daily rhythm, she formed a habit in me that led to many thousands of hours in the company of books. From that moment forward, reading was a natural, accepted part of every single day.

Reading is a habit. It may take a little ingenuity and a sprinkling of discipline to get the habit formed in a child; but once it is, it becomes a regular, centering beat in the life of a home. If you teach children from their youngest days to expect and enjoy the daily rhythm of reading, it will quickly become a settled routine.

A huge part of this habit is to establish family read-aloud times. Hearing a parent read books aloud is one of the central forces that will shape a young child into an active reader. Before my mom ever pulled her naptime/reading switch, I had spent the first six years of my life immersed in a daily world of picture books, naptime stories, bedtime stories, and family reading hours. Before I was born, my mom began collecting picture books and piling them in big, sturdy baskets next to the couch. She tells me that even in the first few months of my life, she read to me daily. As I grew, she sought more intricately illustrated picture books and short readers to read aloud to me, encouraging me to sound out words myself as I began to learn my letters.

This practice ensured that by the time I reached my formal years of school, books were already beloved daily companions. As I entered the more rigorous years of education, it was natural that books become my primary source of learning. Because I was educated at home, I usually spent an hour each morning listening to my mom read aloud from creative history books, nature tales, or our current novel.

My afternoons were often taken up with my usual required hour of reading, plus a lot more as I began to pursue my own interests and ideas. Our family's evening entertainment was often a novel read dramatically by my dad. Story was a literal rhythm in my life.

Another aspect of my reading rhythm was the regular *pattern* of books that I was expected to read. My mom especially made sure that our literary intake was varied and nourishing to every aspect of our education and entertainment. We usually read in a set sequence: history, biography, literature, nature, and always something purely enjoyable to end the cycle (and sometimes to relieve a lag in the middle). Thus, even as I grew accustomed to the regularity of reading, I also came to expect and enjoy a consistent variety of learning.

When children grow up familiar with books and the habit of daily reading, they learn to accept it as a normal part of a wholesome life. In this way, it ceases to become an assignment to resist and turns into an integral, enjoyable part of daily living.

Ideas to Begin

- Establish a regular reading hour every day where everyone goes to his or her own corner to read.

- Replace TV at night with a family read-aloud session.

- Make a weekly trip to the library to stock up on fresh, exciting titles.

- Include a read-aloud time as part of your educational plan.

- Make individual read-aloud dates with each of your children, selecting books that are delightful to them.

- Fill a basket for each of your children with books from a variety of genres.

Make Reading Delightful

It's no secret that if kids think something is boring, they will resist it with every bit of strength they possess. Too often, reading can be seen as a bland, tedious task, especially if a child struggles with comprehension or is uninterested in the subject of the book. I am thankful that my parents never had any qualms about gently enticing me into a love of books.

While reading was a discipline and a habit in my life, I also grew up with a strong sense of its delight. My parents knew I would never continue a practice later on in life that I felt was dull, frustrating, or tinged with a sense of compunction. So they crafted our reading times to be some of the most comfortable, delightful parts of our day.

We often read around the fire, snuggling up in blankets, tucked into a pile of pillows. We might brew a fat pot of tea or stir frothing mugs of hot chocolate to accompany our reading. My siblings and I were allowed to fiddle during read-aloud times; we could build with LEGO blocks, draw, sew, and even squirm (quietly) as long as we could give a successful narration at the end of every chapter.

I have often heard the tale of how my brother Nathan, at age five, wiggled and squirmed his way through half an hour of listening to *The Children's Homer*. Pushed past her usual ease, my mom was sure Nathan hadn't heard a word she said, but when she put the book down she was met by his shrill outrage as he hung upside down on the couch. "Mom, you can't thstop now," he lisped. "I wanna know what happened to Odythseus!"

Another huge part of my learning to delight in reading was my parents' commitment to read aloud. This companionship is a key element in helping any child not only to read, but also to love it. Even when children struggle with learning to read, reading aloud provides them with that daily exposure to words that is so necessary to learning. One of my childhood best friends wasn't able to read fluently until he was twelve years old, but because his mom read aloud to him for hours every day, he was a National Merit Scholar by high school.

In my house, reading aloud continued into high school anyway. My mom continued the habit of "reading dates" for quite a few years. We read *Little Women*, *The Girl of the Limberlost*, and the Little House on the Prairie series in this way. I read numerous classics aloud to my siblings, and we often selected passages to share from favorite books.

As we grew older, my parents looked for ways to invest our enjoyment of reading with a sense of individual ownership. One of the ways my mom found to do this was with our weekly trip to the library. For every couple of educational books we read, she allowed us to choose stories of pure fun.

Our half hour at the library became a treasure hunt as we prowled the aisles in search of a new adventure entirely of our own choosing. I can well remember the delight of finding a new novel or Boxcar Children mystery and toting it home as a prize and much-anticipated treat.

That flavor of anticipation still pervades my reading. As an adult, I consider the reading of almost every book a pleasure, primarily because it was a delight in my childhood. I was first introduced to reading as an entertainment, an adventure, and a treat. By combining a high level of discipline with a high level of pleasure, my parents managed to convince me that reading was a privilege *and* a delight.

Ideas for Making Reading Delightful

- Make reading times cozy with a hot drink of your family's choice.

- Read in different places for fun—by a crackling fire, outside on a quilt on a sunny day, in a coffee shop, etc.

- Create a challenge for your children with a book as prize, and take them on a date to the best local bookstore to choose their reward.

- Make a basket of activities to be enjoyed only during read-aloud sessions. Fill it with crafts, sketchbooks, pencils, Legos—whatever piques your child's interest. Just check from time to time to be sure they are listening!

• Select a book your child will enjoy, and set aside a weekly time for a reading date.

Make Reading Accessible

To this day, if you visit my parents' home, you cannot escape the multitudinous presence of books. They inhabit the house like a vast colony of small, bright people, their covers smiling up at you from every available surface. Seasonal picture books are piled in baskets, fat tomes on art are propped open on table and hearth, tottering stacks of novels or spiritual essays grace the tables—and that's before you even set foot in the library. The family devotion to books is inescapable. This abundance of books was quite a hassle during our moving years (moving company men would walk into our library and groan), but it played a powerful role in shaping me to be an active reader.

I simply couldn't get away from books. No matter how bored I was, there was always something to read right where I was sitting (as my mom never failed to point out). One of the keys to forming the habit of reading in a child is simply to make books accessible. When books are present and inviting, it is natural for a curious child to pick them up. Picture books attract restless eyes with their color, nature magazines offer explanations of the world outside, and good fiction offers an escape from boredom. The process is simple because kids are always in some state of restlessness or curiosity.

But that will only work if there aren't a host of electronic distractions vying for their attention. I was raised on books and magazines *instead* of TV, PlayStation, or endless time on the Internet. A reading home is formed by the choice to make books a sturdy part of its culture, but that means purposefully excluding some other activities. Because our modern culture is so driven by electronic entertainment, it can be hard to foster a reading atmosphere. You just have to choose what sort of culture you will build in your home.

Ideas for Making Reading Accessible

- Start collecting your favorite picture books and set them around the house in book baskets where your kids can reach them.

- Subscribe to a couple of good magazines for kids.

- Prop open art and nature books on a table or hearth where your kids can flip through them.

- Create a book basket for each of your children filled with books they will particularly enjoy.

- Put a bookshelf in your children's rooms on which they can keep their favorite stories. Use Christmas or birthdays to stock it with beautiful, beloved books.

Just Begin

Building a reading culture in your home is really a surprisingly simple process in the end. Don't let the lofty goal of those deep-souled, literate children you are trying to grow fool you into thinking that a life of reading is a complicated or difficult thing. All of the suggestions above are just that—suggestions. There is no formula to a reading life, no law of literariness by which you must live.

The practices described above are some of the influences that I remember as being central to my own formation as a reader. I hope that they will equip you with tools and ideas to use in your own home. Every family has their own way of living by books, and I know that you will find rhythms and delights all your own.

Choose an idea or two from the suggestions above and simply begin.

A Roadmap for Using This Book

There are many little ways to enlarge your child's world.
Love of books is the best of all.

~ Jacqueline Kennedy

Now that you are stocked up on inspiration, it's time to get down to the details of how to use, read, and understand this book as you begin your reading journey. Consider this section a roadmap to the rest of the book. Included are brief explanations of the format and lists in the following chapters, as well as resources, answers to common questions, and a bit about the philosophy behind the selection of the books included in this guide. You're just about ready to go!

Organization of Book Lists

Unless otherwise noted, the book lists in each chapter are organized alphabetically by the author's last name. The chapter on historical fiction and literary biography is organized by time period and series. The index in the back of the book will help you locate specific titles easily.

Selection

With the plethora of books available today, I had a hard time deciding exactly which ones to include in each chapter. In the end, I have opted for quality over quantity, choosing to list only the really best books. I have personally read almost every book listed and have received glowing reviews from trusted sources for those I've not yet read. I want you to be able to open this book, find a title, and be assured of its literary quality and worth before you ever read it. The investment of your reading hours is a serious thing! However, I have tried to include a generous number of titles in each section so that you will have plenty of variety to choose from. In many reviews, I also list several other titles by the same author.

There are also many excellent, classic books that I don't include in *Read for the Heart* simply because they haven't been part of my reading journey. I feel deeply the impossibility of listing every book that deserves space here, but this is simply an ongoing journey into literature. The books I list are mostly the beloved companions of my own childhood. Your reading exploration may begin with the books listed here, but there are hundreds more waiting for your discovery. May the hunt never end!

Book Reviews

Each individual book recommendation includes:

- Author
- Date of original publication
- Award (if applicable)
- Illustrator (if applicable)
- General age category
- A short review
- Cautions regarding mature or questionable content (when needed)

The age categories are simply suggestions as to the general age for which a story was written; they should never limit your choice. Some middle-school books will be enjoyable for the whole family; some picture books become the favorites of older children. I include the categories simply as a guide to the general level of reading comprehension needed to enjoy the story.

The age categories can be defined as follows:

Young Child: Usually picture books, appropriate for very small children up through age 8. (Of course, I still enjoy picture books, so there's no limit on who can read them!)

Elementary: Usually shorter novels or readers, appropriate for ages 8–12.

Junior High: Novels approaching high-school-level reading comprehension with more complex vocabulary and philosophy. Some of the stories contain themes such as war, suffering, or moral dilemmas that are more appropriate to an older, discerning child. Unless specifically noted, however, none of these will contain graphic or objectionable material. Ages 12 and up.

High School: When a book is appropriate for high school reading or could be counted toward a high school reading list, I have included "high school" in the age category.

Family: Appropriate and enjoyable for the entire family; usually great for reading aloud.

Favorites Lists

One of the most frequently asked questions I hear is, "Can you recommend any books for my boys?" Thus, I have included several lists in the back of the book, each targeted to a specific age group or need:

♥ Boys' Favorites
♥ Beloved Girls' Books
♥ Family Read-Aloud Favorites

Audiobooks

A lot of parents want to know whether listening to books on CD or tape can produce the same benefits as silent reading or reading aloud. Audiobooks certainly bestow many of the same benefits, and they help immerse your child in a literary world of rich vocabulary and thought. They can be especially helpful for children who struggle with reading and need a little boost to help them enter a story.

Be sure to look for unabridged readings, as many companies edit older books, removing complex vocabulary and sentences. I have also found that some editions of the classics remove explicit references to faith or belief in God. Unless an audiobook is labeled "complete and unabridged," there is no guarantee you are getting the full story.

Listening should never entirely replace quiet, personal reading, however. The actual act of visual reading requires the brain to assimilate and comprehend information in a unique way that is entirely different from what happens when we hear information. By all means, make audiobooks a great part of your life, but keep up the old-fashioned sort of reading as well.

We listened to audiobooks on many car trips and sometimes in the quiet of our own rooms. They are perfect for long trips, short trips, quiet afternoons, or bored moments. Some of our most hilarious family moments happened in the communal fun of listening to a well-dramatized audiobook.

Places to Find Audiobooks

If you are looking for great audio versions of the classics, here are two of my favorite companies:

Blackstone Audiobooks: We love almost every one of the audiobooks we have gotten from this great family-run company. Most of their recordings were done by a select group of really excellent readers. They are funny, dramatically read, and unforgettable. You can order directly through their website, www.BlackstoneAudio.com, or find their versions on other online audio download sites. In their children's category you can find children's classics while avoiding modern adult novels.

Focus on the Family Radio Theatre: All of us Clarksons are hearty fans of the Focus on the Family radio dramas. Almost every one we've heard has been excellently dramatized, keeping the essence of the book intact, even when it was necessary to shorten the story. With great casts, realistic sound effects, and lovely soundtracks, these dramas have accompanied us on many car trips.

Living Books vs. Textbooks

The books listed in this guide are almost entirely what have come to be identified as "living books." Charlotte Mason, an educator living in England at the turn of the twentieth century, was one of the first to differentiate living books from mere textbooks. Marks of a living book include clear literary quality, the personal conviction and passion of a single author (as opposed to numerous authors with no personal investment in a textbook), and an engaging text that sparks interest and imagination while imparting knowledge. Mason and her educational descendants believe that it is those sorts of books that best waken, inform, and interest the impressionable mind of a child. This guide is really a book full of living books.

Charlotte Mason sums it up:

> I do not hesitate to say that the whole of a child's instruction should be conveyed through the best literary medium available. His history books should be written with the lucidity, concentration, personal conviction, directness, and admirable simplicity which characterizes a work of literary calibre.[17]

Moral vs. Literary Excellence

In choosing which books to review in the following chapters, I have paid attention to several elements. The first is the portrayal of moral, biblical truth. Does the book accurately and insightfully portray the moral nature of the world in which we live? Does it honor goodness and make virtue attractive? How does it portray evil? Does it value beauty?

The second element I consider is its literary quality. To me, this is equally important. Moral excellence ought to be inseparable from creative or literary excellence. However, some people are tempted to gloss over the literary excellence (or lack thereof) of a book in favor of its moral content. While certainly some stories are worth reading just because of the virtue they relate, I think it is vitally important that children be raised primarily on books of literary value.

The inherent beauty or literary excellence of a story aids in the illumination of the moral and spiritual themes it addresses. A blunted vocabulary makes for a clumsily presented idea. A wide, skillfully chosen vocabulary; strong, vivid narrative; and humorous or poignant insight into human nature through character development and intricate plot ought to be present in any story worth the investment of your time. God created us with skill, depth, and insight with which to understand and create. Thus, most of the books I have chosen to include are, as much as possible, excellent in both aspects.

Author's Worldview

In this age of moral confusion, it is perplexing to know what books to allow children to read, especially when the worldview of the author is in question. Many of the greatest works of literature were written by lost, broken people. When dealing with reading choices for children, we may be tempted to censor any story written by an author whose life was less than exemplary, but doing so would cut out a good chunk of the greatest literature available.

As people created in the image of God, all authors are able to portray, reflect, and create things that are inherently true regardless of what they choose to believe. Even while rejecting the reality of God, a determined atheist is still fully able to say true things about the nature of humanity and the created world. Sometimes the unfulfilled hunger and the unanswered desire of unbelievers drives them to grasp the human need for love, redemption, and beauty in a singularly poignant way.

Thus, we have to look at the message, the images, and the implicit truths presented by any book before we judge it exclusively by its author's worldview or life. Your kids might greatly benefit from books written by authors whose hungry hearts drove them to portray the reality of beauty, brokenness, redemption, or even innocence. A good example of this would be E. Nesbit, the author of several children's classics that are recommended later in this book. While flouting biblical ideals of family morality by living in an open marriage, she nevertheless wrote a great number of children's stories with brave, innocent, noble, and tender characters. It is impossible to omit her stories of *The Railway Children* or *The Treasure Seekers* from a list of the most uplifting classic children's literature.

Used and Out-of-Print Books

Watch out! As soon as you start reading these great books, you're going to want to own them. Since it would cost a fortune to buy them all new, and many of them might be out of print anyway, used books are a delightful alternative. There is a whole world of book-crazy people who haunt library sales, bookshops, and online bookstores in search of literary treasures. If you know where to look, you can easily find great quality books at affordable prices. The following list contains some of the many places I have discovered to be excellent venues for finding used book treasures. My only caution: The collecting of books is highly addictive. You have been fairly warned.

Library Sales

Most libraries go through a seasonal cleaning process when dozens of books that haven't been checked out in the last year are discarded for giveaway or sales. Check with your library staff to find out when they have their sales. Also, some libraries have discard copies on sale all the time; my local library has a shelf that I check every time I walk in the library door.

Used Book Stores

With a little computer savvy or a good phone book, you can easily locate used and antique booksellers in your town. Some shops tend to be quite pricey, while others have great bargains. If you are interested in collecting a specific series, these storeowners can be great guides and allies as they specialize in collecting old and out-of-print books and will probably know how to find the title you want. I have beloved memories of several small-town bookstore ladies who always had new suggestions, additional titles by favorite authors, and lots of time to talk and laugh. You should definitely take advantage of (and support!) these lovely around-the-corner bookshops while you can, as they are sadly becoming a rare and dying breed.

Thrift Shops and Goodwill

You wouldn't believe the books people give away. I raid my local Goodwill bookshelves as often as I can and have come out with treasures as diverse as expensive art tomes, illustrated hardcover classics, new-condition favorites, and occasionally a rare Elizabeth Goudge (one of my favorite, hard-to-find authors).

Online Booksellers

Big online book sites are likely to have a listing for almost any book you can think of. Often bringing together a community of bookshop owners under one online identity, these sites give you access to small bookstore owners around the world. My favorites are www.abe.com, www.bibliofind.com, and the Marketplace listings for used booksellers at www.amazon.com.

eBay

Though it takes a bit longer to actually buy the book and you risk the chance of losing it in a last-minute bidding war, eBay is a great way to get high-quality books at affordable prices. With patience and bidding strategy, I have managed to collect most of the out-of-print Dilithium Press Children's Classics, find my favorite rare books by C. S. Lewis and Tolkien, and purchase first-edition picture books for a fraction of their original cost.

5

Picture Books

Books, to the reading child,
are so much more than books—
they are dreams and knowledge,
they are a future and a past.

~ Esther Meynel

It might be my earliest memory. I am curled in the crook of my mother's arm in the evening. Bedtime lurks just around the corner, but for now, the two of us are nestled in the worn cushions of the old brown couch with a battered storybook open between us. My mom is reading, her voice charmingly expressive as she smoothes the glossy pages for me to see. I am entranced. The rhythm of the simple words combines with the whimsical paintings to captivate my little soul. I gaze at it all in bright-eyed wonder until I am compelled to surrender to my bedtime hour. I am only pacified by the knowledge that it will all begin again the next evening.

Over twenty years have come and gone since that night, but the memory came rushing back the other day when I stumbled across the very storybook that had so delighted me as a child. I felt that I was meeting an old friend whose soul was part of my own, and I sat down to renew our old acquaintance. The charm came back as I flipped the bright pages. While the beauty did not surprise me, my grown-up eyes noted the finesse and originality of the drawings with appreciation. I was surprised to find that the illustrations were by Michael Hague, an artist I have admired as an adult, quite apart from any realization that he had illustrated one of my favorite childhood books. I laughed and decided that my taste in art did not seem to have been altered much by growing up.

That thought stopped me in my contemplative tracks. I began to ponder what role such a seemingly insignificant picture book had played in the forming of my artistic and literary taste. How was it that I could still marvel at the beauty of my picture book as an adult with as great an admiration, if of a slightly different kind, as I did when I was just a toddler? Could it be that my exposure as a small child to excellent art and to stories that expressed truth gave me a lifelong value for those qualities in all creative work?

An adult appreciation for artistic excellence is not a coincidence, nor is a heart that hungers for the beautiful. Values such as those must be shaped from early childhood, woven day by day into the fabric of a child's thought. My passionate love of beauty in all artistic forms is due to the faithful effort of my parents to mold my creative appetite throughout my childhood. Their investment of countless hours (and dollars) into that molding is the reason I so highly value great literature and art as an adult.

In their early years, children are sensory sponges, soaking up every drop of sight and sound as they furnish the landscape of their minds. With every picture and illustration they encounter, they are building an internal expectation of beauty against which they will measure all future experiences with art. They are also outfitting the realm of their imagination, setting up that secret world of pictures to which they will turn later in life as they come across great literature that will demand them to furnish images out of the stock in their own minds.

That's why picture books are so important and why they must be chosen so carefully.

They are, after all, the very first bits of art and literature to which the youngest children are exposed. However insignificant they seem, picture books play an incalculable role in the establishing of a child's future ability both to imagine and desire what is lovely in the arts. They are not the end of artistic excellence; they are the beginning—the first course to whet a child's appetite for the feast that is to come.

As a child reads, so he thinks. Not all picture books were created equal. I have a personal vendetta against the plethora of absurd modern picture books. Their insulting, juvenile plainness assumes children to be incapable of deep thought or appreciation of beauty. This is ridiculous.

There is no magical age, however young, at which inanity is nourishing to the soul. Children fed on stick figures, cutesy drawings, and cartoon-like characters will have no appetite for Dickens, Rembrandt, or C. S. Lewis when they are older. Their imaginations will have been so stunted by amusing mediocrity that they will have little desire for the sort of entertainment that actually shapes the soul. Whatever children are given in their earliest years is what they will value when they grow up.

The pervasive mediocrity of modern culture makes it a constant challenge to be sure that children are being nourished by art of the highest quality. In a culture that has lost its definition of beauty, it takes determination to avoid the many books that entertain and distract without leaving any lasting value.

But if a child's first exposure to literature is to books that brim with colorful pictures of fascinating lands and noble, unique characters, then he will grow up valuing the goodness those stories portray. The imaginative, life-affirming stories of Barbara Cooney made me eager to imitate the creativity of the children in her books and spurred me to delve into the similarly imaginative works of Robert Louis Stevenson, George MacDonald, and C. S. Lewis when I was a little older.

Having been immersed in the sweeping beauty of Thomas Locker's picture books and the near-Renaissance art of Margaret Early's classic tales, I grew up to delight in the art of the real Renaissance masters and the landscapes of the Hudson River Valley artists. Charmed as a little girl by the hominess and comfort of the Brambly Hedge and Tasha Tudor stories, I still take great pleasure in all stories of life-giving homes and the families who so colorfully fill them.

Great picture books also protected my innocence. Children need a vast exposure to goodness before they are forced to face the brokenness of our world. The best picture books are compact vehicles of truth and beauty, resized for the wonder of childhood. They entertain, delight, and nourish, but they also shield.

The books listed in this chapter are the same ones on which I was raised—stories whimsical and deep, companioned by pictures that made the created beauty of God's world and the imagined beauty of my heart real and present. I am the writer I am today partly because of these books, but more importantly, they helped awaken my soul to beauty and truth when I was just a tiny girl.

It is never too early to begin.

Hallmarks of a Classic Children's Picture Book

Artful illustration, simplicity of story, and redemptive endings are important hallmarks of classic picture books for children.

Artful Illustration

There is a wondrously wide field of painting, drawing, and artwork that could be considered beautiful in the realm of children's illustration. Some books reflect a near-classical artistry, while others are chock-full of whimsy, fun, and downright silliness. My rule of thumb is to seek out illustrations that reflect God's created beauty, honor the human form, and refrain from too much distortion or the overly absurd.

Simplicity of Story

Part of the delight of a great picture book is its ability to communicate meaning and a heart-affirming story in words simple enough to captivate the mind of a child. The best stories have depth and interest while remaining accessible to a child's growing comprehension and vocabulary.

Redemptive Endings

For the most part, young children should be protected from descriptions of evil. Thus, I have chosen picture books that, while not avoiding the reality of grief and struggle, dwell largely on goodness and end in hope.

Organization and Descriptions of Picture Books

For this chapter only, I am listing books sometimes by author, sometimes by illustrator. Because picture-book stories are told mostly through their artwork, the illustrator is often considered the primary creator. For example, among picture-book collectors, the books illustrated by Barbara Cooney are collectible for their artwork, while books written by Cynthia Rylant are collectible because of their stories.

The Caldecott Medal

The Caldecott Medal is an award named in honor of Randolph Caldecott, an artist and illustrator from the Golden Age of children's literature. The Association for Library Service to Children, a division of the American Library Association, awards the medal annually to the artist of the most distinguished American picture book for children. Discernment is still needed, as a few titles are honored more for their modern values than their literary or artistic excellence. Most Caldecott Medalists, though, are still thoroughly excellent. A complete listing of Caldecott Medalists is provided in the appendix.

Karen Ackerman

Song and Dance Man, 1988. Illustrated by Stephen Gammell.

Up in the attic, a show is about to begin as Grandpa opens his old trunk, dons his hat, and transforms himself into a song-and-dance man of the Vaudeville stage. This is a sing-along, toe-tapping tale swinging with vibrant, zany drawings.

Also written by Ackerman:
♥ *Araminta's Paint Box*

C. W. Anderson (author and illustrator)

Billy and Blaze series, 1936–1971.

This series has provided hearty, innocent adventure stories for several generations of boys. Billy and his pony Blaze are the best of friends, and they find many wondrous adventures. Detailed pen-and-ink drawings complement the text. The series includes:
- ♥ *Billy and Blaze: A Boy and His Pony*
- ♥ *Blaze and the Gypsies*
- ♥ *Blaze and the Forest Fire*
- ♥ *Blaze Finds the Trail*
- ♥ *Blaze and Thunderbolt*
- ♥ *Blaze and the Mountain Lion*
- ♥ *Blaze and the Indian Cave*
- ♥ *Blaze and the Lost Quarry*
- ♥ *Blaze and the Gray Spotted Pony*
- ♥ *Blaze Shows the Way*

Keith Baker (author and illustrator)

The Dove's Letter, 1988.

In her search for the true recipient of a love letter, a faithful messenger dove delivers it to several special people, all of whom assume its heartfelt note was written just for them. A warm-hearted celebration of thoughtfulness in all forms, the story is brought to life by the rustic, whimsical illustrations.

Jill Barklem (author and illustrator)

Brambly Hedge Seasons series, 1980.

After months of studying the customs and traditions of English country life, Barklem set out to craft a series of children's books filled with the hominess she found. The Brambly Hedge series chronicles the colorful days of a cheerful community of mice who love a good feast, an adventurous foray, and the charming company of their families. These are some of my family's favorite read-aloud books. The four seasonal tales were published first as a set, but you can begin with any Barklem title, as each is a stand-alone story.

The Brambly Hedge set includes:
- ♥ *Spring Story*
- ♥ *Summer Story*
- ♥ *Autumn Story*
- ♥ *Winter Story*
- ♥ *The High Hills*
- ♥ *The Secret Staircase*
- ♥ *Sea Story*
- ♥ *Poppie's Babies*

Ludwig Bemelmans (author and illustrator)

Madeline series, 1939–1961.

This enchanting series chronicles the adventures of precocious Madeline in her boarding school in Paris. In the first book, a sudden attack of appendicitis is no match for plucky Madeline. Bemelmans' lyrical verse and bright, impressionistic illustrations display the fun and spunk of lovely little Madeline. The series includes:

- ♥ *Madeline*
- ♥ *Madeline's Rescue*
- ♥ *Madeline's Christmas*
- ♥ *Madeline and the Bad Hat*
- ♥ *Madeline in London*
- ♥ *Madeline and the Gypsies*

Michael Bond

Paddington series, 1958–2008. Originally illustrated by Peggy Fortnum; illustrations vary with different editions.

This series about an adorable little bear from "darkest Peru," who comes with a blue coat, a floppy red hat, and a weakness for marmalade, has been beloved for over fifty years. Found in Paddington Station in London, Paddington is adopted by the friendly Brown family and soon makes a cozy home in England, where he begins a series of adventures and hilarious scrapes. The series includes:

♥ *A Bear Called Paddington*
♥ *More About Paddington*
♥ *Paddington Helps Out*
♥ *Paddington Abroad*
♥ *Paddington at Large*
♥ *Paddington Marches On*
♥ *Paddington at Work*
♥ *Paddington Goes to Town*
♥ *Paddington Takes the Air*
♥ *Paddington on Top*
♥ *Paddington Takes the Test*

Jan Brett (author and illustrator)

Fritz and the Beautiful Horses, 1981.

Jan Brett is known for her intricate drawings with rich, Nordic flavor. This charmingly illustrated book is one of my favorites. In a city known for the surpassing strength and beauty of its horses lives a rugged little pony named Fritz. Though he is sturdy and good-hearted, the people pay him little heed until one fateful day when his humble strength comes to the rescue.

Also written and illustrated by Brett:
♥ *Berlioz the Bear*
♥ *The Hat*
♥ *The Mitten*

❤ *The Three Snow Bears*
❤ *The Umbrella*

Margaret Wise Brown

Goodnight Moon, 1947. Illustrated by Clement Hurd.

The absolute classic of bedtime storybooks, this is a simple, picturesque poem about a bunny who doesn't want to go to bed. Delaying the inevitable moment, he says "goodnight" to everything in his room, including the old woman whispering "Hush."

The Runaway Bunny, 1942. Illustrated by Clement Hurd.

I love this story of the little bunny who could not escape the love of his mother. He says he will be a fish, but she says she will be the fisherman that captures him. He says he will be a boat, but she says she will be the wind that guides him. Reassuring and warm, this story affirms the strength of a mother's love.

Also written by Brown:
❤ *The Golden Egg Book*
❤ *The Little Fir Tree*
❤ *The Little Island*
❤ *Wait Till the Moon Is Full*

Eve Bunting

Train to Somewhere, 1996. Illustrated by Ronald Himler.

An orphan bound for the West on the famed adoption trains of the pioneer days, Marianne yearns to find her mother as she makes the long journey to her adoptive family in Somewhere, Ohio. This heartbreaking but deeply redemptive story is based on the real history of many orphaned children. The book includes impressionistic watercolor illustrations.

Also written by Bunting:
- ♥ *How Many Days to America?*
- ♥ *The Wall*
- ♥ *The Wednesday Surprise*

Nancy White Carlstrom

Does God Know How to Tie Shoes?, 1993. Illustrated by Lori McElrath-Eslick.

With lush, realistic paintings of childhood, this book chronicles a little girl's simple questions about God. A good read-aloud for introducing spiritual concepts to small children.

Also written by Carlstrom:
- ♥ *Glory*
- ♥ *Grandpappy*

♥ Jesse Bear series
♥ *The Snow Speaks*

Barbara Cooney (author and illustrator)

Miss Rumphius, 1982.

With her distinctive illustrations of piquant scenes and children of yesteryear, Barbara Cooney is one of the most-loved children's illustrators around. *Miss Rumphius* is one of her best and is one of my mom's favorite picture books. Alice Rumphius is a spunky little Victorian girl who has decided to do three things when she grows up: see the wide world, live in a cottage by the sea, and fulfill her grandfather's challenge that she leave the world more beautiful.

Roxaboxen, 1991. Written by Alice McLerran.

A favorite in my family that inspired many sessions of make-believe, *Roxaboxen* is the tale of an imaginary town on the edge of the desert. Using cactus, stick horses, and smooth black pebbles, a group of children create their own small but vibrant world. If you read this to your kids, be prepared for a new Roxaboxen to spring up in your own backyard!

Only Opal, 1994. Written by Opal Whiteley and Jane Bolton.

The aching, true tale of Opal Whiteley, an orphan in the early 1900s, this story is a collection of quotes from the journal she kept on thousands of scraps of paper. Companioned in her loneliness by a kind neighbor, a pet mouse she names Felix Mendelssohn, and a beloved tree dubbed Michael Raphael, Opal kept an eye and heart awake to beauty even in the midst of pain.

Also illustrated by Barbara Cooney:
♥ *Chanticleer and the Fox* (adapted by Barbara Cooney from Geoffrey Chaucer)
♥ *Eleanor* (written by Barbara Cooney)
♥ *Emily* (written by Michael Bedard)
♥ *Emma* (written by Wendy Kesselman)
♥ *Hattie and the Wild Waves* (written by Barbara Cooney)
♥ *Island Boy* (written by Barbara Cooney)
♥ *Ox-Cart Man* (written by Donald Hall)
♥ *When the Sky Is Like Lace* (written by Elinor Landor Horwitz)

Marguerite de Angeli (author and illustrator)

Thee, Hannah!, 1940.

De Angeli was known for her hands-on research into the widely varying stories she wrote of children in diverse cultures and historical times. Beloved for her joyful illustrations, her books are often considered collector's items. *Thee, Hannah!*, the first book I read by de Angeli, is the story of a bright little Quaker girl in the dangerous days of the

Underground Railroad. Hannah loves the frills forbidden by her family's plain way of life and longs for the styles of her time. Only when she encounters a runaway slave does she begin to value the simple life and strong faith of her family.

Yonie Wondernose, 1944.

With his father's nickname for him marking his penchant for irrepressible curiosity, little Yonnie Wondernose stumbles into many an adventurous scrape on his family's Amish farm. This is an amusing read-aloud for boys and a colorful portrait of Amish life.

Also written and illustrated by de Angeli:
♥ *Bright April*
♥ *Henner's Lydia*
♥ *Just Like David*
♥ *The Lion in the Box*
♥ *Skippack School*
♥ Ted and Nina series

Tommie dePaola (author and illustrator)

The Clown of God, 1978.

With a folk art style and a love of traditional tales, Paola has carved a niche of great picture books entirely his own. One of my favorites, *The Clown of God* is part of his series on Christian saints and legends. Giovanni is a homeless tramp with a talent for juggling. At first beloved for his painted clown's face and feats of balance, he loses his skill and his heart until a fateful Christmas Eve when he finds refuge and a miracle in a little stone church. Based on an Italian folk tale, this is a beautiful Christmas book. DePaola's series on Christian saints and legends also includes:

- ♥ *Christopher: The Holy Giant*
- ♥ *The Miracles of Jesus*
- ♥ *The Parables of Jesus*
- ♥ *Patrick: Patron Saint of Ireland*
- ♥ *Petook: An Easter Story*

Nana Upstairs & Nana Downstairs, 1973.

Tommy has two Nanas—his grandmother downstairs and his great-grandmother upstairs. This heartwarming story is a lovely picture of the treasure Tommy has in his multi-generational family.

Also by dePaola:
- ♥ *Four Stories for Four Seasons*
- ♥ *Pascual and the Kitchen Angels*
- ♥ *The Quilt Story* (author Tony Johnston)

Roger Duvoisin (author and illustrator)

Petunia series, 1950.

A featherbrained goose with a good heart, Petunia is plagued by restless curiosity. Her adventures in the big city and her thirst for wisdom lead her to discover the true nature of learning. Duvoisin wrote outstanding character lessons into his quirky, humorous Petunia tales, which include:

 ♥ *Petunia*
 ♥ *Petunia, Beware!*
 ♥ *Petunia's Christmas*

Margaret Early (author and illustrator)

William Tell, 1991.

Margaret Early's illustrated retellings of classic stories are worth collecting for the sheer beauty of her intricate artwork. Her filigree-like detail, hand-drawn borders illumined with gold, and paintings in a high artistic style complement classic tales from literature and history. A huge amount of historical research and detail goes into the drawings for these world-famous stories.

This is a beautiful rendition of the historical legend of the skillful archer William Tell, who shot an apple off his son's head and helped to bring about Switzerland's independence. Adventure, history, and great art all in one, this is a fitting read-aloud for school or entertainment.

Also written and illustrated by Early:
- ♥ *Ali Baba and the Forty Thieves*
- ♥ *Romeo and Juliet*
- ♥ *Sleeping Beauty*

Valerie Flournoy

The Patchwork Quilt, 1985. Illustrated by Jerry Pinkney.

When she begins work on her last quilted "masterpiece," Tanya's grandmother must convince her granddaughter of its value. As the quilt grows with patches from costumes, clothes, and memories made in the family, Tanya is captivated; and when Grandmother falls ill, she determines to finish the masterpiece. I am always warmed by this poignant story of family heritage with its realistic watercolor illustrations.

Tanya's Reunion, 1995. Illustrated by Jerry Pinkney.

This sequel to *The Patchwork Quilt* follows Tanya and her grandmother to a family reunion at the old homestead in Virginia. Initially disappointed by the dusty house, Tanya is once again blessed as her grandmother's gift of wonder shepherds her into a love for her own heritage.

Mem Fox

Wilfrid Gordon McDonald Partridge, 1984. Illustrated by
Julie Vivas.

Right next to an old people's home lives an exuberant little
boy who is the proud owner of four names. Miss Nancy, his
favorite old lady, has lost her memory, and he is determined
to find it for her again. The bright, playful illustrations of
this gentle story by well-known Australian author Mem Fox
show the gift of remembrance brought through a little boy's
kindness.

Also written by Fox:
♥ *Harriet, You'll Drive Me Wild!*
♥ *Time for Bed*

Elizabeth Friedrich

Leah's Pony, 1996. Illustrated by Michael Garland.

Set in the dust of the Great Plains during the Depression,
this is the moving story of a girl who sells her beloved pony
to help her bankrupt family. Her act inspires the people of her
town to rally together for what became known as a "penny
auction." Garland's oil paintings are thought provoking and
historically accurate.

Don Freeman (author and illustrator)

Corduroy series 1968–2008.

This tale of the teddy bear Corduroy—who has sat on a store shelf longing for a home, a friend, and a new button, until the day that Lisa finds him—will appeal to all kids who have a particular affection for stuffed animals. The series includes:

♥ *A Pocket for Corduroy*
♥ *Corduroy and Company*

Libba Moore Gray

My Mama Had a Dancing Heart, 1995. Illustrated by Raúl Colón

Told through the eyes of a young girl remembering her mother's dancing heart, this radiant story and its fanciful illustrations capture the joy of a mother who celebrated life throughout the seasons and taught her daughter to do the same.

Also written by Moore:
♥ *When Uncle Took the Fiddle*

Michael Hague (illustrator)

Alphabears: An ABC Book, 1984. Written by Kathleen Hague.

This is one of the first picture books I remember reading. I loved this darling alphabet book, illustrated with Hague's whimsical bears with distinct personalities. Hague's artwork has a touch of timelessness that always catches my eye; his rich colors and busy illustrations fill every corner of the page, and there is a fairy-tale quality to his pictures that makes his books highly collectible. Read this aloud with a little one, and I guarantee delight.

The Children's Book of Faith, 2000. Compiled and edited by William J. Bennett.

Bennett compiled this lovely picture book to "help youngsters learn that we all belong to the Almighty." Hague's engaging pictures add depth to the simply retold tales from Scripture and stories by Tolstoy, Wilde, and other authors. This collection of stories for young children is great for reading aloud and discussion.

Also illustrated by Hague:
- ♥ *Aesop's Fables*
- ♥ *The Children's Book of Virtues* (compiled and edited by William J. Bennett)
- ♥ *The Teddy Bears' Picnic* (written by Jimmy Kennedy)
- ♥ *The Velveteen Rabbit* (written by Margery Williams)
- ♥ *The Wind in the Willows* (written by Kenneth Grahame)

Donald Hall

Lucy's Summer, 1995. Illustrated by Michael McCurdy.

Based on memories from the author's mother, this summer tale of a family in 1900s New Hampshire reveals the yesteryear pleasures of canning a multitude of garden produce, attending Fourth of July parades, traveling to Boston, and witnessing the opening of a hat shop in the family front room. Captivating colored scratchboard drawings give it an earthy, historic feel.

Ox-Cart Man, 1979. Illustrated by Barbara Cooney.
Caldecott Medalist.

Ox-Cart Man is the chronicle of a year in the life of an early American colonial family. The careful illustrations of period farm work, handcrafts, and simple pleasures complement the satisfying tale of a family's joyful work, harvest abundance, and quiet joy in a simple life. This makes a particularly cozy autumn read-aloud.

Also written by Hall:
♥ *Lucy's Christmas*
♥ *The Milkman's Boy*

James Herriot

James Herriot's Treasury for Children, 1992. Illustrated by Ruth Brown and Peter Barrett.

This carefully selected collection of James Herriot's most beloved animal stories is simply retold for a younger audience. The earthy, realistic illustrations greatly enhance the bright charm of Herriot's tales of veterinary life in 1940s England. This book has been a family favorite since my childhood. It is especially satisfying if read on a rainy Sunday afternoon with hot tea.

Hilary Horder Hippely

A Song for Lena, 1996. Illustrated by Leslie Baker.

A haunting song and a mysterious man set the tone for this stirring tale of rural Hungary. When Lena offers a beggar a hot piece of her family's special harvest-time strudel, he responds with a stirring musical gift that touches the family forever. The wistful, expressive pictures and the inclusion of a family recipe for apple strudel make this a gem of a picture book.

Russell Hoban

Frances series, 1960–1970. Illustrated by Lillian Hoban.

I grew up loving the antics and songs of the spunky little badger Frances. Written and illustrated by a husband-and-wife team, these books find Frances in amusing adventures and family events common to many young children. *Bread and Jam for Frances*, my favorite, is about Frances's discovery that being a picky eater isn't all that fun. These funny, practical stories with their lively black-and-white drawings will make your children laugh. The series includes:

♥ *Bread and Jam for Frances*
♥ *A Birthday for Frances*
♥ *Best Friends for Frances*
♥ *A Baby Sister for Frances*
♥ *Bedtime for Frances* (illustrated by Garth Williams)

Katharine Holabird

Angelina series, 1983–2008. Illustrated by Helen Craig.

Little girls will love this series about a dainty mouse who longs to become a ballerina. The first book grants her the beginning of her dream, and the rest of the series follows Angelina through surprises, performances, and scrapes with her family and friends in their close-knit town. The lovely illustrations are based on the artist's childhood in an English village.

The series includes:
- ♥ *Angelina and the Princess*
- ♥ *Angelina at the Fair*
- ♥ *Angelina's Christmas*
- ♥ *Angelina's Birthday Surprise*
- ♥ *Angelina's Baby Sister*

Margaret Hodges

Saint George and the Dragon, 1984. Illustrated by Trina Schart
Rich, elaborate illustrations in a medieval style and haunting, lyrical prose make this version of the legend of St. George irresistible. Deeply beautiful and rich in old English flavor, this book brings to life Princess Una's quest to find a hero to save her castle and country from a cruel and deadly dragon.

Also written by Hodges:
- ♥ *Brother Francis and the Friendly Beasts*
- ♥ *The Kitchen Knight: A Tale of King Arthur*
- ♥ *The Legend of St. Christopher*
- ♥ *Silent Night: The Song and Its Story*

Deborah Hopkinson

Sweet Clara and the Freedom Quilt, 1993. Illustrated by James Ransome.

The hopeful story of a slave girl who used her skill as a seamstress to create a patchwork quilt that mapped out the paths of the Underground Railroad. After her escape, the quilt was left behind so that others could follow its brightly stitched pathway to freedom. Brilliantly colored, realistic paintings enhance the text.

Apples to Oregon, 2004. Illustrated by Nancy Carpenter.

It's 1847, and Papa has decided to move the family west to Oregon, but he can't bear to leave his cherished fruit trees behind. With the help of his plucky daughter Delicious, Papa and the family embark on a rollicking, adventurous trek through the wilderness with a rickety cart of beloved trees. Loosely based on a true story, this exuberant tale offers a slice of history and a whole lot of fun.

Also written by Hopkinson:
- ♥ *Maria's Comet*
- ♥ *A Packet of Seeds*
- ♥ *Saving Strawberry Farm*

Gloria Houston

My Great-Aunt Arizona, 1992. Illustrated by Susan
Condie Lamb.

A lively girl in "long, full skirts and high-button shoes,"
Arizona Hughes loved to dance and sing and dream of
faraway places. Although she became a simple teacher in
the one-room schoolhouse of her childhood, her continuing
enthusiasm for life, dreams, and adventure inspired several
generations of students. The vibrant illustrations capture the
vim of Arizona's spirit and her love of beauty.

The Year of the Perfect Christmas Tree, 1988. Illustrated by
Barbara Cooney.

With Christmas coming in the Appalachians, Ruthie
and her mother must go in search of the perfect tree that
Father marked in the spring before he went to war. A tale of
Christmas hope.

Shirley Hughes (author and illustrator)

Angel Mae, 1989.

This is the story of Angel Mae, a well-meaning but accident-
prone little girl who is cast as an angel in the Christmas
play and who brings the cast and audience to their knees.
Hughes's illustrations thoroughly capture the quirks and
cuteness of small children.

Also written and illustrated by Hughes:
- ♥ All About Alfie series
- ♥ *Dogger*

Tony Johnston

Yonder, 1988. Illustrated by Lloyd Bloom.

A hushed, poignant story poem that follows the life of a young couple as they settle a piece of land and build a home and family. Through the years and seasons, some things change, but many lovely things remain. Subtle poetry, radiant colors, and impressionistic illustrations capture the sweet quiet of family heritage.

Grandpa's Song, 1991. Illustrated by Brad Sneed.

Grandpa has a voice to shake the house down and a love of life just about as big. But when things begin to slip his mind, including his own best song, his grandkids have to help him remember. Jaunty, exaggerated pictures make for a lively, touching tale.

Also written by Johnston:
- ♥ *Amber on the Mountain*
- ♥ *The Harmonica*
- ♥ *Noel*

Steven Kellogg (author and illustrator)

Johnny Appleseed, 1988.

To read a Steven Kellogg book is to enter a matchless imaginative world crammed full of zany, cheerful creatures; tall tales; bigger-than-life heroes; and constant adventure. Based on the life of John Chapman, the big-hearted pioneer who brought apple seeds to many of the early settlers in the Midwest, *Johnny Appleseed is* part history, part legend, and part pure fun. Your kids will love this rollicking tale of Johnny's expansive generosity, courage, and laughter. Other books of American legends by Kellogg include:

- ♥ *Mike Fink: A Tall Tale*
- ♥ *Paul Bunyan*
- ♥ *Pecos Bill: A Tall Tale*
- ♥ *Yankee Doodle*

The Island of the Skog, 1973.

It's National Rodent Day, and Bouncer the mouse along with his team of Rowdies and several of their friends have decided to mount an expedition to escape the persecution of the neighborhood cats. When they land on the Island of the Skog, the mice find evidence of a mysterious creature that they must conquer before they can claim their new home. Humorous and sweet, this is a tale of friendships old and new.

Also by Kellogg:
- ♥ *Can I Keep Him?*
- ♥ *Engelbert the Elephant* (Tom Paxton, author)
- ♥ *If You Made a Million* (David M. Schwartz, author)
- ♥ *Pinkerton, Behave!*

Natalie Kinsey-Warnock

The Bear That Heard Crying, 1993. Illustrated by Ted Rand.

This book is based on the true story of little Sarah Whitcher, who was lost in the wilderness around her family's New Hampshire homestead in 1873. Found after a stranger had a dream about her whereabouts, she claimed to have been protected by a big, black, friendly dog . . . whose prints looked very much like a bear's. Watercolor illustrations.

From Dawn Till Dusk, 1992. Illustrated by Mary Azarian.

This simple book is a nostalgic view of the author's childhood on a Vermont farm. Picturesque woodblock illustrations depict the hearty goodness of maple sugaring accompanied by homemade doughnuts, harvesting the family fields, playing baseball with the fireflies, and gathering in the abundance of harvest for the long winter ahead. An uplifting, joyful reminiscence.

Also written by Kinsey-Warnock:
- ♥ *A Christmas Like Helen's*

- ❤ *A Farm of Her Own*
- ❤ *The Fiddler of the Northern Lights*
- ❤ *Nora's Ark*
- ❤ *The Summer of Stanley*

Patricia Kirkpatrick

Plowie: A Story from the Prairie, 1994. Illustrated by Joey Kirkpatrick.

Written and illustrated by a team of sisters, this is the true tale of their grandmother's childhood on the prairie, focusing on the mystery of a tiny porcelain doll found in her father's fields and the treasure it becomes to each generation. Rustic illustrations vividly depict the time period.

Robert Lawson (author and illustrator)

They Were Strong and Good, 1940. Caldecott Medalist.

This highly entertaining account of several generations of the author's family chronicles the adventures of sailors, farmers, and soldiers, each of whose stories ends with the comment that "they were strong and good." This is a book about heritage and pride in one's roots, with a hearty affirmation of the treasure of a courageous, good heritage. The pen-and-ink illustrations are bursting with action and humor.

Beverly Lewis

Annika's Secret Wish, 2000. Illustrated by Pamela Querin.

Christmas Eve finds Annika deep in the wondrous preparations for her family's Swedish Christmas, especially the making of the rice pudding with a hidden almond that gives a wish to one lucky person. Annika knows exactly what she would wish for...or does she? This is a tender tale of a little girl's compassion, accompanied by luminous, idyllic illustrations of Swedish dress and holiday tradition.

Kim Lewis (author and illustrator)

First Snow, 1993.

The earthy tones of Kim Lewis's illustrations captivated me the first time I saw them. Based on her life on a Yorkshire farm, her books accurately capture the hard work, warm hearth, and wind-swept essence of life on a family farm on the moors. *First Snow* follows a mother and her little girl into the magical chill of autumn's first snow and the search for a lost teddy bear. These family-affirming books are great for cuddle-up read-alouds.

Also written and illustrated by Lewis:
- ♥ *Friends*
- ♥ *Goodnight, Harry*
- ♥ *Here We Go, Harry*

❥ *Hooray for Harry*
❥ *Just Like Floss*
❥ *Little Baa*
❥ *Little Lamb*
❥ *One Summer Day*
❥ *A Quilt for Baby*

Thomas Locker (author and illustrator)

The Boy Who Held Back the Sea, 1987. Co-written with Lenny Hort.

Thomas Locker is a well-respected artist who turned to children's book illustration as a means of exposing children to fine art. His paintings are reminiscent of the Hudson River landscape artists. In this traditional story, Jan is a careless young Dutch boy who avoids school and loves mischief. When his capers lead him to find a leak in the mighty dike near his town, he discovers a courage and grit he didn't know he had.

The Young Artist, 1989.

A gifted young artist, Adrian delights to paint the fields and forests near his home, but his livelihood depends on the portraits he paints for the haughty, nitpicking courtiers in the nearby palace. When the king himself demands a portrait of his court, it seems Adrian may fail . . . until he sets eyes on the princess. Locker's luminescent paintings of palace life are reminiscent of Dutch masters like Vermeer.

Also illustrated by Thomas Locker:
- ♥ *Calico and Tin Horns* (written by Candace Christiansen)
- ♥ *Family Farm* (written by Thomas Locker)
- ♥ *Grandfather's Christmas Tree* (written by Keith Strand)
- ♥ *Home: A Journey Through America* (compiled by Thomas Locker)
- ♥ *The Mare on the Hill* (written by Thomas Locker)
- ♥ *Sailing with the Wind* (written by Thomas Locker)
- ♥ *Snow Toward Evening: A Year in a River Valley* (written by Josette Frank)
- ♥ *To Climb a Waterfall* (written by Thomas Locker)
- ♥ *Washington Irving's Rip Van Winkle* (retold by Thomas Locker with Ashley Foehner)
- ♥ *Where the River Begins* (written by Thomas Locker)

P. J. Lynch (author and illustrator)

The Christmas Miracle of Jonathan Toomey, 1995. Written by Susan Wojciechowski.

Lynch is one of the few illustrators who possess the gift of creating art that is realistic and yet conveys a sense of the ideal—that is warm and beguiling while retaining a sense of simplicity. In this collectible Christmas story, the gloomy Mr. Toomey is hired by a widow and her son to carve them a crèche scene and finds his own heart coming alive along with the crèche scene creations.

When Jessie Came Across the Sea, 1997. Written by Amy Hest.

With a dream-filled heart and fingers skilled in making fine lace, Jessie journeys across the sea to find a good new life. Romantic and heartwarming, this is a tale of the courage and beauty that so many immigrants brought into their new country.

Also illustrated by Lynch:
- ♥ *The Bee-Man of Orn* (written by Frank R. Stockton)
- ♥ *The Gift of the Magi* (written by O. Henry)
- ♥ *Melisande* (written by E. Nesbit)
- ♥ *Oscar Wilde Stories for Children*

Christopher Manson (author and illustrator)

Two Travelers, 1990.

Isaac serves the Emperor Charlemagne and has been sent to make a treaty with the grand Caliph of Baghdad. When the Caliph entrusts Isaac with the gift of a magnificent elephant named Abulabaz, the two begin the journey home in an awkward quiet that ends in a hearty friendship. One of my favorite picture books, this features colorful, realistic illustrations with a storybook feel.

Also illustrated by Manson:
- ♥ *Good King Wenceslas* (traditional carol by John M. Neale)
- ♥ *Over the River and Through the Wood* (poem by Lydia Maria Child)
- ♥ *Till Year's Good End* (written by W. Nikola-Lisa)
- ♥ *The Tree in the Wood* (adapted from nursery song)

Barbara Mitchell

Down Buttermilk Lane, 1993. Illustrated by John Sandford.

My family loves the homey, autumnal illustrations so much that we set out this book every year during the fall. This simple, life-enriching account of a day in the life of an Amish family offers a tour through a world of crimson leaves, chicken potpie, and bumpy rides in a black buggy.

Patricia MacLachlan

All the Places to Love, 1994. Illustrated by Mike Wimmer.

From Mama's windswept hilltop to Grandpa's rafter in the barn, each scene of this story—told through the eyes of the littlest boy—reflects the favorite place of one person in a farming family. The sweeping pictures of countryside and farm capture the beauty and affection so strongly binding the family to each other and their bit of earth.

Through Grandpa's Eyes, 1980. Illustrated by Deborah Kogan Ray.

This is the winsomely written story of one little boy's day spent seeing life through the eyes of his blind grandfather. The lyrical descriptions of a child's wondrous experience of sound, taste, and smell approach poetry. Reveling in the very simplest of meals and activities, the little boy experiences the world in a wholly different way through his grandfather's guidance. A sweet look at a grandfather's love for his grandson as well. Faintly colored pencil drawings.

Also written by Patricia MacLachlan
- ♥ *Painting the Wind*
- ♥ *Three Names*
- ♥ *What You Know First*

Jacqueline Briggs Martin

Snowflake Bentley, 1998. Illustrated by Mary Azarian.
Caldecott Medalist.

With faintly colored woodcuts and fresh, engaging prose, this beautiful book tells the captivating story of the first man to photograph a snowflake. Snowflake Bentley was awed by the beauty he discovered in nature, and he photographed over 5,000 snowflakes, never finding two alike. This historic tale celebrates his exploration of creation.

Also written by Martin:
♥ *Banjo Granny*
♥ *Good Times on Grandfather Mountain*

Robert McCloskey (author and illustrator)

Make Way for Ducklings, 1941. Caldecott Medalist.

Written in the 1940s and '50s, McCloskey's books remain classics to this day. This tale about a mama duck and her little brood making their home in Boston Public Gardens is his best-known book for children. It takes a kind policeman to protect the ducklings as they venture out into the frightening streets of Boston. Make way! Charming pen-and-ink illustrations.

One Morning in Maine, 1952. Caldecott Honor Book.

Based on his family's summer living on a Maine island, this book (and its partner, *Blueberries for Sal*) was inspired by McCloskey's daughter Sarah. *One Morning in Maine* is the lively story of high-spirited Sal, a little girl who has just lost her tooth and is going for a morning sail with her dad. Sal's comic scrapes and questions make the day, and her family's expressions are unforgettable. The ebullient black-and-white illustrations capture a nostalgic view of a simple Maine town, making this a refreshing summer read-aloud.

Also written and illustrated by McCloskey:
♥ *Blueberries for Sal*

- ♥ *Burt Dow, Deep-Water Man*
- ♥ *Lentil*
- ♥ *Time of Wonder*

Ann Whitford Paul

The Seasons Sewn: A Year in Patchwork, 1996. Illustrated by Michael McCurdy.

This book presents the lives and traditions of early America through the history of well-known quilting patterns. Exploring specific quilting designs with names such as "Tea Leaf," "Little Giant," or "Jack in the Pulpit," the author explains the work, celebration, and traditions they represent, patching together a compelling story quilt of her own. The woodcut illustrations are a fit accompaniment to the rustic, historic feel of the book.

Also written by Paul:
- ♥ *Eight Hands Round: A Patchwork Alphabet*

Mildred Phillips

The Sign in Mendel's Window, 1985. Illustrated by Margot Zemach.

A whimsical, topsy-turvy little tale about a Jewish tailor named Mendel who is falsely accused of stealing. His clever wife and the enthusiastic town set out to prove his innocence.

Patricia Polacco (author and illustrator)

Thunder Cake, 1990.

I was browsing a rambling bookstore in Asheville when I first came upon this appealing tale of a grandmother has just the right remedy for her granddaughter's fear of thunderstorms. When the first rumble fills the sky, Grandma announces that it is time to make a thunder cake and draws her granddaughter into the bravery required for the preparation: going out to the barn for eggs, counting the seconds between thunder grumbles, and sitting down to eat just as the storm breaks. Polacco's pencil and gouache (a sort of watercolor) drawings are brimming with life, patterns, and color.

Also written and illustrated by Polacco:
- ♥ *The Bee Tree*
- ♥ *Chicken Sunday*
- ♥ *Ginger and Petunia*
- ♥ *Just Plain Fancy*

❤ *The Keeping Quilt*
❤ *My Rotten Redheaded Older Brother*
❤ *An Orange for Frankie*
❤ *Something About Hensley's*

Cynthia Rylant

When I Was Young in the Mountains, 1982. Illustrated by
Diane Goode. Caldecott Honor Book.

One of our earliest family favorites, this is a simple tale
of a little girl and her brother raised by their grandparents
in the Appalachian Mountains. This family-affirming story
pictures the joy of good meals and outdoor play, as well as
the simplicity of the author's rural childhood.

The Relatives Came, 1985. Illustrated by Steven Gammell.
Caldecott Honor Book.

This rollicking tale of a family reunion and the crazy
delight of a big family is crammed to the corners with
hilarious drawings. The humorous narration brings to life
the boisterous summer adventures of a family reunion and
conveys the deep joy of celebrating life with those we love,
however zany they may be.

The Blue Hill Meadows, 1997. Illustrated by Ellen Beier.

This story portrays four seasons in the life of Willie Meadow
as he grows up in the quiet pastures of Blue Hill, Virginia.

Gently illustrated in pale colors, the book follows Willie through the seasons, each yielding its own simple treasure, whether a fishing trip, a wild blizzard, or the cuddly joy of a new puppy.

Also written by Rylant:
- ♥ *Bunny Bungalow*
- ♥ *Henry and Mudge* series
- ♥ *In November*
- ♥ *Mr. Putter and Tabby* series
- ♥ *The Old Woman Who Named Things*
- ♥ *Thimbleberry Stories*
- ♥ *The Van Gogh Café*

Scott Russell Sanders

Warm as Wool, 1992. Illustrated by Helen Cogancherry.

Based on the true story of a determined young pioneer woman whose heart was set on a flock of sheep to provide her family with soft, warm wool. This is a settler's tale of resolute courage and family spunk, illustrated with warm, realistic paintings.

Aurora Means Dawn, 1989. Illustrated by Jill Kastner.

In the year 1800, the Sheldon family of nine arrived near Aurora, Ohio, in the midst of a raging storm. Loosely based on historical fact, *Aurora* is a heartening, realistic story of the pioneer days, exploring both the exhilaration and hardships of pioneer life. The impressionistic illustrations aptly capture the moods of hope and endurance.

Daniel San Souci (author and illustrator)

North Country Night, 1990.

This book guides its reader through the moonlit woods of the north country of America on a winter's night. Wolves patter through the pine trees, snow gilds the ground, and all is silent, blue, and still. A beautiful glimpse of nature, this book vividly captures the wildness of the nighttime woods.

Also illustrated by San Souci:
- ♥ *Island Magic*
- ♥ *Potter*
- ♥ *Red Wolf Country*

David Shannon (illustrator)

The Acrobat and the Angel, 1999. Written by Mark Shannon.

With drawings that exude a boundless energy in their imaginative portrayals of people and nature, Shannon's books are a treasure trove of radiant yet simple pictures that aptly apprehend the nature of his imaginative tales. His drawings for *Acrobat* poignantly capture the grace and joy of a young boy in a monastery who loves to somersault and dance, whose offering of joy to God became the stuff of legend. A beautiful story, based on an Italian folk tale.

The Bunyans, 1996. Written by Audrey Wood.
Who could have known that the brawny Bunyan family trekked across America and set to work to create some of the great American monuments? A delightful, zany tall tale weaving a story around the legendary John Bunyan and his equally amazing family, this is also a picture book tour of American landmarks. Bright, sweeping illustrations capture the humor and wonder of the fanciful story.

Peter Spier (author and illustrator)

Bored—Nothing to Do!, 1978.
A Dutch artist known for his lively pen, ink, and watercolor drawings, Spier fills his books with busy scenes of the circus, city, or just a child's backyard. If you look closely, you can often find something amusing going on in the background of his pictures. My brothers loved *Bored—Nothing to Do!* for its realistic and madcap portrayal of the adventures of two restless brothers on an afternoon search for entertainment.

Also written and illustrated by Spier:
♥ *Peter Spier's Circus*
♥ *The Erie Canal*

- ♥ *The Fox Went Out on a Chilly Night*
- ♥ *Peter Spier's Rain*
- ♥ *The Star-Spangled Banner*

Sarah Stewart

The Money Tree, 1991. Illustrated by David Small.

Sarah Stewart is a winsome storyteller whose books include her husband David Small's homey, whimsical illustrations. In *The Money Tree*, Miss McGillicuddy has a very strange tree growing in her garden. The bigger it gets, the more people come to beg a few of its leaves. She doesn't mind and just watches from her house with her birds, books, and freshly baked bread. This fanciful tale brings a subtle lesson in contentment.

Also written by Stewart and illustrated by Small:
- ♥ *The Gardener*
- ♥ *The Journey*
- ♥ *The Library*

Cyndy Szekeres (author and illustrator)

The Deep Blue Sky Twinkles with Stars, 1998.

With their cuddly animals and simple tales, Szekeres' books were some of my earliest bedtime stories. Perfectly suited to little children, these amusing stories are all about the capers of bunnies, puppies, and kittens. *The Deep Blue Sky Twinkles with Stars* is a humorous tale of five little bunnies and their bedtime wishes. Hot cocoa and many hugs figure into this good-night story.

Also written and illustrated by Szekeres:
- ♥ *Child's First Book of Poems*
- ♥ *Cyndy Szekeres' Favorite Two-Minute Stories*
- ♥ *Good Night, Sammy*
- ♥ *Sammy's Special Day*
- ♥ *Scaredy Cat*

Tasha Tudor (author and illustrator)

A Time to Keep, 1977.

My mom and I have been endlessly inspired by Tasha Tudor's imagination and determination to live and dress in the old-fashioned way she loved. This illustrated tour through the seasons reflects the reality of Tasha's life, sharing the winsome eighteenth-century traditions that she kept with her family on their Vermont farm. With detailed illustrations of harvest celebrations, garden work, and the puppet shows for which she was famous, this book will spark you to begin new traditions and seasonal celebrations in your own home.

Corgiville Fair, 1971.

The first in Tudor's delightful picture-book series on the village of Corgiville, this is the rollicking tale of the Corgis' annual fair and the naughty rogue dogs who might upset it. The busy, charming illustrations are based on Tudor's own Corgi colony.

Also by Tasha Tudor:
- ♥ *Around the Year*
- ♥ *The Christmas Cat* (with Efner Tudor Holmes)
- ♥ *Corgiville Christmas*
- ♥ *The Great Corgiville Kidnapping*
- ♥ *The Night Before Christmas* (Clement Clarke Moore, author)
- ♥ *1 Is One*
- ♥ *Pumpkin Moonshine*

Chris Van Allsburg (author and illustrator)

The Mysteries of Harris Burdick, 1984.

Van Allsburg's drawings convey a potent tang of mystery; each of his enigmatic pictures whispers a challenge to the reader's imagination. *Mysteries* is a mystifying collection of illustrations supposedly brought to a publisher by a stranger named Harris Burdick, who promises to return the next day but is never seen again. Each picture has only a single opening line. The story is left to the fancy of the reader. The mystery and possibility of this picture book are thrilling.

Also written and illustrated by Van Allsburg:
- ♥ *The Garden of Abdul Gasazi*
- ♥ *The Polar Express*
- ♥ *The Stranger*
- ♥ *The Wreck of the Zephyr*

Audrey Wood

Quick as a Cricket, 1994. Illustrated by Don Wood.

Brimming with a sprightly little boy's exuberance in his own prowess and energy, this book uses big, bright pictures to illustrate his imagination as he compares his speed and skill to a myriad of strange creatures. Good for active boys who love the outdoors.

Jane Yolen

Harvest Home, 2000. Illustrated by Greg Shed.

Shot through with the deep golden light of late summer and the rich rhythm of the harvest season, this book celebrates a way of life almost forgotten in our time. With deeply colored pictures and a lyrical text capturing the simple work, song, and joy of harvest time, it comes close to poetry in its simplicity and depth of beauty.

Honkers, 1993. Illustrated by Leslie A. Baker.

Sent to stay with Grandy and Nana on their farm while her mother is ill, Betsy is greeted with the gift of an unhatched egg that soon opens to reveal the plucky gosling Little Bit. Through the "long and short" days of the summer, Betsy enjoys her new friend and wishes for her mother, but autumn is coming when both she and her Little Bit will have to fly away to their far-off homes. Poignant watercolors in muted tones.

Also written by Jane Yolen:
- ♥ *All Those Secrets of the World*
- ♥ *Owl Moon*
- ♥ *Raising Yoder's Barn*

6
The Golden Age Classics

*A classic is classic not because it conforms to
certain structural rules, or fits certain definitions
(of which its author had quite probably never heard).
It is classic because of a certain eternal
and irrepressible freshness.*

~ Edith Wharton

On a storm-blown Sunday afternoon in a creaky old manor house in England, I rediscovered the timeless delight of classic children's books. It took me by surprise. I was one of about thirty international students studying and living in England for the summer, and this was our first British teatime all together. A shy, awkward silence had fallen about us as we tried our best to balance philosophy, sophistication, and hot mugs of tea, when one of our tutors said something that sent us all staring.

"Let's read *Winnie-the-Pooh.*"

A swift current of suppressed mirth ran the length of the room, but we were up for some fun, and the tutor assigned each person a part in the story. Pooh's expedition to the North Pole was the story of choice, and before we knew what was happening we were immersed in the comical, compact world of the Hundred Acre Woods. The story had all of us—tutors, college students, post-graduates, old, and young—laughing until our sides literally ached.

Amidst my giggles, I marveled at the ageless cleverness of the tale and the artfully captured personality of each animal (with resemblances to a few humans I could name). That unexpected hour brought back to me all the delight of the imaginative stories that so shaped my childhood. I left that day intent on rereading my old favorites.

Such is the peculiar charm of the children's classics. They have a staying power and a timeless beauty that endears them to adult and child alike. Of the many books I read throughout my childhood, these were the stories that most delighted and formed me. I almost can't imagine childhood apart from these books.

In the last few years, though, I have found that knowledge of the children's classics is increasingly rare. It took only a brief conversation with a Canadian flight attendant who regularly flew in and out of the famed Prince Edward Island but had never heard of *Anne of Green Gables* for me to realize that the classics need reviving. That startling encounter helped me to see that in an age of media entertainment, the Golden Age books have lost their charming reputation.

Perhaps you are in the same boat as my flight attendant friend. Maybe you have never come face to face with the delight of *Winnie-the-Pooh, The Secret Garden, The Wind in the Willows,* or *Peter Pan.* If so, then you and your children are in for a marvelous adventure. These imaginative books contain some of the most beautiful stories ever written for children. I love these tales so much that I would tell you to choose them if you could only pick one type of books to read. Even if you never read any other genre of literature, your soul would be rich simply from the beauty and imagination that fill these graceful stories.

The history of these children's classics reveals some of the reason for their singular power and beauty. Written primarily in a historic blossoming of imagination during the mid-to-late nineteenth century, these books defined an era of writing that became known as the Golden Age of children's literature. The result of an unprecedented combination of social thought, artistic renewal, and fresh imagination, they broke new literary ground by being the first stories ever written specifically for the delight of children.

The birth of children's stories as a distinct literary genre was a fairly recent event, dating only to the early 1800s. Although there were some books for children before this time, they were written primarily for moral or educational instruction. The philosopher John Locke (1632–1734) was a great advocate of childhood education, but he believed children's stories should primarily educate and instruct, leaving children with a small selection of virtue tales that sacrificed any imagination or aesthetic excellence to a pointed (sometimes pedantic) morality. Folktales saw a resurgence when they were turned into "fairy tales" by French author Charles Perrault (1628–1703). His stories of Cinderella, Sleeping Beauty, and Puss in Boots are among the best-known fairy tales of all time and greatly influenced the other famous authors of the fairy-tale genre, most notably the Brothers Grimm. In 1744, John Newbery wrote a whimsical little book, *A Little Pretty Pocket Book*, that was full of games and fun verses. Written to instruct through delight, it was unique in the history of books for children to that time.

But by the mid-1800s, a unique convergence of cultural changes set the stage for the birth of a new, almost revolutionary form of literature. The first major influence was Victorian society's passion for home and family. Queen Victoria, crowned in 1838, ushered in a new era of reformed morals and respectability with her marriage to Prince Albert and her determination not to repeat the scandalous affairs of previous monarchs. The large royal family (Victoria and Albert had nine children), along with Prince Albert's strong sense of duty and decorum, shaped Victorian society. The Victorians idealized the home as a small, near-perfect world and children as innocent souls to be formed within its walls by affection, courage, and beauty. The stories written during this period reflect a spiritual atmosphere that prized nobility in word and deed, loyalty to family, the purity of childhood, and a general love of uprightness.

Another major influence was the spirited philosophy of the Romantics, who rejected the strict rationality and reason so prevalent in the Enlightenment thought that preceded it. Romanticism's passionate defense of ideal beauty and its embrace of deep emotion and unhindered imagination led to a new breed of artists, writers, and musicians who sought to imbue their creations with the full force of their imaginative ideals. As this renewed value for imagination and beauty infiltrated society, it combined with that era's Victorian ideals to foster the view that children were perhaps the only human beings untainted by cynicism and uninhibited in their experience of the world's inherent beauty. William Wordsworth, a major Romantic poet, believed that children had a purer, more intuitive existence than adults. The cultivation and entertainment of these small souls, unspoiled by adult skepticism, became a focus for skilled writers.

Some of the first writers to delve into the riches of this new cultural imagination were Christian pastors and teachers who combined their desire to pass their faith on to their children with a deep passion for beauty. Norman MacLeod, a pastor and editor of a literary periodical for children called *Good Words for the Young*, wrote a winsome spiritual allegory for children called *The Gold Thread*. Published in 1860, it was one of the first stories that used literary form and imagination specifically for children. Soon after that, *Good Words* also provided a publishing home for the spiritual fantasy of George MacDonald, a prolific Victorian writer and pastor. *At the Back of the North Wind*, a tale MacDonald wrote to convey an idea of heaven to his eleven children, was first serialized in *Good Words*.

The most dramatic historical turn came in 1865 with the publication of the now-famous *Alice's Adventures in Wonderland*. Lewis Carroll (the pseudonym of Anglican clergyman Charles Dodgson) sent the whole literary establishment plunging into Wonderland. Entirely unconcerned with moral instruction, its sole purpose was delight and the amusement of children. At the time, it was a startling new creation.

The great success of *Alice* (its first printing sold out within months) opened the door to a whole new genre of literature: children's. The new possibilities kindled the imaginations of some of the most skilled, insightful writers of the time, as well as their wealthy publishers. With a growing middle class and the greater availability of books, people saw artistic and financial possibility in stories for children. Once the door of children's literature was opened, nothing could hold back the rush of writers. *Alice* was followed within the next twenty years by such favorites as *The Princess and the Goblin, Heidi, Treasure Island,* and *Little Women* (in America). The widespread enthusiasm for these books sparked an international hunger for children's stories. The result was a feast that lasted roughly from 1865 to 1914.

The books that most characterize this era possess an atmosphere of idealized beauty, innocence, and freshly unhindered imagination. Whether set in fantastical realms or realistic settings, these stories tend to portray the secret, inner world of the imagination in which children find adventure and beauty and learn nobility. Stories such as *Peter Pan* (first published as *Peter and Wendy*), *The Wind in the Willows*, *The Story of the Treasure Seekers*, *The Water-Babies*, and *The Secret Garden* reflect that love for secret, beautiful places and the new life and growth to be discovered within them.

Robert Louis Stevenson began writing adventure stories for boys, such as *Kidnapped*, *Treasure Island*, and *The Black Arrow*. Soon there was a wide range of adventure books, including Rudyard Kipling's *The Jungle Book*, Howard Pyle's *The Merry Adventures of Robin Hood*, and Charles Kingsley's *Westward Ho!* Girls had their own beguiling heroines in such works as *Little Women*, *The Little Princess*, *Heidi*, and *Anne of Green Gables*. Beatrix Potter began a beloved set of animal tales with her bestselling work *The Tale of Peter Rabbit*. It was soon followed by Kenneth Grahame's *The Wind in the Willows* and the unforgettable and much-adored *Winnie-the-Pooh* by A. A. Milne.

That first exploration and expansion of the new frontier of children's literature lasted until around the beginning of the First World War. To this day, these stories are considered the classics of children's literature. They are remarkable for their sheer imagination, vivid beauty, and compelling, childlike adventures. To echo the words of Edith Wharton, I believe these books are classic because of their unfettered reach of imagination, the nobility and innocence of their child heroes and heroines, and the simple themes of quest, beauty, bravery, and compassion.

They are also classics because they portray true things about the world and the human heart. Though secular scholars don't always recognize it, I believe that these books are classics in large part because they portray truth, goodness, and beauty. They clearly portray moral and aesthetic goodness; they celebrate what is lovely. In these stories there is no ambiguity regarding right or wrong. Virtue, honesty, and courage are portrayed as noble and worthy of pursuit, and innocence is presented as desirable and worthy of protection.

Though they are children's tales, they have a spiritual insight, a soul-striking poignancy that is remarkable in literature of any genre. They offer a solidity of spiritual truth that satisfies our souls and shapes the way we look at the world. It is not often that moral and artistic excellence combine so well, and it is a rare thing in history for children and family to be so deeply valued. Books such as these have a far more long-lasting impact than that of mere entertainment. They picture what is true and beautiful again and again for each succeeding generation.

I hope that a love for the Golden Age children's classics will be revived in my generation and in those to follow. We need these stories to help form a culture that values the true, the good, and the beautiful. Such is the legacy of the Golden Age books. As you discover them with your children, may it be yours as well.

Children's Classics Collections

If you are interested in gathering a high-quality set of children's classics to last your children into adulthood, finding some beautiful collections is quite easy. My dad began searching for *The Children's Classics* (Dilithium Press) when I was small and now has the complete collection. He's just waiting for grandkids now. There is an endless variety in bindings, illustrations, size, and price. If you are going for the long term, look for a hardbound series with acid-free paper, high quality binding, and illustrations by the classic illustrators. I highly recommend the following:

- *The Children's Classics, Dilithium Press* (hardcover)

- *Everyman's Library Children's Classics* (hardcover)

- *The Children's Library, Penguin Classics Complete Collections* (paperback)

Golden Age Illustrators

Hot on the heels of the visionary authors of the children's classics came equally visionary artists and illustrators, intent on capturing the enchantment portrayed in the stories. The whimsy and imagination of the illustrations that accompanied the first or other early editions of many of the classics add to their enduring charm. If you possibly can, get editions that include artwork by the original illustrators or the great Golden Age artists. In the following reviews, I have included the name of an illustrator if one of the Golden Age artists was

121

linked with that book. In any case, look for books illustrated by these artists:

- Walter Crane

- Edmund Dulac

- Kate Greenaway

- Arthur Rackham

- Jessie Wilcox Smith

- John Tenniel

- N. C. Wyeth

Further Reading

If you are interested in finding out more about the Golden Age of children's literature, take a look at the following books:

- *Children's Literature: An Illustrated History,* edited by Peter Hunt

- *Behold the Child: American Children and Their Books* by Gillian Avery

Louisa May Alcott

Little Women, 1868. Illustrated by Jessie Wilcox Smith.
Elementary through Junior High.

Meg, Jo, Beth, and Amy March are four of the most beloved sisters in literary history. This tender, humorous story of four girls with vastly differing personalities growing up in New England is still one of the favorite books of girls worldwide. With a brave father fighting in the Civil War and a wise, gracious mother called Marmee, the March girls grow up in a whirl of drama, sisterly squabbles, family idealism, unhindered creativity, and an abiding love for each other. Based on Louisa May Alcott's own family, this is a wonderful mother-daughter read-aloud.

Little Men, 1871. Elementary through Junior High.

Continuing the tale of *Little Women, Little Men* centers on the lively school run by Jo and her husband, Professor Bhaer. With her sisters and their children close by, Jo becomes Mother Bhaer to a mischievous household of orphan boys, raising them with the vim and grace characteristic of Marmee's training. Ideal for boys, this book is filled with the escapades and thrills of daydreamer Demi (Meg's son); plucky, rebellious Dan; and musical Nat. There are characters to match any boy's personality. When my mom read this book aloud, my brother Nathan said he wanted a gang of boys just like the little men.

Jo's Boys, 1903. Elementary through Junior High.

This story starts ten years after the end of *Little Men*. There is a somber note to this heartwarming tale of Jo's boys as they venture into life. They continue to turn to the grace and compassion of Mother Bhaer to help them through new loves and near tragic struggles as they seek to find their place in the world. But find their place they do—one as a musician, one as a sailor, and one as an adventurer in the unexplored West. A satisfying conclusion to the saga of the March family.

J. M. Barrie

Peter Pan, 1911. Elementary.

A celebration of childhood, *Peter Pan* is the tale of a young boy who has decided never to grow up. Hungry for friends, he whisks three children away from their home in London to visit him in Neverland, a country of perpetual childlike imagination. Battling pirates, dancing with Indians, swimming with mermaids, and fascinated by a fairy named Tinker Bell, the children revel in this strange land of childish imagination. Eventually they must decide if they will stay or return home to grow up. The sequel is *Peter Pan in Kensington Gardens*, illustrated by Arthur Rackham.

Frances Hodgson Burnett

The Little Princess, 1905. Elementary.

Sara Crewe is the adored daughter of a wealthy, widowed father when she is sent to London for boarding school. Imaginative and enigmatic, she charms her peers, nettles her teachers, and dazzles the daily life of the school. When tragedy comes, however, she must decide how she will meet it and what it means to be a princess even when she is forgotten. This cherished story for girls illumines the true nature of dignity, beauty, and self-worth.

The Secret Garden, 1911. Elementary.

My personal favorite by Burnett, *The Secret Garden* is the story of Mary, an orphan transported from India to her uncle's old mansion on the windy moors of Yorkshire. Lonely and bad-tempered, Mary discovers the key to a forgotten, secret garden with a mystery surrounding its overgrown beauty. Through the friendship of young Colin and his animal friends, the good-natured ministrations of maid Martha, and the enigmatic wisdom of gardener Ben Weatherstaff, both Mary and her secret garden find their inner spaces blossoming anew. The edition with Tasha Tudor's quaint illustrations is one of my favorites.

Little Lord Fauntleroy, 1886. Elementary.

Cedric is a "charming little fellow" living with his demure, widowed mother in Brooklyn when he receives the astonishing news that he is the grandson of an English earl and heir to a vast estate. Transported across the sea to be raised by a grandfather he has never met and who refuses to even speak to his mother, Cedric must use all his simple courage to win the old man's affection, protect his mother, and defend his title against an imposter. A runaway best seller when it was first published.

Lewis Carroll

Alice's Adventures in Wonderland, 1865. Illustrated by John Tenniel. Elementary.

The book that turned the literary world upside down, *Alice* is the topsy-turvy, fantastical adventure of a little girl who falls into Wonderland, a realm peopled by perpetually late white rabbits, foolish knights, and tyrannical queens. Some readers find allegory and symbolism; some find the strange delight of pure whimsy. But all find this book to be a classic of childish imagination. The sequel is *Through the Looking-Glass.*

Mary Mapes Dodge

Hans Brinker, or, The Silver Skates, 1865. Elementary through Junior High.

Set in the countryside of the Netherlands, *Hans Brinker* is the story of a selfless young boy. While Hans and his sister Gretel dream of entering the great winter skate race and competing for the prize of the silver skates, they must scrape pennies together just to support their family and injured father. When a brilliant but gruff doctor comes to town, Hans must make a choice between two dreams. This noble, riveting tale offers an intriguing glimpse into the colorful customs and culture of the Netherlands.

Kenneth Grahame

The Wind in the Willows, 1908. Illustrated by Ernest H. Shepard. Young Child through Elementary.

Down by the river beneath the willows live a clan of friends: bumbling, adorable Mole; clever, capable Mr. Ratty; the mysterious and rather frightening Mr. Badger; and the madcap, incorrigible Toad. *The Wind in the Willows* is the chronicle of their adventures from picnics and boating on the river to the pursuit and rescue of the reckless Mr. Toad from a gang of weasels. This timeless story is imbued with a comforting spirit of friendship and wonder. While the

Shepard illustrations are classic, Michael Hague's illustrations are equally enchanting and might be my favorite.

The Reluctant Dragon, 1898. Elementary.
    When a young English boy discovers a clever, mushroom-loving dragon in the hills near his home, the two become fast friends. But when the nearby townspeople find out about the dragon, they call in an elderly St. George to slay him. A sympathetic knight, a fake joust, and echoes of English legend complete this charming little tale.

Charles Kingsley

The Water-Babies, 1863. Illustrated by Jessie Wilcox Smith. Elementary through Junior High.
    A fanciful allegory written by an Anglican clergyman (who was appointed as Canon of Westminster by Queen Victoria), this tale of the woeful young chimney sweep Tom imaginatively pictures the journey of redemption in an underwater world. When the Queen of the Fairies transforms Tom into a water baby, he is whisked away through the waves to meet Mrs. Doasyouwouldbedoneby and Mrs. Bedonebyasyoudid, just two of the delightful menagerie of characters who aid in his transformation from a dirty chimney sweep with no awareness of his soul to a noble, cleansed young man. This is a thoroughly odd but wondrous tale.

Rudyard Kipling

The Jungle Book, 1894. Elementary.

The most famous of Kipling's collection of jungle animal tales set in India is the yarn of Mowgli, a boy raised by wolves. His best friends Baloo the bear and Bagheera the panther help him escape the murderous tiger Shere Khan. Each story portrays a noble character quality, and most are accompanied by Kipling's intriguing poems.

Also written by Kipling:
- *Just-So Stories*
- *Kim*

Charles and Mary Lamb

Tales from Shakespeare, 1878. Elementary.

A brother-sister team modified twenty Shakespeare plays (including fourteen comedies) in content and vocabulary for younger readers. This is a wonderful way to shepherd children into the wit and wonder of Shakespeare and whet their appetites for his full genius later on.

George MacDonald

At the Back of the North Wind, 1871. Illustrated by Jessie
Wilcox Smith. Elementary through Junior High.

One of my favorite authors, George MacDonald was
gifted with the rare skill of clothing spiritual concepts in
word-pictures. His confidence in and devotion to God's love
shone through in every story he wrote. C. S. Lewis said that
no writer he had ever read seemed closer to the Spirit of
Christ. Using his love for fairy tales and his vivid Scottish
imagination, MacDonald wrote to illuminate God's truth and
reality to his eleven children.

At the Back of the North Wind is the haunting tale of a little
boy named Diamond who comes to know the beautiful
and frightening woman who is North Wind. Carried by
her throughout the world, Diamond witnesses her acts of
blessing and justice, and for a short, blissful time, visits the
unforgettably beautiful country at her back. This poignant
allegory pictures the mystery of God's Spirit as it moves
within the world and us. A sense of the longing for heaven
imbues this beautiful book, making it one of my favorite
children's classics of all time.

The Princess and the Goblin, 1872. Illustrated by Jessie Wilcox
Smith. Elementary through Junior High.

Irene is a plucky young princess living on a mountain with
goblins beneath her house and a mysterious woman in the
attic. When the goblins hatch a plot to kidnap her, Irene must

journey with Curdie, the son of a humble miner, through the dark caves. They both must follow the nearly invisible thread that will lead them back to the light and safety of the castle tower and Irene's wise great-great-grandmother. A fairy tale that radiantly pictures the light of God as it leads us out of darkness.

The Lost Princess, 1875. Retold and illustrated by Karen Mezek. Young Child through Elementary

This story of the spoiled Princess Rosamond pictures the journey of a selfish young soul as it is transformed by the gentleness, grace, and severity of wisdom. Kidnapped by the cloaked Wise Woman, Rosamond wanders the halls of her mysterious house, climbing into different pictures in which she learns patience, self-control, and gentleness of heart. If you can find it, the illustrated version of this story published by Eerdmans brings the tale to life.

Also written by George MacDonald:
The Golden Key
The Light Princess
The Princess and Curdie
*The Gifts of the Child Christ: And Other Stories and
    Fairy Tales*

Norman MacLeod

The Gold Thread, 1860. Elementary through Junior High.

A literary allegory, this story of young Prince Eric and his journey through a dangerous forest bears all the mystery of a good fairy tale, while artfully instructing its reader in the virtues of honesty, loyalty, and purity of heart. With only a slim golden thread for guidance, Eric must ignore every temptation to let it go if he is ever to reach the center of the forest and find his heart's desire.

A. A. Milne

Winnie-the-Pooh, 1926. Illustrated by Ernest H. Shepard.
Young Child through Elementary.

Winnie-the-Pooh, a stuffed bear of "very little brain," is the beloved friend of Christopher Robin. Milne's delightful cast of characters includes the incorrigible Tigger, skeptical Rabbit, timid but loyal Piglet, and the endearingly pessimistic donkey Eeyore as they explore and enjoy life in the Hundred Acre Wood.

Also written by Milne:
- ♥ *The House at Pooh Corner*
- ♥ *Now We Are Six*
- ♥ *When We Were Very Young*

Lucy Maud Montgomery

Anne of Green Gables series, 1908–1921. Elementary through Junior High.

Anne of Green Gables is the beloved first book about Anne Shirley, a spunky, imaginative, red-haired orphan sent to live with prickly spinster Marilla Cuthbert and her gentle brother Matthew on their farm in Prince Edward Island, Canada. Anne's buoyant love of life and penchant for scrapes and unexpected friendships transforms Marilla, Matthew, and the little town of Avonlea. Every girl simply must read the Anne books. There is no match for Montgomery's winsome prose as it expertly illumines the foibles of human hearts, the passionate wonder of imagination, and a young girl's love of beauty. Once you begin, you'll have to continue with the rest of the series:

- ♥ *Anne of Avonlea*
- ♥ *Anne of the Island*
- ♥ *Anne of Windy Poplars*
- ♥ *Anne's House of Dreams*
- ♥ *Anne of Ingleside*
- ♥ *Rainbow Valley*
- ♥ *Rilla of Ingleside*

The Story Girl, 1911. Elementary through Junior High.

Of all her books, Montgomery said this charming tale was her favorite. Sara has a wondrous gift for bringing stories to life as she tells them to her lively cousins on the King

Farm on Prince Edward Island. This lovely read-aloud is a perfectly woven tapestry of rambunctious adventures that celebrates childhood friendships, poignant stories, and the simple goodness of a family farm.

The Golden Road, 1913. Elementary through Junior High.
　　This sequel to *The Story Girl* continues the growing up of the King Cousins as they begin to imagine what they will find on "the golden road of youth." Wistful and hopeful as the world begins to expand in possibility for all the different children, the story ends with an unforgettable afternoon ramble just before Sara's father returns to take her back with him to Europe.

Also written by Montgomery:
- ♥ *Emily of New Moon*
- ♥ *Emily Climbs*
- ♥ *Emily's Quest*
- ♥ *Jane of Lantern Hill*
- ♥ *Magic for Marigold*

E. Nesbit

The Story of the Treasure Seekers 1899. Elementary.
　　This is the story of Dora, Oswald, Dicky, Alice, Noel, and Horace Octavius (H.O.) Bastable as they attempt to recover the fallen fortunes of their motherless family. An ingenious

little group, they hatch numerous plans for financial expansion, including excavation in the backyard, highway robbery, and pleas to the rich. Told entirely in the frank, unconsciously humorous voice of an unnamed Bastable child, this is a hilarious family tale. Its sequels include *The Wouldbegoods* and *The New Treasure Seekers.*

The Railway Children, 1906. Elementary.

Sent to live in the country with their mother after their father mysteriously disappears, Roberta, Peter, and Phyllis must learn to be very brave in their poky old cottage and decidedly poorer lifestyle. But with the whole countryside to roam and the fascinating train to watch every day, they soon find friends and adventures enough to keep them busy until they can figure out a way to bring their father home. I love this story for its portrayal of the joy that is possible even in the midst of a family's struggle.

Eleanor Porter

Pollyanna, 1913. Elementary through Junior High.

The much-beloved story of a little girl whose unassailable joy in life infects a whole town, *Pollyanna* could best be called a tale of gladness. Sent to live with grim and dutiful Aunt Polly, Pollyana determines to keep up the "glad game" taught her by her father before he died. Despite her grief, Pollyanna determinedly finds joy in every possible situation. Her lively spirit wins its way into the hearts of the town, including the stubborn invalid, Mrs. Snow, and the crotchety old bachelor, Mr. Pendleton. It takes a great tragedy, however, to finally touch the frozen depth of Aunt Polly's heart and lead her to give Pollyanna the tenderness she needs.

Just David, 1916. Elementary through Junior High.

Written just three years after *Pollyanna, Just David* was meant to be a boy's companion to the girl's story, but the outbreak of World War I and a paper shortage ensured this beautiful tale was quickly forgotten. David is a joyful little boy who has lived with his father in a mountain cabin until a sudden crisis sends them on an unexpected journey into the valley. With the sudden and mysterious death of his father, David is left to the care of a crusty old farming couple. David's stunning gift as a violinist perplexes the town, while his kindness and innocence bring about a slow redemption in the lives of his friends. A perfect family read-aloud and one of our all time favorites.

Gene Stratton Porter

Freckles, 1909. Junior High.

Set in the swamps of the Indiana forest, this story is rich with the author's love of the natural world. A "plucky waif," Freckles is a red-haired orphan in desperate search of work and belonging when he is hired to be a timber guard of the valuable trees in the Limberlost Forest. Befriended by the eccentric Bird Woman, Freckles struggles to outwit the timber thief named Black Jack, earn the love of a girl he calls simply "The Swamp Angel," and learn the truth of his history.

Girl of the Limberlost, 1909. Junior High.

Elnora has grown up on the edge of the strange and beautiful Limberlost Swamp with a mother who blames her for her father's death. Determined to gain an education, she attends the high school in the local town, paying her way by selling the ethereal moths she captures in the Limberlost. Through the kindness of her childless old neighbors and the mentorship of the Bird Woman, Elnora discovers her gift for music, revels in her education, and begins an unexpected process of redemption with her mother. This is one of my favorite books.

The Keeper of the Bees, 1925. Junior High.

Jamie is a World War I veteran with a wound that will not heal but a heart still full of grit when he decides to abandon his dank hospital room and strike off on his own up the sunny coast of California. A chance meeting with an old man in trouble lands him as the keeper of a cottage and caretaker of several thousand bees. The healing he finds in the fresh, earth-centered living of his new home and the spiritual peace he gains prepare him for another adventure with a beautiful, troubled girl. This is a story that celebrates God's creation.

Beatrix Potter

The Tale of Peter Rabbit, 1902. Young Child through Elementary.

An eccentric, artistic spinster living with her parents in London, Beatrix Potter was shocked when her little nature tales for children became national bestsellers within months of their publication. Her observation of nature led to the intricate, humorous illustrations that fill her books. With bunny mothers, gullible ducks, mischievous mice who take over a doll's house, and the famous Peter Rabbit, Potter's books are ideal for young children and soon became the best beloved bedtime stories for generations of families. Potter's stories and illustrations have been conveniently bound into one volume, *The Complete Tales of Beatrix Potter*, but there are also picture-book editions of her individual stories, including:

- ♥ *The Tale of Benjamin Bunny*
- ♥ *The Tale of Mrs. Tiggy-Winkle*
- ♥ *The Tale of the Flopsy Bunnies*
- ♥ *The Tale of Jemima Puddle-Duck*

Howard Pyle

The Merry Adventures of Robin Hood, 1883. Elementary.

Every adventurous boy ought to read Pyle's classic retelling of the medieval Robin Hood legends. With jolly Friar Tuck as an ally and the love of the winsome Maid Marian, Robin Hood robs the rich to feed the poor, keeping justice and faith alive in a kingdom yearning for the return of its courageous king. Strong, skillful drawings enhance the story.

The Story of King Arthur and His Knights, 1903. Elementary.

This excellent retelling of an old legend chronicles the valiant doings of "the most honorable, gentle Knight who ever lived in all the world" and his brotherhood of the world's fairest and bravest knights who gather at the Round Table in Camelot. This original model for knightly chivalry, adventure, and courage will feed the budding gallantry of any young boy.

Caution: Families who are concerned by these elements should know that the King Arthur stories include a fair amount of good and evil magic. The source of the magic is never fully explained, though the good knights all pray to God and are considered faithful Christians.

Christina Rossetti

Sing-Song, 1872. Elementary.

The sister of famous artist Dante Gabriel Rossetti, Christina Rossetti was a prolific poet with a deeply held Christian faith. This collection of poems and songs for children reflects her whimsy, wonder, and devotion. It was considered an example of the rising quality of children's writing when it was published.

Anna Sewell

Black Beauty, 1877. Elementary through Junior High.

Originally meant as a novel for horse-lovers, this book quickly became a favorite children's story because of its winsome narrator and hero, the stallion Black Beauty. This tale of his life from birth on a farm to his work as a prize horse, a London cabby, and a packhorse teaches kindness to animals and the merit of integrity. With memorable characters such as the fiery mare Ginger, the plucky pony Merrylegs, and the simple-hearted boy Joe, this tale is sure to delight any animal-lover.

Johanna Spyri

Heidi, 1880. Illustrated by Jessie Wilcox Smith. Elementary.

One of the best-known pieces of Swiss literature, *Heidi* is the story of an orphaned little girl who lives with her crusty grandfather high on the slopes of the Swiss Alps. Affection slowly blossoms between them as she revels in her grandfather's hut, his goats, and the friendship of the herder Peter. When Heidi is suddenly taken away, her grandfather realizes the depth of his love for her. A redemptive story with clear spiritual themes of grace and restoration, the book is also highly descriptive. I can still remember the accounts of toasted cheese, fresh mountain winds, and Heidi's little nest in her grandfather's attic.

Robert Louis Stevenson

Treasure Island, 1883. Illustrated by N. C. Wyeth. Elementary through Junior High.

A swashbuckling, high-seas adventure set in the eighteenth century, *Treasure Island* is the ultimate pirate's tale. Jim Hawkins, son of an innkeeper, has accidentally stumbled upon the legendary pirate treasure map of the infamous Captain Flint. Jim's wealthy friends eagerly set up a sea voyage in search of the treasure, hiring the best sailors that they can find. But as they near the mysterious Treasure Island, it becomes clear that pirates are aboard and a battle is going to be fought, led by the charismatic, one-legged cook, Long John Silver.

Caution: Though never graphic in nature, this classic pirate novel does have quite a bit of sword and gun play, with quite a few bad guys (and several good ones) meeting an early death.

Kidnapped, 1886. Illustrated by N. C. Wyeth. Elementary through Junior High.

This is the tumultuous tale of young David Balfour, stranded in the highlands of Scotland and forced to seek his fortunes during the Jacobite Rebellion. Betrayed by a greedy uncle, David is kidnapped and set on a ship where he falls in with the daring and audacious Alan Breck, a fierce Scottish highlander who drags him on a mad journey through the highlands. It takes a mighty amount of valor and a trek through the English countryside before David can figure out how to reach his home and reclaim his fortune. I read this aloud to my siblings one autumn, and we could barely stand the suspense between reading times.

Also written by Stevenson:
- ♥ *The Black Arrow*
- ♥ *David Balfour*

Mark Twain

The Adventures of Tom Sawyer, 1876. Junior High.

Mark's Twain's boisterous "hymn" to the "idyll of childhood" follows mischievous young Tom through the hot, lazy days of a southern town in summer. With his penchant for trouble and a love of showing off, Tom gets tangled up in a murder trial and a hunt for treasure buried in a cave, all while wooing the lovely Becky and escaping his aunt's strict ministrations. An exuberant picture of boyish summer fun.

Caution: A key element of the plot is a murder in a graveyard, witnessed by Tom and his friend.

The Prince and the Pauper, 1881. Junior High.

Young Prince Edward (son of Henry the VIII) and the beggar boy Tom Canty have almost nothing in common—except their identical looks. After a chance meeting at the palace gates, the boys embark on a daring adventure by switching places. Tom Canty is immersed in the noble life for which he has yearned, while the prince tastes the struggle of life as a beggar and the cruelty of the English courts. But when the real king dies, Edward must find a way to get back to the palace and convince the nobles that he is their true king.

Caution: Mark Twain vividly recreates life in the 1500s, including the gruesome and cruel punishment practiced by the English courts at that time, which included burning at the stake, dismemberment, and torture.

Also written by Twain:
♥ *Adventures of Huckleberry Finn*

Kate Douglas Wiggin

Rebecca of Sunnybrook Farm, 1903. Elementary.

Rebecca is a little girl sent to live with her two great-aunts in small-town Maine at the end of the nineteenth century. With one aunt stern and one sweet, Rebecca is immediately immersed in a challenging whirl of a new life. But her zest, love, and best friend Emma help her to prevail and win over her new family in the end.

7
Children's Fiction

Imagination has brought mankind through the Dark Ages to its present state of civilization. Imagination led Columbus to discover America. Imagination led Franklin to discover electricity. Imagination has given us the steam engine, the telephone, the talking-machine, and the automobile; for these things had to be dreamed of before they became realities. So I believe that dreams—daydreams, you know, with your eyes wide open and your brain machinery whizzing—are likely to lead to the betterment of the world. The imaginative child will become the imaginative man or woman most apt to invent, and therefore to foster, civilization.

~ L. Frank Baum

I could feel the spring warmth of the Colorado day as I knelt behind a stand of scrub oaks, their new leaves just shielding my face. As the quiet of the mountain settled round me, I watched, intent on the hillside just ahead. All was still except for the usual jabbering of the magpies shattering the whoosh of the wind. Joy, my five-year-old sister, crouched beside me.

"Do you hear dem, Sabah? I can't see dem yet."

"Shhh. Just wait a minute . . ."

A sudden cacophony of outlandish yells emerged from the bushes as Joel (age thirteen) bounded through the thick branches, with Nathan (age eleven) hot on his heels, brandishing a long stick with alarming zeal.

"I'll catch ye, ye Jacobite spy!" he yelled in a British accent.

But Joel had gained the hilltop and faced his opponent with a formidable broadsword of gleaming tubes and silver duct tape.

"Ye'll never catch me alive!" he challenged, rolling his r's. "Scotland forever!"

Just when it seemed that Joel had been wounded, Joy and I rushed from our hiding spot. Brandishing her shawl with great vigor, Joy rushed at Nathan, yelling at the top of her lungs. He threw up his hands in mock terror and retreated as I very seriously dressed Joel's wound.

"We must get back to the fort; we must hide!" gasped Joel, breathing hard.

We set off quickly through the bushes, we girls holding our shawls over our heads with one hand and lifting our dirndl skirts with the other. Joel wielded his sword as he ran, lest any enemy accost us before we tumbled into the pine forest and collapsed in relief in our stone fort. Another skirmish won. Scotland forever!

As I look back at that moment, I think we really half-believed we were hero warriors and maidens in a desperate battle for the freedom of our beloved country. There was a strange and sudden courage pounding in our hearts, a thrill of determination. We felt that make-believe or not, we could do anything.

Such is the power of imagination.

Growing up, my siblings and I were almost constantly in the throes of some imagined story—shipwrecked travelers, desperate orphans, disguised royalty, westward pioneers. After our obligatory hour of reading, our afternoons were often spent outdoors in worlds available only through the creative power of our minds—worlds often introduced through the stories we had read. On the particular day above, we had just finished a chapter of *Kidnapped* and were intent upon living out the grand struggle for freedom in the Scottish highlands.

In the past few years I have come to the conclusion that those hours of imagination gave me far more than just good memories. As I have begun writing my first books and done just a bit of speaking, numerous people have asked me what gave me the ability to dream, what drove my desires and shaped my goals.

The answer is simple: God, family, and . . . imagination.

Imagination is too often described as a "childish" thing—attributed only to the young, the very creative, or the "artsy" and impractical. But in reality, imagination is a transformative force that is common to all people who dream deeply enough to accomplish something of worth with their lives. At its core, imagination is the ability to envision the future we desire, the force enabling us to pursue a dream whose reality is radically different from the present. We cannot set out on a road of great hopes and determination if we have no concept of what it is we are journeying toward. Imagination drives inspired action.

A robust imagination must, in large part, be carefully cultivated. Children are born with the raw material of imagination, the conception of the world as being unfettered in its possibilities. But it is an ability that must be nurtured, coddled, and nourished daily if it is to become a source of inspiration that will drive the goals and dreams of a growing soul.

Imagination is also necessary to education. The goal of a truly excellent education ought to be a whole person with a soul driven by a potent dream and a mind equipped with the knowledge and skill necessary to pursue it. Thus, it is absolutely necessary that children be given the means to dream. Children can be filled up with facts, equipped with a wide knowledge, and trained to embrace a correct understanding of reality. But if their imagination has died in the process, they will have no energizing dream on which to base a vision-driven life.

Children must be given the means to cultivate the full potential of their imaginations through the treasury of books—not textbooks or instruction manuals, but living, thought-expanding story. Children need a lavish spread of colorful worlds and compelling characters to show them what is possible, to give them a vision for what they can become.

Throughout my childhood and youth, I read literally hundreds of children's novels. While usually written a little later than the Golden Age classics discussed in the last chapter, the children's fiction listed here encompasses stories of people, countries, and histories from around the world. These books first exposed me to cultural traditions, unique homes, and dynamic families, as well as a new world of work and vocational possibilities that I had never dreamed existed. They stretched my comprehension of what nobility and courage look like as they were lived out in different circumstances and cultures. They introduced me to the drama of life in all its grandeur and grief, heroism and beauty. By expanding the reach of my imagination, those books significantly enlarged the reach of my goals.

You cannot read the story of Robbie Bruce, act out his courage, and walk down the hill to dinner unchanged. Stories like that enter into your soul and thought as a challenge, convincing you that you also have some brave and noble deed to accomplish in your own few years.

The books listed in this chapter nourish the imagination and provide that feast of story so necessary to crafting strong goals and creating a sense of drive and purpose in the hearts of active children. These tales will spur their imaginations into picturing the grand stories they intend to live out in their lives.

The Marks of Good Children's Fiction

Moral Discernment

As children enter the elementary and junior high years, their comprehension of and ability to deal with the reality of good and evil expand. The stories they encounter in history and fiction will have much clearer, more developed pictures of virtue and vice than the simplicity of picture books. This is a natural progression. I am careful to recommend books where the lines defining right and wrong are clearly displayed. Stories play powerfully in the development of an inner conception of morality; so for me to call a book good, it must clearly distinguish between goodness and evil.

Second, as children prepare to enter adulthood, it is healthy for them to begin encountering the reality of a fallen world in tales of war, hunger, or struggle. It prepares them to be brave and compassionate. But it is not healthy for them to encounter it in graphic description. A good work of children's fiction can relate a real story of adversity without resorting to explicit descriptions of violence or sensuality.

Literary Excellence

There is no denying the fun of a Nancy Drew mystery. It could be argued that the plot clearly outlines good and evil and that the characters are courageous. While I did read dozens of them growing up, they were a rare treat, occasionally inserted into a steady diet of more literarily excellent books. Most of the books listed in this chapter combine excellence with entertainment because every book read in childhood sets the appetite. The majority of reading should be stories of literary quality containing a well-developed plot, multidimensional characters, and words to enrich and expand vocabulary rather than limit it.

The Newbery Award

The Newbery Medal was named in honor of eighteenth-century writer, educator, and bookseller John Newbery. As the author of one of the first books written specifically for children, he is considered one of the fathers of children's literature. The Association for Library Service to Children, a division of the American Library Association, presents this award to the author of the most distinguished contribution to American literature for children each year. Newbery Honor Awards are also bestowed on runners-up. While many of the books on this list are really excellent, a few not-so-great titles have crept in. Some of the more modern books contain politically correct themes of religious tolerance and adult issues that really don't need to be present in a children's book. I recommend that you review and research any title before reading. A complete listing of Newbery Medalists is provided in the appendix.

The Carnegie Medal

Established in 1936, the Carnegie Medal is named in honor of philanthropist Andrew Carnegie. A self-made businessman who made a fortune during the Industrial Revolution,

Carnegie donated much of his money to establish libraries that would make books available to people from all classes. The Medal is awarded annually by the Chartered Institute of Library and Information Professionals to the writer of an exceptional children's book.

The PEN/O. Henry Prize

An annual award established to encourage the art of the short story, the PEN/O. Henry prize is named in honor of William Sydney Porter, the author of the well-known "The Gift of the Magi," who wrote under the pseudonym O. Henry. Originally started by a small society as a "monument to O. Henry's genius," the prize is now awarded by a juried editorial team from Random House, which then gathers the winning stories into an annual collection for publication as *The O. Henry Prize Stories*. Beginning in 2009, Random House partnered with a literary and human rights organization called the PEN American Center, and the stories are now released as *The PEN/O. Henry Prize Stories*.

Joan Aiken

The Wolves of Willoughby Chase, 1963. Elementary.

When the cunning Miss Slighcarp comes to care for plucky Bonny and her cousin Sylvia while Bonny's parents are away, the girls discover her sinister plot to steal the family estate. With the help of a brave boy from the forest and their own intrepid spirits, the girls determine to foil her plan. Set in the author's fictional history of Britain in the early 1800s when dangerous wolves have invaded the countryside, this is a delightfully adventurous tale.

Also written by Aiken:
- ♥ *Black Hearts in Battersea*
- ♥ *Nightbirds on Nantucket*

Edith Martha Almedingen

Ellen, 1970. Elementary.

This captivating author's stories are based on the life of her grandmother, an Englishwoman in Russia. Ellen is an imaginative child in a topsy-turvy but very happy family home near Canterbury, England. Her mother's death prompts her restless father to whisk his family on a gypsy tour through Europe that ends in the cold and mystery of Russia. Filled with unforgettable characters and scenes from old Europe.

Also written by Almedingen:
- ♥ *Candle at Dusk*
- ♥ *Katia*
- ♥ *Young Mark*

Richard Atwater

Mr. Popper's Penguins, 1938. Newbery Honor Book.
Elementary.

Mr. Popper has always dreamed of travel, but the most exotic thing in his life so far is a pet penguin. When Captain Cook (the penguin) gets lonely, the Poppers end up with a zany brood of penguins that give Mr. Popper a rather brilliant idea. Laugh-aloud funny.

Natalie Babbitt

Tuck Everlasting, 1975. Junior High.

This is the curious tale of the Tucks, a family who accidentally become immortal after a drink from an unusual spring. When a curious young girl named Winnie happens upon the spring, they try to stop her from drinking the immortal waters, even as Jesse Tuck comes to love her. But when a stranger also learns their secret, the Tucks must fight to protect themselves and their friend. This thrilling story imaginatively explores the nature of human frailty and the human desire for immortality. It will open up some fascinating family discussions.

B.B. (Denys Watkins-Pitchford)

The Little Grey Men, 1942. Carnegie Medalist. Elementary.

A classic in England, this is the tale of four brothers who are the last of the "little people." When one of the four, named Cloudberry, goes missing, the other three must set out on an epic search to find him. Filled with rich descriptions of flowers, trees, animals, and fields, this book is a slice of the legend, lore, and natural history of the English countryside.

Carol Ryrie Brink

Caddie Woodlawn, 1935. Newbery Medalist. Elementary.

Brink was a prolific and highly engaging writer of children's stories, and *Caddie Woodlawn* is one of her best. Caddie is an incorrigible tomboy with an irrepressible spirit who lives on the Wisconsin frontier in the 1860s. Her spunk and bravery catapult her into numerous adventures of midnight rides, fire fighting, and making peace with a local Indian tribe. For more Caddie adventures, read the sequel, *Magical Melons*.

Winter Cottage, 1968. Elementary.

When their car breaks down halfway through a road trip, Minty, Eggs (short for Eglantine), and their dad take shelter in a little holiday cottage and end up staying through the winter. Surviving largely on pancakes, poetry, and imagination, Minty and Eggs barely notice their Depression poverty amidst the fun and magic of the Winter Cottage.

Also written by Brink:
- ♥ *Goody O'Grumpity*
- ♥ *Two Are Better Than One*

Alice Turner Curtis

A Little Maid series, 1913–1927. Elementary.

An earlier version of the *American Girls* sort of books, these heartwarming tales of young girls are set mostly in the early American colonial and Revolutionary War days. I read *A Little Maid of New England* several times over, loving the story of a spirited little girl living bravely with an adoptive family while waiting for her father to return from war. Each story focuses on a historical place or event in early American history. The series includes:

- ♥ *A Little Maid of New England*
- ♥ *A Little Maid of Provincetown*
- ♥ *A Little Maid of Boston*
- ♥ *A Little Maid of Maryland*
- ♥ *A Little Maid of Old Philadelphia*
- ♥ *A Little Maid of Ticonderoga*
- ♥ *A Little Maid of Old New York*
- ♥ *A Little Maid of Old Maine*
- ♥ *A Little Maid of Massachusetts Colony*

Alice Dalgliesh

The Bears on Hemlock Mountain, 1952. Newbery Honor Book. Elementary.

"There are no bears on Hemlock Mountain," everyone tells Jonathan, but when he finds himself on the mountain one dark winter's night, it seems that everyone is wrong! With the help of an iron pot and a good dose of spunk, Jonathan manages to conquer his fear and the mountain.

Also written by Dalgliesh:
♥ *The Courage of Sarah Noble*
♥ *The Silver Pencil*

Marguerite de Angeli

Henner's Lydia, 1936. Young Child through Elementary.

With this popular book, the beloved children's author Marguerite de Angeli began the habit of experiencing the settings of her stories firsthand. She spent time as a guest in an Amish community before writing this tale of a lively, distractible little Amish girl desperate to finish her hooked rug so she can go to the market with Father. Brimming with scenes of wagons, apple-butter making, and Grandmother's storytelling, this book offers an authentic taste of Amish life.

The Lion in the Box, 1975. Young Child through Elementary.

Christmas has come to a fatherless family deep in New York City and with it, the children's wishes for presents despite their poverty. But when a huge, mysterious box appears on the front door with the deliverymen hinting it might be a lion, the children find their wishes more than fulfilled. A lovely tale of generous Christmas spirit.

Also written by de Angeli:
- ♥ *The Copper-Toed Boots*
- ♥ *Petite Suzanne*
- ♥ *Skippack School*

Meindert De Jong

The Wheel on the School, 1954. Newbery Medalist. Elementary.

When the storks that come every year to the little Dutch village of Shora fail to show up, six children mourn their absence and hatch a daring plan to get them back. Their ingenuity and faith intrigue the entire town and weave a poignant story of childhood determination.

Also written by DeJong:
- ♥ *The House of Sixty Fathers*
- ♥ *Shadrach*

Kate DiCamillo

Because of Winn-Dixie, 2000. Newbery Honor Book.
Elementary through Junior High.

Kate DiCamillo has quickly become beloved for her stories of children and animals. *Because of Winn-Dixie* is the heartwarming tale of a motherless little girl and her beloved stray dog. Together, they unwittingly kindle the hearts of the lonely, forgotten people of their southern town.

Also written by DiCamillo:
♥ *The Miraculous Journey of Edward Tulane*
♥ *The Tale of Despereaux*

William Pène du Bois

The Twenty-One Balloons, 1947. Newbery Medalist.
Elementary through Junior High.

After long years of teaching math, Professor William Waterman Sherman decides to plunge into his lifelong adventurous dream of flying around the world in a hot-air balloon. His wild ride lands him on the secret island of Krakatoa, whose zany inhabitants welcome him into their unforgettable world. A tale of unfettered imagination.

Elizabeth Enright

Thimble Summer, 1938. Newbery Medalist. Elementary.

When Garnet discovers a silver thimble in the dirt of her family's Wisconsin farm, she is sure that it is bringing the good luck of rain and the daily adventures of her memorable summer. Enright's skillful narrative captures the rich, simple goodness of a Wisconsin farm during the Depression.

Eleanor Estes

The Moffats, 1941. Elementary.

This diverting story of a rambunctious, fun-loving family is based on the author's childhood memories. Set during World War I, this is the tale of a fatherless family of four children who bear a strong love for each other and an equally strong penchant for adventures in their close-knit neighborhood. Entertaining, heartwarming, and downright fun. Sequels include *The Middle Moffat* and *Rufus M.*

Also written by Estes:
♥ *The Hundred Dresses*

160

Paul Gallico

The Snow Goose, 1941. O. Henry Prize Winner. Junior High.

   The Snow Goose is the plaintive World War II story of Philip Rhayader, a hunchback artist and recluse living in a lighthouse on the English coast. When the young girl Fritha brings him a wounded snow goose for healing, they begin a friendship in which more is healed than the just the bird. But change comes crashing in when Rhyader bravely sails off one dark night to aid in the rescue of the soldiers stranded at Dunkirk.

Also written by Gallico:
   ♥ *The Small Miracle*

Doris Gates

Blue Willow, 1940. Newbery Honor Book. Elementary through Junior High.

   Janey Larkin has one treasure: a blue willow plate with a pastoral scene of a house in a picturesque valley. Constantly on the move as her father searches for work during the Great Depression, Janey has clung to this one possession that pictures her dream of a stable life and lovely home. But when her mother becomes ill and the rent must be paid, it seems that Janey might lose her treasure. A realistic yet hopeful story of the Depression era.

Jean Craighead George

My Side of the Mountain, 1959. Newbery Honor Book. Junior High.

With a penknife, forty dollars, and a bit of flint and steel, Sam Gribley runs away from his city home to his family's abandoned farm in the Catskill Mountains. For over a year, he lives with only a falcon for companion, learning to live off of the land until late one Christmas night when his father comes to find him. This book richly portrays the wonder of nature and the strength of a boy's courage in encountering its beauty and challenges alone.

Frank B. Gilbreth and Ernestine Gilbreth Cary

Cheaper by the Dozen, 1948. Elementary through Junior High.

One of my family's all-time favorite, laugh-aloud books, this is the true tale of the eccentric Gilbreth parents, both trained as efficiency experts, and their twelve high-spirited children. With their father full of an irrepressible number of ideas and jokes and their mother nearing sainthood, the twelve Gilbreth children grow up in a merry tumult of train trips, language lessons, family epidemics, and fun. It's hard to find a more family-affirming, hysterical tale. Especially good for car trips.

Caution: There is one brief instance of God's name being taken in vain.

Belles on Their Toes, 1950. Elementary through Junior High.

In this sequel to *Cheaper by the Dozen*, the Gilbreth family learns to thrive even after the death of their beloved father. Because Mother is determined to continue Father's work and the children are resolved to keep up his lively love of life, the Gilbreths muddle through. With an amazing amount of laughter and sibling loyalty, the family weathers the changes of adulthood, marriage, and the beginning of new families.

Elizabeth Goudge

The Little White Horse, 1946. Carnegie Medalist. Junior High.

Elizabeth Goudge is one of my favorite authors. A master of descriptive narrative, she is an idealist with uncanny insight into the hearts of humankind and the beauties of creation. In this adored story for children, little red-haired orphan Maria is sent to live with her second cousin, Sir Benjamin Merryweather, in his castle called Moonacre Manor. Amidst the legend-haunted hills of Devonshire, Maria finds unexpected friends and stumbles upon a dark family mystery that she feels bound to solve.

Caution: While always affirming the Christian faith, Goudge freely includes elements of legend, mystery, and hints of the supernatural in some of her stories. These are never out of the bounds of wholesome imagination, but they might be troublesome to some children.

Also written by Goudge:
- ♥ *Henrietta's House* (a.k.a. *The Blue Hills*)
- ♥ *Linnets and Valerians*

Marguerite Henry

Misty of Chincoteague, 1947. Newbery Honor Book.
Elementary through Junior High.

Set in the Chincoteague Islands of Virginia, this is the story of the wild pony Phantom, her beautiful foal Misty, and the determination of the Beebe siblings, Paul and Maureen, to capture them at the annual Pony Penning Day. Vivid, well-crafted prose captures the wildness and beauty of the historic Chincoteague horses that so fascinate the imagination.

Stormy, Misty's Foal, 1963. Elementary through Junior High.

In this sequel to *Misty of Chincoteague*, Misty herself is about to have a foal, but the storm of the century is looming on the horizon, threatening the wild ponies, coastal farms, and maybe even Misty's life. An exciting story, based on true events.

Also written by Henry:
- ♥ *Black Gold*
- ♥ *Justin Morgan Had a Horse*
- ♥ *King of the Wind*

Jennifer L. Holm

Boston Jane: An Adventure, 2001. Junior High.

Prim, city-raised Jane Peck sails to Oregon in the pioneer days to marry her true love. At first dismayed by the unexpected realities of ship rats and smoky cabins, Jane learns spunk and gradually falls in love with the dramatic beauty of her new land. Themes of courage and endurance permeate this first book in a loosely historical series about a dauntless young woman.

Also written by Holm:
♥ *Our Only May Amelia*

Brian Jacques

The Redwall series, 1986 to Present. Elementary through Junior High.

Set in medieval times within the splendor of Redwall Abbey, this imaginative series about the adventures of brave mice, intrepid rabbits, and other valiant animals has charmed children around the world. With characters and plots based on Jacques's admiration for the men and women of Liverpool who fought and worked in World War II, these stories heartily commend courage, self-sacrifice, and the jovial celebration (not to mention mouthwatering feasting) of this brave and fun-loving race of animals. Whether they are defending their beloved abbey from the cruel weasels or celebrating the return of a brave explorer, their literary world seems almost tangibly real. *Redwall* is the first in the series, though each is a stand-alone tale as well. The series includes:

- ♥ *Redwall*
- ♥ *Mossflower*
- ♥ *Mattimeo*
- ♥ *Mariel of Redwall*
- ♥ *Salamandastron*
- ♥ *Martin the Warrior*
- ♥ *The Bellmaker*
- ♥ *Outcast of Redwall*
- ♥ *The Pearls of Lutra*
- ♥ *The Long Patrol*
- ♥ *Marlfox*
- ♥ *The Legend of Luke*
- ♥ *Lord Brocktree*
- ♥ *Taggerung*
- ♥ *Triss*
- ♥ *Loamhedge*
- ♥ *Rakkety Tam*
- ♥ *High Rhulain*
- ♥ *Eulalia!*
- ♥ *Doomwyte*

Eric P. Kelly

The Trumpeter of Krakow, 1928. Newbery Medalist. Junior High.

A mysterious crystal and ruthless thief set the Charnetski family on a perilous journey to medieval Krakow, Poland, where they must fight to protect their treasure. Power-hungry spies, greedy merchants, and curious alchemists all attempt to own it, convinced of its secret power. A vivid exploration of medieval Krakow, this unforgettable tale combines mystery with history.

E. L. Konigsburg

From the Mixed-Up Files of Mrs. Basil E. Frankweiler, 1967. Newbery Medalist. Elementary through Junior High.

When siblings Claudia and Jamie Kincaid run away to the Metropolitan Museum of Art in New York City, they are riveted by the statue of a beautiful angel. Determined to discover the history of their statue, they begin a sleuthing chase that lands them in the mysterious home of Mrs. Basil E. Frankweiler, the wise and humorous narrator of this highly entertaining story. This is a great book for car trips or read-aloud.

Selma Lagerlöf

The Wonderful Adventures of Nils, 1906–1907. Junior High.

Originally commissioned as a geography reader for public schools in Sweden, this fanciful tale quickly became an adored children's book. When the naughty young Nils breaks his agreement with an elf, he becomes a little person himself and ends up catching a wild ride on the back of a white goose that gives him a whirlwind tour of Sweden and helps him to earn the character he lacks. Full of gentle poetry in its descriptions of Sweden's natural beauty and the distinctive flavor of the different provinces, this delightful book is an education in history, nature, and character.

Elizabeth Lewis

Young Fu of the Upper Yangtze, 1932. Newbery Medalist. Junior High.

Amidst the turmoil and change of China in the 1920s, Young Fu and his mother move to the big city where he is apprenticed to Tang, a master coppersmith. Young Fu must shoulder his new responsibilities, walk the narrow line between old China and the new, and learn to be a man in this vivid story of his native country.

Patricia MacLachlan

Sarah, Plain and Tall, 1985. Newbery Medalist. Elementary through Junior High.

Sarah Wheaton, a woman "plain and tall," has journeyed all the way from Maine to the plains of Kansas in answer to widower Jacob Witting's plea for a mother for his children. During a trial month on the prairie, she must win the love of the lonely Anna, who yearns for her dead mother, befriend the mischievous Caleb, and come to terms with the barren grace of the prairie. A wistful story of grace and redemption. Sequels include *Skylark* and *Caleb's Story*.

Ralph Moody

Little Britches series, 1950–1968. Junior High.

Beginning in the late pioneer days of Colorado, this auto-biographical series centers on a boy nicknamed "Little Britches" as he comes of age in the exciting and difficult days of the settlers. The father and son's strong relationship is central to this story of a young man's struggle to work, learn, and grow up as he travels west and back and west again. Strong, moving writing makes these excellent books greatly worthwhile.

Caution: There are several instances of God's name being taken in vain, as well as mild bad language that reflects the roughness of the cowboy life.

The series includes:
- ❤ *Little Britches*
- ❤ *Man of the Family*
- ❤ *Home Ranch*
- ❤ *Mary Emma & Company*
- ❤ *The Fields of Home*
- ❤ *Shaking the Nickel Bush*
- ❤ *Dry Divide*
- ❤ *Horse of a Different Color*

Walt Morey

Gentle Ben, 1965. Junior High (and into High School).

Morey's tales of the wild glory of Alaska and the Northwest have inspired pioneer spirits since the publication of his first famous story of a captive bear, *Gentle Ben*. When young Mark Anderson befriends an enormous Alaskan brown bear, his small fishing village and family watch the strange camaraderie with skepticism. When Gentle Ben attacks his former owner, Mark must decide what to do with the wild creature that is his friend.

Peopled by troubled youngsters, friendly or fearsome bears, wolves, and dogs, Morey's stories have deep themes of redemption and portray the endurance to be learned through experiencing nature. These are great books for older, adventurous kids with a taste for the wild.

Caution: Morey's books, including *Gentle Ben*, are probably best for kids approaching high school, as they deal with coming-of-age struggles, including kids in difficult family situations and boys who get in trouble with the law.

Also written by Morey:
- ♥ *Gloomy Gus*
- ♥ *Home Is the North*
- ♥ *Kavik the Wolf Dog*
- ♥ *Run Far, Run Fast*
- ♥ *Runaway Stallion*
- ♥ *The Year of the Black Pony*

Sterling North

Rascal, 1963. Newbery Honor Book. Elementary through Junior High.

When a raccoon named Rascal enters young Sterling's life, he provides the friendship and zest Sterling needs to help him navigate the death of his mother and his troubled relationship with his father. Basing this story on his childhood, North called this book a "memoir of a better era," when a boy could still roam and find solace in the countryside.

Robert C. O'Brien

Mrs. Frisby and the Rats of NIMH, 1971. Newbery Medalist.
Elementary through Junior High.

When poor little mouse Mrs. Frisby finds that her home is about to be destroyed by the farmer, she gathers up all her courage to ask help of the powerful Rats of NIMH. With secret laboratories and great daring, these intelligent rats, escaped from nearby researchers, have become scientists themselves; and it is to their skill that Mrs. Frisby must trust herself and her babies. This fanciful tale of curiosity prompts some interesting philosophical questions, while also being a highly entertaining read.

Katherine Paterson

Bridge to Terabithia, 1977. Newbery Medalist. Junior High.

This bittersweet story follows quiet, artistic Jesse Aarons through his friendship with Leslie, a spirited and imaginative tomboy. In the deep forest near their houses, they create a wondrous world dubbed Terabithia; but when Leslie is tragically killed, Jesse must use the passion, imagination, and courage he gained from their friendship to face his grief. Gently leads children through the frightening reality of death.

Caution: Based on the true experience of the author's son in losing his best friend, the book deals directly with the death of a beloved character and may be upsetting to some children.

Arthur Ransome

Swallows and Amazons series, 1930–1936. Elementary.

The first book in the much-beloved British series, *Swallows and Amazons* pictures an idyllic children's summer in the Lake District of England. When the Walker and Blackett siblings join together in a boating adventure to a nearby island, they begin a foray into an adventurous, half-imaginary, half-real world of fishing, camping, piracy, and endless escapades. The series includes:

- ❤ *Swallows and Amazons*
- ❤ *Swallowdale*
- ❤ *Peter Duck*
- ❤ *Winter Holiday*
- ❤ *Coot Club*
- ❤ *Pigeon Post*

Marjorie Kinnan Rawlings

The Yearling, 1938. Pulitzer Prize winner. Junior High (and into High School).

I didn't read this American classic until just a year ago, but as soon as I did, I was sorry not to have encountered the wry wisdom of Penny Baxter and his son Jody sooner. A realistic depiction of pioneer life in the Florida Everglades, this story of Jody and his love for a wild, young fawn revolves much around the daily grapple for food and the fight with nature for health and prosperity that made quiet heroes of early settlers. The story is told with a depth of insight and a grace of prose that nears poetry and will not leave you unchanged.

Caution: While beautiful, this story deals with the gritty realities of pioneer life, including the slaughtering of farm animals, the danger of wild animals, and the death of two main characters.

Wilson Rawls

Where the Red Fern Grows, 1961. Junior High.

I challenge anyone to read this book without tears. Billy longs for two coon dogs of his own; and he puts muscle, sweat, and grit into finally buying Old Dan and Little Ann. A pair of hounds imbued with matchless skill and affection, they and Billy take the forest and the coons by storm, winning the awe of the countryside as they do. Even tragedy can't strike out the depth of their friendship, and their story is marked by the miraculous growth of a rare red fern. A beloved, tender tale.

Caution: The accidental death of a young boy could be upsetting to children.

Summer of the Monkeys, 1976. Junior High.

One of the favorite read-alouds of my childhood, this book tells of a lively boy in the Ozark Mountains who discovers a band of runaway monkeys and coaxes them into a tenuous friendship. With a crippled little sister and a sympathetic grandfather, he spends a riotous summer taming his wild and mischievous monkeys.

Louis Sachar

Holes, 1998. Newbery Medalist. Junior High.

Stanley Yelnats is a luckless boy who finds himself interned at a reform camp in Texas for a theft he didn't commit. But it seems that adventure at least has followed him, as he and the other boys are forced to dig countless holes in search of a legendary treasure. With quirky, memorable characters both good and bad, this is a family favorite.

Caution: For those concerned with themes of magic, the mystery in the story centers on the Yelnats' family legend of a curse given by an old woman for a young man's ungratefulness.

George Seldon

The Cricket in Times Square, 1960. Newbery Honor Book. Elementary.

Chester is a talented young cricket from the countryside who comes to New York City seeking adventure. Befriended by Tucker the mouse and Harry the cat, Chester explores the city and ends up being adopted by Mario Bellinni, whose parents run a newspaper stand in Times Square. When the Bellinnis discover Chester's musical talent, the cricket becomes the darling of New York City and manages to help his friends out of trouble at the same time. *Tucker's Countryside* is the sequel to this funny, imaginative tale.

Kate Seredy

The Good Master, 1935. Newbery Honor Book. Elementary through Junior High.

A prolific writer, Seredy drew many of her stories from the Hungarian tales she heard in her childhood. *The Good Master* was one of my favorite books. Set on the windswept plains of Hungary and framed by the lively traditions and riveting legends of the countryside, this is the sweet, vibrant tale of a mischievous little girl who finds acceptance with her adoptive family.

Also written by Seredy:
- ♥ *The Chestry Oak*
- ♥ *The Singing Tree*
- ♥ *A Tree for Peter*
- ♥ *The White Stag*

Monica Shannon

Dobry, 1934. Newbery Medalist. Junior High.

The child of hard-working farmers in Bulgaria, Dobry has grown up learning to be diligent and carry out the work of his family. But he harbors a secret dream: he wants to be a sculptor. This inspiring story of a boy's creative determination demonstrates the value of artistic passion.

Margaret Sidney

The Five Little Peppers series, 1881–1916, Elementary through Junior High.

The beguiling tale of the five fatherless Peppers whose pluck and good spirits make life in their little brown house lovely, however poor. When Phronsie, the littlest girl, is kidnapped by an organ-grinder, the Peppers meet brave young Jasper, who just might turn their lives around. Margaret Sidney considered the series completed with the publication of the fourth book, but pressure from her fans worldwide compelled her to continue the Five Little Peppers series. I have listed the primary titles below; there are eleven titles in all:

- ♥ *The Five Little Peppers and How They Grew*
- ♥ *Five Little Peppers Midway*
- ♥ *Five Little Peppers Grown Up*
- ♥ *Five Little Peppers: Phronsie Pepper*

Virginia Sorensen

Miracles on Maple Hill, 1956. Newbery Medalist. Junior High

Marly and her family move to the country to help her father, who is just home from being a prisoner of war, recover. With the generous Chris family who run a maple-sugaring farm as neighbors, Marly and her family come to love the country and throw themselves into helping old Mr. Chris when he falls ill. The making of maple syrup weaves in with the remaking of hearts to create a year of miracles.

Patricia St. John

Treasures of the Snow, 1950. Elementary through Junior High.

Patricia St. John was a missionary to Morocco as well as a beloved author of spiritually powerful children's stories. Her best-known book, *Treasures of the Snow*, is the tale of crippled little Danny and his sister Annette, who bears a

178

bitter grudge toward Lucien, the boy who caused Danny's injury. This skillfully woven story of bitterness, forgiveness, and redemption told against the backdrop of blizzards, stars, and chalet hearths in the Swiss Alps is a perfect family read-aloud.

Also written by St. John:
- ♥ *Rainbow Garden*
- ♥ *The Runaway*
- ♥ *Star of Light*
- ♥ *Twice Freed*

Svenson, Andrew (pseudonym, Jerry West)

The Happy Hollisters series, 1953–1969. Elementary.

A rambunctious family with five children, the Hollisters are a gang of young detectives who seem to stumble constantly upon mysteries in their family travels and adventures. Innocent, family-friendly tales that affirm sibling camaraderie while providing an engrossing mystery read for kids. The series begins with the title book, *The Happy Hollisters*, and includes over thirty titles, a few of which include:
- ♥ *The Happy Hollisters on a River Trip*
- ♥ *The Happy Hollisters at Sea Gull Beach*
- ♥ *The Happy Hollisters and the Indian Treasure*
- ♥ *The Happy Hollisters at Mystery Mountain*
- ♥ *The Happy Hollisters at Snowflake Camp*

Sydney Taylor

All-of-A-Kind Family, 1951. Elementary.

Right in the heart of New York City's Lower East Side live five rambunctious sisters in a tight-knit Jewish family. With quirks and escapades galore, they grow up amidst the rich celebrations of their family's Jewish heritage, making fun and goodness wherever they go. A great glimpse into the beautiful celebrations and rich traditions of Judaism.

Also written by Taylor:
- ♥ *All-of-A-Kind Family Downtown*
- ♥ *All-of-A-Kind Family Uptown*
- ♥ *More All-of-A-Kind Family*
- ♥ *A Papa Like Everyone Else*

P. L. Travers

Mary Poppins, 1934. Elementary.

This is the famous story of the mysterious, severe, and rather vain nanny, Mary Poppins, who is blown by the East Wind into the household of the Banks family. With her carpetbag and hidden charm, Mary Poppins leads the children through a round of adventures with chimney sweeps and tea parties on the ceiling, leaving them better behaved and very sorry to see her go. Classic.

Gertrude Chandler Warner

The Boxcar Children series, 1942–1974, Elementary.

Hiding out in a boxcar after the death of their parents, the Alden children (Henry, Jessie, Benny, and Violet) gain their peculiar name and begin their penchant for tumbling into mysteries. Adopted by their kindhearted grandfather, the close-knit siblings seem to find unsolved riddles in every place they visit. Old-fashioned and fun, this series of mystery stories is full of sibling escapades and innocent adventures. The series includes nineteen titles; I have listed the first five below.

Caution: While these are never truly upsetting, there are references to mysteries including possible ghosts and past crimes. Use discretion for younger children.

The series includes:
- ♥ *The Boxcar Children*
- ♥ *Surprise Island*
- ♥ *The Yellow House Mystery*
- ♥ *Mystery Ranch*
- ♥ *Mike's Mystery*

Dr. Joe Wheeler

Great Stories Remembered, volumes 1–3, 1996–2000. Family.

One of America's leading anthologists, Dr. Joe Wheeler is a champion for old-fashioned tales that affirm family and faith.

Having gained his love for inspirational tales and poems from his mother, he went on to study literature, eventually becoming the world's foremost authority on the western writer Zane Grey. Along the way, he began collecting stories from what he calls the "Golden Age of Judeo-Christian literature," from 1870 to 1950, when many writers still celebrated family, faith, and the old-fashioned virtues of duty, courage, and nobility. He eventually compiled the best of those stories into the attractive *Great Stories Remembered* series. There are now three volumes of creative, heart-warming tales drawn from as far back as the Victorian age right up to the present day. Excellent read-alouds, these stories are perfect for family times—they will delight and challenge all at the same time.

E. B. White

Charlotte's Web, 1952. Newbery Honor Book. Elementary through Junior High.

This tale of a runt pig saved by the love of the little girl Fern and the sagacity of a wise and verbose spider is a perennial favorite. Wilbur the pig is an affectionate soul who adores the regal spider Charlotte. Perched on her well-woven web in his stall, Charlotte coaches Wilbur in etiquette, character, and the joys of articulateness. When Wilbur's fate hangs in the balance, it is her brilliance that saves him. A tender, entertaining story.

The Trumpet of the Swan, 1970, Elementary through Junior High.

Louis is a trumpeter swan who has just one problem: he's mute. With the help of Sam Beaver, a young boy who discovers him when he is still a nestling, and the aid of his determined father, Louis learns to read and write. He even manages to obtain a trumpet, which lands him jobs from camp counselor to club singer. The only thing he lacks is the affection of Serena, a beautiful young swan whom he loves. Told in the wry, humorous voice of White, this was a favorite audiobook for my family.

Stuart Little, 1945. Elementary through Junior High.

When the second son of the Little family of New York arrives, they are startled to discover that he has the face and stature of a mouse. The family—even Snowball the cat—soon adjust to their "little" brother, with his mouse-like reserve and polite manners. But when Stuart's best friend, Margalo, a bird who lives near his house, disappears, Stuart sets off on a grand quest to find her. Crisp prose, a valiant little mouse, and adventures galore make this a delightful book.

Laura Ingalls Wilder

Little House on the Prairie series, 1932–1941. Elementary.

This was the first series my mom read aloud with me just as I was beginning to learn to read. The story of brown-haired, spunky little Laura Ingalls Wilder and her pioneering family has become a beloved picture of American history. Set in Wisconsin, the first book, *Little House in the Big Woods*, chronicles Pa's decision to move his family West, where there's "still room to breathe." The subsequent books follow the Ingalls family through blizzards, dugouts, scarlet fever, and the eventual marriage of Laura, as the family fights to carve out a good, new life for themselves in the prairies of the West. This classic series includes:

♥ *Little House in the Big Woods*
♥ *Farmer Boy*
♥ *Little House on the Prairie*
♥ *On the Banks of Plum Creek*
♥ *By the Shores of Silver Lake*
♥ *The Long Winter*
♥ *Little Town on the Prairie*

Elizabeth Yates

The Journeyman, 1990. Junior High (and into High School).

In the rolling hills of New Hampshire during the colonial days lives a pale, sensitive boy named Jared who was born with the soul of an artist. When his father apprentices him to a journeyman painter, Jared is filled with joy at his new life of adventurous, itinerant artistry. His only regret is that he must leave his love Jennet, but he vows to return one day to claim her. Yates's books are always marked by a keen perception of history and her talent at crafting a near-tangible literary world. *Hue and Cry* is the sequel to *The Journeyman*.

Laurence Yep

Dragonwings, 1975. Elementary.

Young Moon Shadow, an eight-year-old boy from China, makes a long journey to join his father, Windrider, in the new land of America. While he and his father dream of building an airplane, they struggle to make a home and friends in their new land. A vivid picture of Chinese culture in San Francisco set amidst the drama of the 1906 San Francisco earthquake. Hopeful and imaginative.

8

Fairy Tales and Fantasy

"Fairy tales are more than true;
not because they tell us that dragons exist,
but because they tell us that dragons can be beaten."

~ G. K. Chesterton

The debate was about to begin. A howl of winter wind circled the house as the six of us perched in various corners of couch and hearth in the shadow dance of a merry fire. Beside us were book stacks, notebooks, magazines, and article clippings in varying degrees of toppled organization. Fortified with fat mugs of hot chocolate and armed to the teeth with research and our own very decided opinions, we waited for the signal to begin what promised to be a historic and very lively discourse in the history of Clarksondom.

It was the great fairy tale debate.

With the three older kids moving into their teenage years, my dad had decided to call a family conclave regarding the presence of fantasy and fairy tale literature in our home.

Though we had grown up familiar with C. S. Lewis and Hans Christian Andersen, we were now moving into new realms of fantasy with books by Tolkien, MacDonald, and L'Engle. By including us in the decision-making process that would govern our literary choices, my dad helped us to comprehend and discern what sorts of fantasy literature would strengthen our souls and why. At his signal, we sprinted off in pursuit of the fairy tale balance.

In the years since that night, I have rehashed the fantasy literature debate in countless similar discussions with strangers and friends. Many people, especially parents of young children, feel uneasy with the whole idea of fantastical stories. While the value of a stellar work such as The Chronicles of Narnia is clear to most, they aren't sure about the rest of the genre. I understand this entirely; fantasy and fairy tale are potent spiritual influences. But it is precisely because they are so powerful that I am their hearty advocate.

The famous family discussion on that long-ago night was the beginning of a deep conviction in my heart that imaginative, fantastical stories are a gift. While great discernment is imperative in this genre, the right imaginative literature can illumine spiritual reality in such a way that it makes biblical truth clearer. Great fantasy and fairy tales uniquely capture the soul-shaking reality of the spiritual world.

Books such as The Chronicles of Narnia, *The Lord of the Rings*, and *A Wrinkle in Time* illuminate spiritual concepts such as good and evil, moral courage, sacrifice, and heroism.

In an increasingly secular culture, the point of good fairy tales or fantasy is to prick our souls awake to spiritual reality. These stories can help flesh out what it means to be good into a clear-cut realm of beauty, battle, and the momentous consequences of our moral choices.

The Bible frequently describes the spiritual world with simile, symbol, and metaphor. Similarly, Christ-centered writers of fantasy and fairy tales (though not divinely inspired) take the substance of transcendent spiritual reality and clothe it in story, character, and form that will bring it to life in our hearts. The point of great fantasy and fairy tales is to guide us back to the reality of a loving God and His story of redemption. These marvelous stories picture the battle that must be fought, the quest that must be started, and the good choices that must be bravely made.

As I mentioned in the introduction, when I was a teenager questioning every aspect of my faith, *The Lord of the Rings* helped to clarify my spiritual turmoil. In that sweeping story of a brave little hobbit sacrificing his life, of kings fighting for their people, and of elves protecting what beauty they could, I realized what it meant to be brave. I saw my own need to commit my life to the true quest of the world—loving God and making him known. Far from obscuring the reality of my own world, Tolkien's fantasy shed a new, clarifying light on the impact of my choices. That story gave an epic scope to my understanding of the world, providing that touch of the eternal, transcendent, and holy for which we all long.

Because that longing in our hearts is so potent, however, we have to be painstakingly careful to satisfy it with stories that will lead us toward the God who will fill all longings. That is why discernment is especially necessary in this genre. It doesn't mean you never read fantasy; it just means you choose it wisely. It will be different for every family; parents must decide what they believe is nourishing to the heart of their children. With this in mind, there are several foundational considerations in choosing good imaginative literature that can help guide you into a wise choice for your family.

First is the age of your children. In their young, formative years, any literature that children encounter should add to their store of beauty and goodness. They need a thorough grounding in what is right before they encounter the darkness and evil of what is wrong. Of course, they will come across mean characters or sadness in their tales, but these are simply part of life and are very different from adult struggles with complex issues of morality. Stories by writers such as Hans Christian Andersen, the picture books of George MacDonald, or the classic Chronicles of Narnia are appropriate fare.

As they grow older, children will eventually move beyond the simplicity of nice and naughty into the reality of a broken world. They will become aware of the sin in their own hearts and the brokenness of other people. They may be challenged by negative influences in culture and their desire to please their peers, as well as their growing need for independence. At this point more complex, mature tales of spiritual

190

imagination become powerful mentors because they give clear, flesh-and-blood imagery to the sometimes elusive idea of what it looks like to be good, brave, or pure. Stories such as *The Lord of the Rings, Dangerous Journey*, or *A Wrinkle in Time* are now appropriate. The villains in these books clearly portray the deception and destruction caused by evil choices, while their heroes and heroines can be role models offering vivid pictures of sacrifice, courage, or humility.

The second thing to consider is worldview. The fantasy world of any author portrays his understanding of moral and spiritual reality. An author who creates out of a void of truth may very skillfully portray a fascinating imaginative reality, but it will also be a profoundly confusing one. Because it is based on a view of the world other than one of absolute truth, good and evil will be portrayed as relative ideas instead of unchangeable, eternal realities.

Children should not be immersed in an imaginative world based on a framework of self-fulfillment or self-reliance, where the hero determines his own morality. Nor should they invest their minds in a story where the line between good and evil, light and dark, is constantly changing based on the circumstances or desires of the characters. A great fairy tale or fantasy should always be built on the framework of real, absolute truth that gives meaning to its characters' choices.

Many of the fantasies by Christian authors are considered classics in both the Christian and the secular world because a moral universe is necessary to a good fairy tale. There can't be a hero without a clear good side and an equally clear bad one, and there can't be right and wrong without some suggestion of a moral order. The concept of heroism is meaningless if there's really no reason for a character to choose one way or another. Works such as *The Lord of the Rings* or The Chronicles of Narnia are classic precisely because of the clearly portrayed dichotomy between good and evil.

The final thing to consider is the use of symbolism in the stories you select. This is where older folklore and ancient fairy tales have value. In his excellent book *A Landscape with Dragons* (1998), Michael O'Brien argues that the use of symbols in literature, both in Scripture and folklore, has always been a means of instructing people in the nature of good and evil. In many of the world's oldest fairy tales, stories passed down literally through centuries, certain images have a universally agreed-upon meaning.

Light, beauty, angels, princesses, and unicorns have always been associated with goodness. Dragons, darkness, black, ugliness, and monsters have always been associated with evil. O'Brien argues that these symbols in the fairy tales passed down from mother to child around the fireside were the means that past generations used to teach their children to recognize the good and evil present in their own world.

This is why I include several collections of folklore and fairy tales in this chapter. While not as explicitly Christian as many more recently written fantasy books, these stories maintain a basic dichotomy between good and evil. With some parental discernment, it can be fascinating for a child to see how clearly goodness has been portrayed throughout the centuries. Because of some pagan roots of the old legends, elements of superstition certainly exist in some of them; because of this, I highly recommend parents prescreen any books for their kids. But overall, the old fairy tales are fascinating pictures of good and evil battling it out through the centuries.

The modern tales, however, are a different matter altogether. In the past few decades, many secular writers of fairy tales have turned the symbols upside down. Dragons become misunderstood outcasts; ogres are portrayed as jolly souls who just need a little patience. You are just as likely to find a prince who is spoiled, selfish, and evil as one who represents true heroism. The traditional "good" symbols get switched, with beauty being disparaged as shallow, while purity is often portrayed as little better than prissiness. While there is nothing wrong with the use of wide creativity in telling a compelling story, I agree with O'Brien that the upending of traditional, deeply meaningful symbols creates confusion. Since symbolic images are meant to picture spiritual reality clearly, seeing them increasingly blurred is disturbing.

The books I have listed below are some of the very best imaginative tales ever written. Each conveys a powerful picture of spiritual reality clothed in adventure, beauty, and whimsy. The elements of worldview, correct symbolism, and creative excellence are present in all of them. While each of you will come to your own decisions regarding each story, I hope that these books will be a source of spiritual encouragement and great delight to your family. I hope that you too will draw close to the fireside to warm both hands and heart by the mystery of these tales.

Further Reading

With the profusion of fantasy being written today because of our cultural fascination with it, several insightful writers have tackled the issue of the effect it has on the heart of a child. These books greatly influenced my own thoughts regarding this genre, and I commend them to you:

- *Landscape with Dragons: The Battle for Your Child's Mind* by Michael O'Brien

- *Tending the Heart of Virtue: How Classic Stories Waken a Child's Moral Imagination* by Vigen Guroian

- *God of the Fairy Tale: Finding Truth in the Land of Make-Believe* by Jim Ware

Lloyd Alexander

The Chronicles of Prydain, 1964–1973. Junior High.

Based loosely on Welsh mythology, with characters and drama drawn from the *Mabinogion* (an ancient book of Welsh myth and legend), this quality literary series has been deeply loved since its publication. It is powerful in its presentation of good and evil and subtle in its exploration of the moral dilemmas that all would-be heroes and heroines must face.

In the first volume, *The Book of Three*, Taran, an Assistant Pig Keeper in the realm of Prydain, is a restless young man yearning for adventure and heroism. When his charge, the pig Hen Wen, runs away, he is catapulted into an adventure that will start him on the road to becoming a hero. Accompanied by the sharp-tongued princess Eilonwy, the eccentric bard Fflewddur Fflam, and the forest creature Gurgi, Taran begins a quest to foil the evil Horned King's plans to conquer the beautiful land of Prydain.

Caution: This is a fantasy series, based in a fantasy world where magic is a normal part of daily life.

The series includes:
- ♥ *The Book of Three*
- ♥ *The Black Cauldron*
- ♥ *The Castle of Llyr*
- ♥ *Taran Wanderer*
- ♥ *The High King*
- ♥ *The Foundling and Other Tales of Prydain*

Hans Christian Andersen

Fairy Tales, 1835. Elementary.

"Every man's life is a fairy tale written by God's own fingers." With thoughts like that in his wondrously creative brain, Andersen wrote a collection of some of the world's most-loved fairy tales which convey deep themes of virtue. Whether exploring the self-sacrifice of a girl for the lives of her enchanted brothers or the repentance of the selfish little mermaid, these stories are gems in their literary beauty and poignant moral ideas. There are countless versions available, but I especially recommend the following:

♥ *Michael Hague's Favorite Hans Christian Andersen Fairy Tales*

♥ *The Classic Treasury of Hans Christian Andersen* illustrated by Christian Birmingham

John Bunyan

The Pilgrim's Progress, 1678. Junior High through High School.

This classic spiritual allegory pictures the journey of faith that each believing soul makes. Christian's dangerous journey through Vanity Fair, the Slough of Despond, and many other dark places on his way to the Celestial City has inspired generations of Christians to perseverance and faith. First published over three hundred years ago, it has never been out of print. It provides timeless insight into the sin and moral struggles of the common Christian, vivid personification of vice and virtue, and a compelling portrayal of hope.

Dangerous Journey, 1985. Arranged by Oliver Hunkin. Junior High.

Oliver Hunkin retells *Pilgrim's Progress* for a modern audience. While retaining much of the original wording and staying wholly true to the author's intent, this abridged edition slightly simplifies some of the old language and adds dramatic illustrations that capture the images presented in the story. My family loved this version for its pictures; we read it aloud many times.

Caution: Alan Parry's illustrations are vivid, intense, and at times disturbing as they portray the vices of the world or the outright evil of Apollyon (Satan). Use discernment when reading to younger children.

Andrew Lang

Fairy Book series, 1889–1910. Elementary.

Andrew Lang's compilations of folk and fairy tales are among the best. His love for the English borderland fairy tales he heard in his youth led him on a hunt to find great folktales in countries around the world. With some of his discovered tales being published for the first time, these collections give their readers a taste of the highly distinctive folk legends original to countries from Europe, Asia, and Africa, while also observing the recurrence of some themes and story forms throughout all ages and civilizations.

Caution: As with all fairy tales, good and evil fight it out in more or less troublesome ways. Also, because these are old stories from diverse countries, quite a few bear the superstitious elements of earlier times and various religious cultures, including witches, genies, magic, ogres, etc. Many fairy tales can be downright strange and, at times, upsetting. I recommend that parents review these books before handing them to young children. These stories do, however, maintain the near-universal symbols of good and evil that so clearly illustrate the human need for clearly defined morality.

The series includes:
- ♥ *Blue Fairy Book*
- ♥ *Red Fairy Book*
- ♥ *Green Fairy Book*
- ♥ *Yellow Fairy Book*
- ♥ *Pink Fairy Book*
- ♥ *Grey Fairy Book*
- ♥ *Violet Fairy Book*
- ♥ *Crimson Fairy Book*
- ♥ *Brown Fairy Book*
- ♥ *Orange Fairy Book*
- ♥ *Olive Fairy Book*
- ♥ *Lilac Fairy Book*

Madeleine L'Engle

A Wrinkle in Time, 1962. Newbery Medalist. Junior High.

Stubborn Meg Murry hates her glasses, her school, and the fact that her father is missing. When she and her brother Charles Wallace meet three mysterious old women, they find that they alone have the power to find and free their father. Whisked through time and space to the far-off planet where their father is held prisoner, Meg and Charles must struggle to free him and themselves from the powerful, streamlining force of It, an intelligence who demands that all beings obey his powerful pulse. A vivid, triumphant picture of the power of love to conquer evil, this story will challenge you to live with courage, love, and endurance.

Caution: Some readers have found fault with L'Engle's characters for their confusing symbolism. For example, a character called Mrs. Which (one of a trio including Mrs. Who and Mrs. Whatsit) appears dressed like a witch as a joke on her name. In another case, the children visit a planet to meet the Happy Medium (notice the wordplay), who shows them what is happening across the universe. While these two situations could be confusing to young children, the book never endorses magic or witchcraft; with parental explanation, I feel that the spiritual impact of this story is so powerfully good that it should not be missed.

C. S. Lewis

The Chronicles of Narnia. Elementary through Junior High.

When four ordinary English children are swept into a strange, vibrant world called Narnia, they discover talking animals, a winter wasteland, dryads and fauns, and a prophecy that they seem created to fulfill. But it is the rumor of the great lion Aslan that sets their hearts tingling with hunger to meet this being who called them out of their own world to know him better in Narnia. Each book conveys deep spiritual truths reflecting the Christian gospel, but the whole series is so subtly crafted that the world of Narnia seems like a real, beloved place. This classic series should be read over and over, both alone and aloud.

The Lion, the Witch, and the Wardrobe, 1950.
   In this first book, the four Pevensie children—Peter, Susan, Edmund, and Lucy—discover a world that they enter from the back of an old wardrobe. Swept up in the fight between a witch who desires to keep the world in winter and the servants of the great lion Aslan who has come to bring spring, the children must decide which side they will join. Edmund betrays the others, and a great sacrifice must be made to win him back. The classic beginning to the Narnia adventures, with one of Lewis's more explicit depictions of the gospel.

Prince Caspian, 1951.
   Called back into Narnia by a desperate plea for help, the four Pevensie children tumble back into their beloved world only to find that hundreds of years have passed since their last visit. With Narnia now at war, they must find the rightful prince, young Caspian, and fight to set him back on the throne before his cruel uncle Miraz destroys the old Narnia and sends the talking beasts back into hiding.

The Voyage of the Dawn Treader, 1952.

A strange picture transports Lucy, Edmund, and their whiny cousin Eustace back into Narnia on board Caspian's ship of exploration. With the new young king determined to find the lords banished by his evil uncle and the "utter east" where Aslan dwells, the children are caught up in a grand and dangerous voyage through unknown islands, right to the edge of Aslan's own country. This is one of my favorite Narnia books; I love the poignancy with which it conveys the hunger and thrill of the heart as it journeys toward God.

The Silver Chair, 1953.

Eustace and his friend Polly literally tumble into Narnia and into a grievous mystery. They find Prince Caspian an old man who has gone in search of his only son, missing now for ten years. Entrusted by Aslan with a series of signs that will lead them to the missing prince, the two children begin a journey that takes them into the wild lands of the north and then deep into the strange places beneath the earth. Rich with themes of remembrance, loyalty, and endurance, this Narnia tale illumines the nature of relentless faith.

The Horse and His Boy, 1954.

A departure from the Narnia of the earlier stories, this tale begins in the southern and eastern realms of hot, pagan Calormen. Shasta, a bright young boy who has never loved his cruel father, meets a talking warhorse, and they decide to escape to the free lands of the north where the beautiful

Narnia is said to exist. Picturing the spiritual journey of conversion through the physical road that Shasta must take with his horse Bree and the runaway princess Aravis, this is a fast-paced, exciting tale.

The Magician's Nephew, 1955.

A prequel to the first five books, this is the tale of Narnia's creation as a world sung into existence by the great, loving Aslan. When Digory and Polly end up in an enchanted wood, they discover that the many pools on the forest floor lead to different worlds. While trying to escape from a destructive queen, they tumble together into a newborn world where they must fight to keep evil from corrupting its fresh, innocent beauty. Themes of the power of new creation and the consequences of choice pervade this earliest history of Narnia.

The Last Battle, 1956.

In this final, apocalyptic book, every human character from the previous books comes back to Narnia as it reaches the end of its days. From a peaceful, beautiful land, Narnia has become a realm of grief and war as the Narnians are deceived by a clever ape. When the invading Calormenes bring with them their evil god Tash, the end has come and only Aslan can restore his loyal people and beautiful land.

This last book wherein Lewis imagines the end of the world encourages and heartens my spirit every time I remember it.

Lois Lowry

The Giver, 1993. Newbery Medalist. Junior High.

This book pictures a utopian world in which all pain, grief, and struggle have been erased and, along with them, human emotion and color. When young Jonas reaches the age when all citizens are assigned a lifelong work, he is shocked to discover the existence of one man chosen to keep the memories of pain and beauty for all generations. Even more shockingly, Jonas has been chosen to replace him. His lessons with the Giver prompt him to question the reality of his sterile world and eventually require him to make a heart-rending choice. A powerful, haunting story, this is an excellent read-aloud for parents with their older children as the story leads into deep moral and spiritual questions.

Caution: This is definitely a story for older kids as it deals with issues such as euthanasia, infanticide, and the abdication of moral responsibility. There is a section dealing with Jonas's passage into adulthood when he is given pills to suppress any unwanted "feelings."

P. J. Lynch (illustrator)

The Candlewick Book of Fairy Tales, 1993. Edited by Sarah Hayes. Young Child.

Illustrated by the matchless P. J. Lynch with realistic but fanciful pictures bursting with color and action, this is an enjoyable fairy tale read-aloud to be treasured for its beauty. These fresh, concise retellings of the most familiar European fairy tales offer an introduction to the classic canon of fairy tales that forms a foundational part of the modern imagination.

George MacDonald

See Chapter 6 for reviews of *At the Back of the North Wind*, *The Lost Princess*, and *The Princess and the Goblin*.

David and Karen Mains

Kingdom Tales, 1983–1996. Junior High.

Deep in the fiery heart of the Enchanted City, where people work by night and sleep by day, live the orphan Scarboy and his little brother. Haunted by fear of the Fire Lord and his servants, Scarboy decides to escape the city for the nearby forest where ancient stories say a kind and generous king lives in exile, waiting to return and claim his people. Adopted by a benevolent group of forest-dwellers, Scarboy discovers that he has fallen in with the king's own people. But it is only when they step through the circle of sacred fire that their real souls, and Scarboy's own, are truly seen.

This highly symbolic series with its clever portrayals of evil and good and its captivating servant king are a beautiful picture of Christ's love as He rescues us from Satan's enchantment and sends us back to rescue others. The final book with its theme of a returning, sacrificial king took my breath away. Look for the editions with illustrations by Jack Stockman, as his amazing pictures greatly enhance the beauty of the story. The series includes:

♥ *Tales of the Kingdom*
♥ *Tales of the Resistance*
♥ *Tales of the Restoration*

Alan and Linda Parry

The Evergreen Wood, 1992. Elementary.

This charmingly illustrated retelling of Bunyan's *Pilgrim's Progress* tells the tale of Christopher Mouse as he makes his arduous journey through the Dark Wood with its weasels and snares to the bright beauty of the Evergreen Wood. A great spiritual story for young children, the book is full of amusing, bright pictures and colorful examples of moral strength; it makes a great read-aloud.

J. R. R. Tolkien

The Lord of the Rings, 1954–1955. Junior High through High School.

This epic, heroic, heartrendingly beautiful tale is one of my greatest spiritual influences. Considered by many devoted readers to be the zenith of faith-driven fantasy, this sweeping adventure story is the tale of a simple hobbit (a little man) who stumbles upon a simple gold ring that is the only thing that Sauron, the most evil power in the world, needs to enslave the whole world. With the brave, long-suffering elves fighting to keep beauty alive and the kingdom of men struggling to hold back the dark power, Frodo the hobbit must begin an arduous journey into the darkest land on earth to destroy the powerful ring. He must protect his fellowship of sworn companions from the ring's dark power and resist the temptation to take it for himself.

This tale is matchless in the intricacy of its imagined world, the vivid reality of its characters, and the different races of elves, dwarves, men, ents, and hobbits. Its portrayal of the most fundamental Christian virtues, its stark presentation of good and evil, and its mighty description of the battle that must be waged against evil make this a classic. I can't do justice to the beauty of this story.

Caution: This trilogy is for older children. While never explicit, it includes numerous battles with evil creatures, dragons, and darkness. Also, some readers object to the portrayal of a "wizard" as a good character, but in reality, the wizards of the story are so named only as a convenience and should be most closely compared with spiritual shepherds or archangels. Tolkien considers epic problems of good, evil, choice, and doom, and the characters and battles reflect the grand scope of his deep spiritual insight. Thus, even while being readable by younger children, it is perhaps better to save it for children old enough to consider and be challenged by its powerful spiritual themes.

Due largely to post-war paper shortages, the novel was published in three volumes:

- ♥ *The Fellowship of the Ring*
- ♥ *The Two Towers*
- ♥ *The Return of the King*

The Hobbit, 1937. Junior High.

The more simply told precursor to *The Lord of the Rings* trilogy, *The Hobbit* is the humorous tale of Bilbo the hobbit and his unexpected journey to defeat a dragon. Told in many ways like a traditional fairy tale, full of the earthy charm of dwarves and forest elves, this is an amusing and adventurous read that retains echoes of the heroism and greatness of its sequel. A great read-aloud.

Caution: Again, this is a vivid fantasy world peopled by fantastical creatures such as a dragon which causes great danger to the heroes of the tale. Use caution when reading to younger children.

Paul Zelinsky (author and illustrator)

Rapunzel, 1997. Caldecott Medalist. Young Child.

Rich, colorful drawings complement the spirit of timeless fairy tales with a wealth of detail and intricacy. With startlingly beautiful art and old tales retold in a fresh, simple voice, Zelinsky's picture books are ideal for read-aloud.

Also by Zelinsky:
- ♥ *Hansel and Gretel* (Caldecott Honor Book)
- ♥ *Rumpelstiltskin* (Caldecott Honor Book)

9

History and Biography

A library, to modify the famous metaphor of Socrates,
should be the delivery room for the birth of ideas—
a place where history comes to life.

~ Norman Cousins

My enjoyment of history has a definitive beginning: It dates to the moment I discovered that knights and fair maidens had actually lived and that the enjoyment of their tales constituted study. Discovering the academic worth of something your imagination already loves is always a good way to begin. I was eight years old and captivated by the illustrated *Saint George and the Dragon* by Margaret Hodges when I heard my mom mention to a friend that I was studying medieval history.

I was momentarily shocked. It had never occurred to me that my avid delight in the near-magical world of my books would qualify as serious study. I hadn't consciously realized that I was studying a period of history or even that my reading was a form of education. When I became aware that the engrossing stories of monks, fair maidens, and kings could constitute history, I was won. If this was history, then history was simply one of the best stories I had ever read.

Because of that, I have always understood history within the context of story and thus have found it to be fascinating. I think, though, that I am among the fortunate few. Far too often the first reaction that kids have to the study of history is disinterest. To them it seems dry and remote—a boring collection of facts about dead people and long-forgotten events. When history is studied solely through textbooks—disconnected from the particular, colorful stories of individual lives—it loses the luster of its deep emotion and becomes simply a recitation of obscure dates.

History is really the epic, true story of the world, and it ought to be told with the same skill and delight inherent in any great tale. Children need to be absorbed by the real drama of history so that they will be able to understand the vast consequences wrought by the actions of a single person. As they mature, they will need to comprehend the forces of power, ideology, and passion that crafted the present so that they will be equipped to similarly craft the future. This will only happen if their imagination and thus their interest have been sparked by history.

That's where historical fiction and biographies take the stage.

When the record of the world is introduced to children as a rip-roaring tale peopled by humorous, dramatic, and highly entertaining souls whose spunk shaped the world in which we now live, it becomes a fascinating subject. Literary biographies and well-written historical fiction introduce children to history (as well as philosophy, religion, and geography) as an engaging, fascinating experience of real people with very human desires, feelings, and hopes.

Textbooks, the standard tools for teaching history, simply can't offer this keen flavor of story. They are severely limited in their ability to convey the intricate weave of individual stores that make up history because they are required to be broad in scope and generalized in tone, with a vocabulary limited to what a classroom of a dozen or more children can easily grasp in a lesson. Fact based, group-oriented, and often written by several people, they are only the skeleton of fact upon which the blood, muscle, and breath of history is built. Historical fiction or well-researched biographies by a single author offer the viewpoint of a writer with a specific interest and passion for the time period in which the stories are set. The quality of language, story content, and subject are more literary in tone, uninhibited by a stunted vocabulary list or politically correct agenda.

If you want your children to grasp the fierce glory of the Scottish struggle for independence, then give them *The Scottish Chiefs*. For the Civil War, give them the distinctive story of *Rifles for Watie* or the heart-rending *Across Five Aprils*. If you want them to understand and remember George Washington, Joan of Arc, and Martin Luther, give them the imaginatively formed stories by skilled writers that illuminate the gritty, funny, passionate souls that were driven to life-altering action.

It is entirely possible to teach history primarily through literature. With some guidance and a little factual framing, well-written historical fiction, memoirs, and biographies can impart a living, breathing picture of past times that will help your children comprehend the depth and drama of history in an unforgettable way. Historical literature imparts an imaginative experience in which the reader encounters the spice of curry, the clank of armor, the mellow music of a lute, and the raucous laughter of a medieval feast. A good historical tale sets its reader right in the minds of characters experiencing historic events as they happen, giving insight into the passions and causes of great wars or rising kingdoms.

Children need to understand the people and events of history as pertinent to their preparation for life. If they are used to thinking of history as merely factual and therefore boring, that can take some convincing. But it shouldn't be too hard if you hand them a good story. Give your boys a copy of *The Red Keep,* or your girls a copy of *Number the Stars,* and watch their inner historians emerge.

Study Guides

I highly recommend the historical study guides by Beautiful Feet Books and Greenleaf Press. Beautiful Feet guides especially employ a wide variety of outstanding fiction as part of their historical courses. Both companies have a wide selection of historical fiction by time period.

Beautiful Feet Books: www.bfbooks.com
Greenleaf Press: www.greenleafpress.com

Ancient History: Creation–A.D. 400

Ruth Beechick

Adam and His Kin, 1990. Junior High through High School.
   This dramatized and entertaining account of the first eleven chapters of Genesis brings creative insight to the creation story while maintaining loyalty to the biblical text. Beechick recreates the earliest years of man, including great amounts of historic fact surrounding the biblical stories.

Jeanne Bendick

Archimedes and the Door of Science, 1962. Junior High through High School.
   The mathematical, philosophic, and scientific research of the ancient Greek scientist Archimedes influenced the theories of countless scientists in the centuries after his death.

With insight and humor, Bendick illuminates his ancient world, his work, and the brilliance of his discoveries.

Galen and the Gateway to Medicine, 1962. Junior High.
A Roman medical researcher, Galen developed theories of the human body that became foundational to the thinking of medicine for the next thousand years. With humor and a story filled with little-known facts, Bendick introduces her reader to this pivotal doctor of the Roman era.

Padraic Colum

The Children's Homer, 1918. Elementary through Junior High.
Colum has condensed for children the ancient Greek classics of *The Iliad* and *The Odyssey*, which many scholars consider to be the world's greatest stories. Retaining much of the intricacy of the originals, Colum skillfully recounts the story of the Trojan War, its heroes, and their epic journeys home in clear, beautiful language. A great introduction to the ancient classics that will whet the appetite for the real stuff later on.

Eloise Jarvis McGraw

Mara, Daughter of the Nile, 1953. Junior High.

Brave and intelligent, the young slave Mara is embroiled in danger when her talent for translation prompts her master to offer her freedom in exchange for her services as a spy. Set in the lush royal palace of the Egyptian queen Hatshepsut, this is an engrossing portrait of ancient Egypt.

The Golden Goblet, 1961. Newbery Honor Book. Junior High.

As a porter in a goldsmith shop, Ranofer has put his keen eyes to use in observing and learning the trade. When his cruel half-brother forces him to become involved in a sinister plot to steal gold, he must figure out a way to escape and learn the papyrus trade he loves from a man called the Ancient. A great introduction to Egyptian history and culture.

Caroline Dale Snedeker

Theras and His Town, 1924. Elementary.

Lauded author Caroline Dale Snedeker's books are set mostly in ancient Greece and are classics in their genre. When his father is killed in battle and his mother loses her position of work, Theras is forced to leave his beautiful Athens for the strange land of Sparta. Longing for his mother and home, Theras befriends another boy, and they plot together to make the journey to home and freedom.

Lysis Goes to the Play, 1962. Elementary.

Immerse yourself in the grandeur and excitement of Greek drama at the time of its writing. When young Lysis sneaks himself and his sister into the performance of a new play, he gets a taste of the legendary Euripides.

The White Isle, 1940. Elementary.

When Lavinia's father is exiled, she and her family must make the long, arduous journey to the strange White Isle (England), where the new religion of Christianity is just taking hold. An insightful look at Great Britain and the early church, as well as life in the Roman world.

Elizabeth George Speare

The Bronze Bow, 1961. Newbery Medalist. Junior High through High School.

Daniel wants nothing more than to spill the blood of the Romans who destroyed his family. A member of an outlaw band from his early teens, he ventures back into the confines of Jerusalem after meeting an old friend. There he encounters his timid sister Leah and is caught up in the drama surrounding Jesus. As his interest in Jesus grows, Daniel finds himself torn between his hatred and Jesus' proffered love. Speare's excellent, literary writing and skilled narrative vibrantly portray Jerusalem in Jesus' time, while poignantly tracing the redemption of a young man's soul.

Diane Stanley

Cleopatra, 1994. Elementary.

Stanley combines careful historic research with detailed, intriguing illustrations and a storyteller's delight in the outlandish tales surrounding the life of Cleopatra, the dramatic and beautiful queen of Egypt who stole the hearts of Julius Caesar and Mark Antony. An unforgettable picture book of the legendary queen and her tumultuous times.

Patricia St. John

Twice Freed, 1971. Elementary through Junior High.

Based on Paul's biblical letter to Philemon, this vividly imagined story follows Onesimus, a rebellious young slave who is on the run from his master. From the gladiator rings of Nero's Rome to the earthquake in Laodicea, Onesimus searches for adventure and freedom, but he cannot seem to escape the followers of the strange new religion of Christ. A spiritually poignant tale that accurately depicts the world of the early church with its social tensions and tumultuous times.

217

Rosemary Sutcliff

The Eagle of the Ninth, 1954. Junior High through High School.

Considered one of the best writers of historical fiction, Sutcliff skillfully weaves the tumultuous history of Roman Britain into a set of novels that are remarkable for the factual accuracy of the worlds they imagine, as well as their literary quality and engaging characters and plots. The first book, *The Eagle of the Ninth,* introduces the reader to young, restless Marcus, the son of a Roman commander whose legion disappeared in the wilds of Britain. Determined to restore the honor of his lost father and to enter combat, Marcus begins a quest accompanied by an odd companion with a colorful past.

The Silver Branch, 1957. Junior High through High School.

Set a hundred years after *Eagle,* this book follows the trek of two brave cousins who set out to oppose a tyrant who has set himself up as ruler and has broken ties with Rome. Continuing the theme of the famous Ninth Legion, this adventure story gives an accurate portrayal of Great Britain in the Roman days.

The Lantern Bearers, 1959. Carnegie Medalist. Junior High through High School.

Set in the frightening days of the Saxon invasion of Britain, this is the story of Aquila, a Roman soldier who courageously

218

stays behind to defend his home when the Romans retreat before the savage Saxons. When he and his sister are kidnapped and enslaved, he struggles to gain his freedom, striving to keep alive the light of dignity and civilization in his land and in his own heart.

Caution: This is a bleak story, dealing with issues of war, brutality, and irrevocable loss; therefore it is best suited for older children nearing high school.

Joanne Williamson

Hittite Warrior, 1960. Elementary through Junior High.

A young boy finds himself caught up in the struggle between the Hebrew army of Barak and Deborah and the Hittite army. This story of a boy's search for shelter and truth vividly portrays the religion and culture of a vital period of Hebrew history.

God King: A Story in the Days of King Hezekiah, 2002. Elementary through Junior High.

With the young Egyptian pharaoh Taharka as its hero, this book dramatically portrays the reign of King Hezekiah as he alone holds out against the cruel Assyrian attacks under Sennacherib. Brings ancient and biblical history to vivid life.

Also Recommended for This Time Period:
♥ *Joel: A Boy of Galilee* by Annie Fellows Johnston

♥ *The Librarian Who Measured the Earth*
   by Kathryn Lasky
♥ *The Ides of April* by Mary Ray
♥ *The Forgotten Daughter* by Caroline Dale Snedeker
♥ *The Spartan* by Caroline Dale Snedeker
♥ *A Triumph for Flavius* by Caroline Dale Snedeker
♥ *The Runaway* by Patricia St. John
♥ *The Wanderings of Odysseus* by Rosemary Sutcliff
♥ *Black Ships Before Troy* by Rosemary Sutcliff
♥ *The Queen Elizabeth Story* by Rosemary Sutcliff

Medieval Period: A.D. 400–1500

Aliki

A Medieval Feast, 1983. Young Child.

Detailed, whimsical illustrations in radiant hues depict the creation of a medieval feast. With text detailing all sorts of historical facts regarding cooking, gardening, clothes, manners, and traditions of a medieval house, this book is sure to inspire delight in the pageantry and color of medieval times.

James Daugherty

The Magna Charta, 1956. Junior High through High School.

An artist and champion of the "wit and taste, beauty and joy" that are the legacy of a free people, Daugherty poured his passion into spirited historical books for children. *The Magna Charta* traces the tangle of kings, popes, and wars that led to the writing of an unprecedented document declaring the rights and freedoms of a people. Set in the days of Robin Hood and Richard the Lionheart, this book illustrates how the Magna Charta became the founding document for the idea of a country ruled by a constitution. Illustrated by the author.

Marguerite de Angeli

The Door in the Wall, 1949. Newbery Medalist. Junior High.

With his father away in the Crusades and his mother off in service to the queen, young Robin waits at home, dreaming of knighthood until the day he falls ill with the deadly plague. Left a cripple, he must learn how to live life anew and become a hero in his own right with the help of the kind Brother Luke. This award-winning story of medieval England is chock full of knights, fair ladies, and gallantry.

Elizabeth Janet Gray

Adam of the Road, 1942. Newbery Medalist. Junior High.

The son of an itinerant minstrel, eleven-year-old Adam Quartermayne has inherited his father's musical gift and sets out with him on a journey to follow in the training of a knight. Through tournaments and fairs, cities and castles, Adam pursues music and his lost dog, getting a vivid tour of the medieval world in the process. A unique view of this time period.

Allen French

The Red Keep: A Story of Burgundy in the Year 1165, 1938. Junior High.

Conan is a young page in service of the noble Baron Roger, one of the few goodhearted rulers in a land of robber barons. When Conan helps his lord to rescue Anne, the only daughter of a baron murdered by the cruel Sauval brothers, Conan begins a journey to avenge her and reclaim the ruined Red Keep. A swashbuckling tale of medieval France, the book is illustrated with black-and-white pictures by the famous artist Andrew Wyeth.

The Story of Rolf and the Viking Bow, 1904. Junior High.

Set amidst the cold and drama of a newly Christian Iceland, this tale is woven in the epic style of an old Norse saga. From being named an outlaw for defending his father to being captured by Vikings to finally becoming a slave of a haughty Icelandic boy, Rolf traverses the high seas, striving to vindicate his father and make his way back home. Rich with themes of vengeance versus forgiveness, this is a scintillating portrait of medieval Iceland.

Jonathan Hunt

Illuminations, 1989. Young Child.

This oversized picture book is brightly illustrated in the style of medieval illuminations, the intricate drawings with which medieval monks illustrated their sacred texts. Using the alphabet of the medieval world, each page illumines some aspect of castle, monastery, or peasant life. Great for reading aloud.

Eleanore M. Jewett

Big John's Secret, 1962. Junior High.

There's a mystery to Big John's past, but only Old Marm knows it; and she is determined to educate the poor boy and teach him courtly manners. When Old Marm dies, Big John becomes page to a knight of the Crusades. In his journeys, he meets a compassionate man named Francis who has come to tell the Saracens about Christ.

Katherine Paterson

Parzival: The Quest of the Grail Knight, 1998. Elementary through Junior High.

With royal blood in his veins and a desire for knighthood in his heart, the young peasant Parzival sets out for the court of King Arthur. This retelling of the legend of Percival and his quest for the Holy Grail (the cup of Christ from the Last Supper) weaves Camelot's adventure and thrill with a clear presentation of Christian ideas. A classic, chivalric tale.

Jane Porter

The Scottish Chiefs, 1810. Junior High through High School.

This famous novel explores the Scottish fight for independence from England led by William Wallace and Robert the Bruce in the thirteenth and fourteenth centuries. Focusing on the lives of Scotland's favorite heroes, this is an epic tale of engaging character and heart-tugging love along with a stirring portrayal of sacrifice, patriotism, and heroism.

Howard Pyle

Otto of the Silver Hand, 1888. Junior High.

Raised in a monastery after the death of his mother, Otto is reclaimed by his baron father when he is twelve years old.

Thrust into a world of feuding and battle, Otto is captured by a cruel knight and falls in love with the knight's daughter. Told in strong, old-fashioned prose, this story of medieval Germany has at its heart the belief that character is stronger than any sword.

Men of Iron, 1891. Junior High.

With a blind father and a tarnished family heritage, Myles Falworth is determined to become a knight and reclaim his family's honor. With dialogue that authentically captures medieval wording and expression, and a captivating portrayal of the workings of a medieval castle and tournament, this adventure story has strong themes of courage and endurance.

Kate Seredy

The White Stag, 1937. Newbery Medalist. Junior High.

Fascinated by the myths of the Huns and Magyar tribes that were the founders of her own country, Hungary, Seredy set out to retell the myth of her country's founding and bring a spark of humanity to the infamous Attila the Hun. Written with her spare, lovely prose and a storyteller's gift of insight into history, this slim tale pictures a little-known part of the settling of medieval Europe.

Robert Louis Stevenson

The Black Arrow, 1883. Junior High.

When young Richard Shelton falls in with the outlaws whose sign is the black arrow, they cause him to question the circumstances of his father's death. With a treacherous uncle and a constant tumult of battles to contend with, Richard joins with outlaws and runaways to claim justice and rescue his lady, Joanna Sedley. Set in England during the Wars of the Roses.

Mark Twain

Joan of Arc, 1896. Junior High through High School.

Mark Twain, the famous author of *Adventures of Huckleberry Finn,* considered this book on the French saint his best work. Spending over twelve years in research, he eventually published this creative account of Joan's life, writing it from the point of view of her childhood friend. An engaging telling of the true story of the young medieval girl who heard God call her to defend France against the English, this is a beautiful account of a young woman's unshakable faith.

Barbara Willard

Augustine Came to Kent, 1963. Junior High through High School.

In the year 597, Pope Gregory sent a band of missionaries to re-evangelize Britain. Told through the eyes of young Wolf, a member of the party who makes the journey, this story of early Christian Britain is insightful and exciting as Wolf comes to love the young girl Fritha and finds his faith and his place in a strange world.

If All the Swords in England, 1961. Junior High.

Separated after the tragic death of their parents, twins Simon and Edmund end up as servants to two archenemies, King Henry and Thomas Becket, the Archbishop of Canterbury. Through their eyes, the reader experiences the story of a raging king and a holy, stubborn priest who became a martyr for his defense of the church.

Son of Charlemagne, 1959. Junior High.

This is a captivating imagining of the life of Charlemagne, the early medieval Frankish king who created an empire of smaller kingdoms ruled by his children. Fact-filled but story-driven, this is a delightfully personal tale, portraying Charlemagne's love for his family even as he strove to expand his empire.

Also Recommended for This Time Period:
- ♥ *The Sword in the Tree* by Clyde Robert Bulla
- ♥ *The King's Swift Rider* by Mollie Hunger
- ♥ *The Trumpeter of Krakow* by Eric Kelly
- ♥ *Twelve Bright Trumpets* by Margaret Leighton
- ♥ *The Merry Adventures of Robin Hood* by Howard Pyle
- ♥ *The Story of King Arthur and His Knights* by Howard Pyle

The Renaissance: 1500–1650

Jeanne Bendick

Along Came Galileo, 1999. Elementary through Junior High.
 One of the foremost of the brilliant Renaissance scientists, Galileo was a genius in mathematics, astronomy, and science. This insightful, absorbing biography brings to life the story of a gifted man whose theories turned the world upside down.

Janie B. Cheaney

The Playmaker, 2000. Junior High.
 Determined to grant his mother's dying wish and find his father, fourteen-year-old Richard must figure out how

to survive the danger and drama of London in 1597. He joins a company of actors called Lord Chamberlain's Men and befriends one in particular named Will. His friendship with the budding playwright becomes central to his life as he battles mysterious attackers and searches for his father. A captivating introduction to the life and times of Shakespeare.

Elizabeth Borton de Treviño

I, Juan de Pareja, 1965. Newbery Medalist. Elementary through Junior High.

When the young slave Juan is given to the great painter Velasquez as a servant, a deep, artistic friendship begins. As Juan grows to love his kind, quiet master, he discovers his own gifts in art and slowly begins to express them. This novel brings to life the times of the Spanish masters.

Charles Kingsley

Westward Ho!, 1855. Junior High through High School.

Headstrong young Amyas Leigh is full of energy, hates the Spanish (as do all good Englishmen of his generation), and hungers to set to sea. In a round of adventures encompassing sailing with Sir Frances Drake, fighting with Raleigh in Ireland, and sailing against the Spanish Armada, Amyas sees the world. Along the way, he fights his way to manhood and gains a worthy heart full of love for the beautiful Ayacanora. A swashbuckling classic.

Robert T. Reilly

Red Hugh, Prince of Donegal, 1957. Junior High.

A brave Irish prince and heir to a great castle, young Hugh, Prince of Donegal, is kidnapped by the English and imprisoned in Dublin. His daring escape and wholehearted love of his country take him on a wild journey in the company of brawny Irishmen and his brave mother, Ineen. An enthralling slice of Irish history during the reign of Elizabeth I.

Also Recommended for This Time Period:
- ♥ *Good Queen Bess* by Diane Stanley
- ♥ *Bard of Avon: The Story of William Shakespeare* by Diane Stanley
- ♥ *The Prince and the Pauper* by Mark Twain

The Reformation: 1500–1650

Scott O'Dell

The Hawk That Dare Not Hunt By Day, 1975. Junior High through High School.

A young smuggler on a ship that regularly crosses the English Channel, Tom sees William Tyndale and his dangerous desire to get the Bible into the hands of common men as another way to get rich. But as the kind Tyndale exposes Tom to the life-giving words of Scripture, Tom's heart begins to change. This stirring story of the brave martyr William Tyndale is told with intrigue and grace by an award winning author.

Louise A. Vernon

Reformation series, 1967–1977. Junior High.

Told through the eyes of various unexpected and engaging characters, this series of books on the heroes of the Reformation chronicles the lives and times of such great reformers as Martin Luther, William Tyndale, and Gutenberg with his printing press.

   ♥ *The Beggars' Bible* (Wycliffe)
   ♥ *The Bible Smuggler* (Tyndale)
   ♥ *Ink on His Fingers* (Gutenberg)

❤ *The Man Who Laid the Egg* (Erasmus)
❤ *Thunderstorm in Church* (Luther)

N. A. Woychuk

The British Josiah, 2001. Elementary through Junior High.

Crowned at nine years old and king for just six years, Edward VI had an extraordinary love for Scripture. Likened to the biblical king Josiah for his sincere faith and earnest searching of Scripture, this young man readied England for the Reformation and left a legacy of godliness that influenced the spiritual center of his country. This novel tells his fascinating though little-known story.

American Colonial Period: 1600–1775

Gary Bowen

Stranded at Plimoth Plantation 1626, 1994. Young Child through Elementary.

When the good ship *Sparrowhawk* is wrecked near Plimoth Colony in the New World, thirteen-year-old Christopher Sears is lodged with the family of William Brewster. Throughout his winter there, he keeps a journal vividly picturing the solemnity, heartiness, and faithful daily lives of the Plimoth Pilgrims. This picture book history of Plimoth Plantation is superbly illustrated with the author's woodcuts.

Joseph Bruchac

Squanto's Journey: The Story of the First Thanksgiving, 2000. Young Child through Elementary.

Sweeping gouache paintings and a painstakingly researched story make this picture book history of Squanto's life insightful and inspiring. His remarkable journey from young tribesman to slave and back to freedom is compellingly told, revealing the compassion of the forgiving man who willingly helped the Pilgrims in their time of need.

Clyde Robert Bulla

Squanto: Friend of the Pilgrims, 1954. Junior High.

A captivating and much-beloved writer for children, Bulla brought his story-telling skill to this insightful biography of Squanto, the Indian who aided the starving Pilgrims when they first came to Plimoth. With skillful narrative and empathy, Bulla weaves this true, incredible story into a literary classic. Originally titled *Squanto: Friend of the White Men*.

Pocahontas and the Strangers, 1971. Junior High.

With the young Algonquin Indian girl Pocahontas as its heroine, this story weaves imagination with fact to illumine the incredible friendship that Pocahontas forged with the early colonial settlers, despite their strange, unsettling ways. Based on the few facts we have on Pocahontas, this story is rich with historic detail regarding the lives of both Indian and white man and is a skillful imagining of a mysterious piece of American history.

A Lion to Guard Us, 1981. Elementary.

When Amanda, Jimmy, and Meg are left alone after the death of their mother in England, they determine to sail to America and find their father. Courageously boarding a boat bound for the New World, they are shipwrecked on the shores of Bermuda as they make their way toward the new colony of Jamestown. Told with Bulla's usual creativity and color, this is a great historical adventure.

James Daugherty

The Landing of the Pilgrims, 1950. Junior High.

This keenly written story of the Pilgrims is based on the journals of William Bradford. Tracing their first years of settlement and their mutually honorable relationship with the Indian Squanto, this story brings great insight into the hopeful yearning that drove the Pilgrims to seek a new world.

Lois Lenski

Indian Captive, 1941. Newbery Honor Book. Junior High.

This book is based on the true story of Mary Jemison, a young girl whose family was captured by Seneca Indians during the French and Indian War. Separated from her family and adopted by her Indian captors, Mary is shown unexpected kindness and quickly learns the ways and work of her new home. When faced with the possibility of rescue, she finds her heart strangely torn by conflicting loyalties. With meticulous historical detail and compelling characters, this story offers a compelling glimpse into a turbulent time in American history.

Andrea Davis Pinkney

Dear Benjamin Banneker, 1994. Young Child through Elementary.

This is a fascinating illustrated biography of the brilliant Benjamin Banneker—inventor, mathematician, astronomer, and America's first African-American scientist. Born in 1731, Banneker had a remarkable gift for scientific discovery and influenced such great minds of his day as Thomas Jefferson.

The book is beautifully illustrated with rustic, realistic paintings.

Elizabeth George Speare

The Witch of Blackbird Pond, 1958. Newbery Medalist. Junior High through High School.

One of my favorite writers of historical fiction, Speare has a gift for bringing history to life through her brave, vibrant characters. When the spirited orphan Kit Tyler comes from Barbados to live with her uncle's strict religious family, she rankles under their many rules. Befriended by a kind Quaker woman, Kit is accused of witchcraft as her New England village is caught up in the deadly wave of fear that characterized the Salem Witch Trials. This captivating story of a young woman's bravery vividly illustrates the nature of real righteousness while bringing to life a dark period of colonial history.

Calico Captive, 1957. Junior High through High School.

Based on a true story, this is the tale of beautiful young Miriam Willard from New Hampshire who is captured in a raid by the Abenaki Indians. Sold for ransom to the French, she becomes the maid for a wealthy family in Montreal, where she catches the eye of a daring young Frenchman. Torn between this love, the struggle to keep her family together, and her love for the man she was going to marry before her capture, she strives to keep her hope alive, becoming a dressmaker as she works for her freedom. I couldn't put this book down when I first read it.

The Sign of the Beaver, 1983. Junior High.

When Matt's father leaves him behind in their new cabin in the wilds of 1768 Maine, he promises to return in seven weeks. While waiting, Matt sprains his ankle, falls into a river, and is rescued by an Indian chief. Out of gratitude, Matt agrees to teach the chief and his son to read, soon forging a deep friendship with the two. After many months of waiting, Matt must decide if he will join the Indian tribe or wait for his family to find him.

Kate Waters

Pilgrim series, 1989–1996. Young Child through Elementary.

This series of photographic picture books is a fascinating glimpse into the day-to-day realities of life during Pilgrim times. Each book focuses on a day in the life of an individual child, using photographs of actual historical reenactors to illustrate the clothing, work, food, entertainment, and general life of children in early colonial times. The series includes:

♥ *Sarah Morton's Day: A Day in the Life of a Pilgrim Girl*
♥ *Samuel Eaton's Day: A Day in the Life of a Pilgrim Boy*
♥ *Tapenum's Day: A Wampanoag Indian Boy in Pilgrim Times*

N. C. Wyeth (illustrator)

The Pilgrims, 1991. Family.

A marvelous picture book based on murals N. C. Wyeth completed in the 1940s, this eye-catching work is filled with lush, idealized paintings. With informative text by Robert San Souci, the book offers an insightful, moving glimpse into the lives of the Pilgrims.

Also Recommended for This Time Period:
♥ *The Courage of Sarah Noble* by Alice Dalgliesh
♥ *Three Young Pilgrims* by Cheryl Harness
♥ *Jamestown: New World Adventure* by James Knight
♥ *Stories of the Pilgrims* by Margaret B. Pumphrey
♥ *The Pilgrims of Plimoth* by Marcia Sewall

American Revolution: 1775–1800

Esther Wood Brady

Toliver's Secret, 1976. Elementary.

When ten-year-old Ellen's grandfather sprains his ankle, it falls to her to deliver a secret message to the American patriot soldiers. Disguising herself as a boy, timid Ellen must maneuver her way through spies, redcoats, and a long journey to deliver her precious report and play her part in the Revolutionary War.

Charles Carleton Coffin

The Boys of '76: A History of the Battles of the Revolution, 1877. Junior High through High School.

A strong Christian with a passion for history, Coffin wrote history books in the late 1800s, but there has been a renewed interest in them because of their vivid historical accounts and strong moral sense. *The Boys of '76* is a rousing battle-by-battle account of the American Revolution told through the eyes of the valorous soldiers who fought it.

Also written by Coffin:
♥ *The Story of Liberty*
♥ *Sweet Land of Liberty*

Esther Forbes

Johnny Tremain, 1943. Newbery Medalist. Junior High.

This story of Johnny Tremain, a printer's apprentice in Boston, explores the events leading up to the war with boyish intrigue, excitement, and passion. A classic novel of the Revolutionary War.

Also written by Forbes:
♥ *America's Paul Revere*

Marguerite Henry

Benjamin West and His Cat Grimalkin, 1947. Elementary.

Before he became one of the first great American artists, Benjamin West was a little Quaker boy who loved painting so much that he made brushes out of his pet's hair and dug colors from the dirt. This imaginative biography of the creative little boy who grew up to become one of the first American masters makes a delightful read-aloud. My parents read this aloud to my family while we were holed up in a mountain cabin during a blizzard, and I have always remembered the story.

Jean Lee Latham

Carry On, Mr. Bowditch, 1955. Newbery Medalist. Junior High.

This novel, based on the life of Nathaniel Bowditch, a learned sailor and scholar famous for his navigational guide for seamen, is full of high-seas adventure and the thrill of scientific discovery.

Robert Lawson

Ben and Me: An Astonishing Life of Benjamin Franklin by His Good Mouse Amos, 1939. Elementary.

The highly entertaining account of the remarkable life of founding father, inventor, and statesman Benjamin Franklin, this biography is told from the view of his good friend Amos the Mouse, who claims to have originated many of Ben's discoveries. Hilarious and highly educational.

Constance Savery

The Reb and the Redcoats, 1961. Elementary.

A fascinating glimpse of the Revolutionary War, this story is told from the rare viewpoint of a British family entrusted with an American patriot prisoner of war. With empathy for both sides involved, the author weaves a tale of compassion and friendship.

Elizabeth Yates

Amos Fortune, Free Man, 1950. Newbery Medalist. Junior High.

This is a true, inspiring tale of a slave in colonial New England named Amos Fortune, who earned his freedom and professed faith in God despite his slavery. A man of compassion and resolve, he earned enough money to free his sister and the woman he loved, leaving a legacy of kindness and freedom after his death.

Also Recommended for This Time Period:
- ♥ *The Arrow over the Door* by Joseph Bruchac
- ♥ *The 4ᵗʰ of July Story* by Alice Dalgliesh
- ♥ *The Cabin Faced West* by Jean Fritz
- ♥ *Early Thunder* by Jean Fritz
- ♥ *Young John Quincy* by Cheryl Harness
- ♥ *The Swamp Fox of the Revolution* by Stewart Holbrook
- ♥ *The Winter at Valley Forge* by James Knight
- ♥ *Silver for General Washington* by Enid LaMonte Meadowcroft
- ♥ Young American Patriots series by Susan Olasky
- ♥ *Guns for General Washington* by Seymour Reit
- ♥ *The 18 Penny Goose* by Sally Walker

American Expansion and Settlement: 1800–1920

Bess Streeter Aldrich

A Lantern in Her Hand, 1928. Junior High through High School. Spanning her life from starry-eyed bride to old woman, this is the story of Abbie, a girl with a gift for music and a love for beauty. When her husband moves her to the wilds of Nebraska, she pours the force of her creativity and spirit into her children and enters the struggle for life and joy in the unsettled West. This is a life-affirming story of endurance and grace.

James Daugherty

Daniel Boone, 1939. Junior High.

A detailed, informative biography of the legendary Daniel Boone by an award-winning author. With his bold exploration of wild lands and adventurous pioneering, the daring life of "Dan'l Boone" is sure to captivate any boy's imagination.

Sid Fleischman

By the Great Horn Spoon!, 1963. Young Child through Elementary.

This humorous, fast-paced adventure story tells of a smart young boy and a wily butler named Praiseworthy who dash out to join the California gold rush to strike it rich for dear old Aunt Arabella.

Laurie Lawlor

Addie Across the Prairie, 1986. Elementary.

As her family settles in the Dakota territories, Addie struggles to adjust to the stark new life on the plains. But when a wildfire sweeps across the prairie, she becomes an unexpected heroine.

Ralph Moody

Little Britches series, 1950–1968. Elementary through Junior High.

This classic series is based on the true story of Moody's childhood in the West in the early 1900s. See full review in chapter 7.

Brinton Turkle

Obadiah series, 1965–1978. Elementary.

This tender, funny series about a young Quaker boy growing up in the early 1800s is filled with engaging historical detail and insight into the life of a simple people. These joyful books illustrate history while spinning darling stories about a mischievous young boy. Included in the series:
- ♥ *Obadiah the Bold*
- ♥ *Rachel and Obadiah*

♥ *Thy Friend, Obadiah*

Laura Ingalls Wilder

Little House on the Prairie series, 1932–1941. Elementary School.

The all-time classic story of a little pioneer girl and her family as they move westward from Wisconsin to the prairie, from a little cabin in the woods to a dugout on the plains. See full review in chapter 7.

Also Recommended for This Time Period:
♥ *Black-Eyed Susan* by Jennifer Armstrong
♥ *The Ballad of Lucy Whipple* by Karen Cushman
♥ *Brave Buffalo Fighter* by John Fitzgerald
♥ *Boston Jane: An Adventure* by Jennifer Holm
♥ *Sarah, Plain and Tall* by Patricia MacLachlan

American Civil War: 1861–1865

Albert Marrin

Virginia's General: Robert E. Lee and the Civil War and
Unconditional Surrender: U. S. Grant and the Civil War, 1994.
Junior High through High School.

An excellent historian and skilled writer, Marrin has written biographies that are classics in each era they cover. These two biographies of the opposing generals of the American Civil War, Robert E. Lee and Ulysses S. Grant, insightfully portray the equally ardent passions and opposing values that drove the lives and loyalties of these great men.

Jeri Ferris

Go Free or Die, 1988. Elementary through Junior High.

This excellent biography of the intrepid escaped slave woman Harriet Tubman tells the story of the dangerous Underground Railroad and the woman who risked her life to help slaves escape. Inspires and educates at the same time.

Carl Sandburg

Abe Lincoln Grows Up, 1928. Junior High through High School.

The classic biographical story of the young years of Abe Lincoln told by a famous American poet. Sandburg eloquently brings to life the formative years of one of America's greatest presidents.

Irene Hunt

Across Five Aprils, 1964. Newbery Honor Book. Junior High.

This heartrending story of a family living in the border lands that divided Union from Confederate portrays the profound, secret struggles of conviction that separated families during the Civil War. One of my favorite novels of this time period.

Harold Keith

Rifles for Watie, 1957. Newbery Medalist. Junior High.

Young Jeff Bussey from Kansas marches off to join the Union army but is hijacked by several unexpected friendships that leave him with loyalties on both sides of the Mason-Dixon Line. Shaped by his encounters with the stout Confederate General Stand Watie and the beautiful Lucy Washbourne, sister of a Cherokee Indian fighting for the Confederates, Watie finds himself torn between two passionate worlds. A fascinating look at the Civil War, including the true, little-known story of the Cherokee Indians' involvement with the Civil War, this engrossing novel provides its reader with a rare point of view and a rip-roaring good story.

Also Recommended for This Time Period:
♥ *Brady* by Jean Fritz
♥ *Follow the Drinking Gourd* by Jeanette Winter

World War I: 1914–1918

Michael Foreman

War Game: Village Green to No-Man's-Land, 1993. Young Child through Elementary.

Based on the lives of the author's four uncles, this beautifully illustrated picture book chronicles England's patriotic fervor on the verge of World War I, as four eager young men enlist to defeat the Kaiser. With expressive watercolors that capture the essence of both battlefields and beauty, the author weaves a story of war, heartbreak, endurance, and surprising joy. A beautiful read-aloud.

Linda Granfield

In Flanders Fields, 1996. Young Child through Elementary.

A moving, radiantly illustrated version of the famous World War I poem written by a soldier from the trenches of Flanders Fields. It is accompanied by an introduction to the life and times of the poet John McCrae.

Where Poppies Grow: A World War I Companion, 2001. Young Child through Junior High.

This vivid scrapbook-style history of World War I includes photographs, old war letters, propaganda posters, and snippets of history. A great companion to the study of the First World War.

John McCutcheon

Christmas in the Trenches, 2006. Elementary.

The true story of a miraculous truce between the Germans and the British on Christmas Day in 1914, this book describes the sacred urge for peace that led to a day-long cease-fire, with opposing sides joined together on the battlefield to play ball, drink toasts, and sing far into the night. A moving picture of compassion amidst war, the story is complemented by joyous, colorful illustrations.

Lucy Maud Montgomery

Rilla of Ingleside, 1921. Junior High.

The last book in the famous *Anne of Green Gables* series, this is Montgomery's poignant history of Canada's heroism and heartbreak as they gave their sons to a faraway war. Told through the eyes of Anne's youngest daughter, this is an excellent chronological history of World War I but also a heart-tugging glimpse into the bravery and grief of the women and families left behind.

Norman Jorgenson

In Flanders Fields, 2003. Young Child through Elementary.

The tale of a homesick young soldier who risks his life to free a robin caught in the barbed wire of a battlefield. With only his white silk scarf knotted on his bayonet for protection, he ventures into no-man's-land in an act of compassion that inspires both sides of the battlefield. Moving illustrations in muted tones.

Kate Seredy

The Singing Tree, 1940. Elementary.

This fascinating glimpse of World War I is set on a family farm in Hungary and is the sequel to Seredy's beloved book *The Good Master. The Singing Tree* finds tomboy Kate and her cousin Jancsi forced to grow up quickly as Jancsi's father is summoned to fight and the farm becomes a refuge for German orphans and Russian POWs. Seredy's excellent writing makes this poignant story a fascinating and moving read.

World War II: 1939–1945

Louise Borden

The Little Ships, 1997. Young Child through Elementary.

This account of the rescue of thousands of English soldiers at Dunkirk is told through the eyes of a little girl and her fisherman father. Answering the call of their country, they set out in a little boat, rescuing the stranded soldiers and looking for their own son and brother. Watercolor illustrations keenly set the mood of danger, courage, and daring that pervaded that historic day.

Maureen Daly

The Small War of Sergeant Donkey, 1966. Elementary.

Having lost his own beloved donkeys to the Germans at the beginning of the war, Chico is elated when a whole slew of the creatures come in with the new troops, and he ends up owning one that he names "Sergeant Donkey." When danger approaches, Chico and his "Sergeant" must prove their mettle and cement their friendship. An entertaining account of the late days of World War II Italy.

Lois Lowry

Number the Stars, 1989. Newbery Medalist. Junior High.

When the Nazis hunt Annemarie's Jewish best friend and her family, Annemarie and her parents risk their lives to help them. A poignant portrait of the heroism and ingenuity of the Danish people, this book illustrates the sacrifice and historic courage that enabled Denmark to save most of its Jews from the Nazis.

Albert Marrin

World War II series, 1980s. Junior High through High School.

Marrin's historical books and biographies are outstanding in their detail, accuracy, and engaging text. Each of the four books listed below covers a different aspect of World War II, exploring the causes, the cultural clashes, and the stories of the people who shaped this era in history. His World War II books include:

- ♥ *Hitler*
- ♥ *Stalin: Russia's Man of Steel*
- ♥ *Victory in the Pacific*
- ♥ *The Yanks Are Coming*

Marie McSwigan

Snow Treasure, 1942. Elementary.

Peter and his friends have been recruited for a daring plan: Right under the Nazis' noses, they are to smuggle millions of dollars of gold out of Nazi-occupied Norway, keeping the country's wealth out of the hands of its enemies. Fast-paced and suspenseful, this adventurous story was actually written during the war.

Johanna Reiss

The Upstairs Room, 1972. Elementary.

Based on the experiences of the author, this story follows two brave little Jewish girls who must hide with a simple peasant family in the Holland countryside. With the insight of experience, Reiss poignantly pictures the long, dull days of hiding, the ache of family separation, and the simple friendship and courage of the Dutch people who saved their Jewish neighbors.

Constance Savery

Enemy Brothers, 1943. Elementary through Junior High.

Kidnapped as a child, young Max has been raised to be a loyal Nazi until the day he is captured by a British airman named Dym. Transferred to England until his true family can be discovered, Max struggles to decide who he will be, fighting both bitterness and love as he encounters these opposing forces in himself and the people near him. A fascinating glimpse into the opposing ideas that drove World War II.

Ian Serraillier

Escape from Warsaw (originally published as *The Silver Sword*), 1958. Elementary.

When the Nazis capture their parents, Ruth, Bronia, and Edek begin a perilous quest to escape German-occupied Poland. Driven by the simple courage of three brave children, this is a story of ingenuity, family connectedness, and the will to endure and survive.

Hilda van Stockum

The Winged Watchman, 1963. Elementary.

This fast-paced, exciting tale of a family of mill keepers in Nazi-occupied Holland considers the exceptional courage of ordinary people who chose to actively resist the Nazi invasion.

Also Recommended for This Time Period:
- ♥ *Jacob's Rescue* by Malka Drucker and Michael Halperin
- ♥ *Lily's Crossing* by Patricia Reilly Giff
- ♥ *The Endless Steppe: Growing Up in Siberia* by Esther Hautzig
- ♥ *When Hitler Stole Pink Rabbit* by Judith Kerr
- ♥ *The Little Riders* by Margaretha Shemin

Historical Children's Series

Ingri and Edgar Parin d'Aulaire

Biography series, 1930–1970. Elementary.

This talented husband–wife team combined their tremendous artistic skills (Edgar studied with Matisse) to create a series of historical picture books for children that won numerous awards and are now a standard for children's history education. Beginning with tales of Ingri's native Norway, they eventually turned to tales of their new country and wrote big, eye-catching picture books on the lives of American legends from Leif the Lucky to Buffalo Bill. With vivid, detailed lithographs, they bring to life the times about which they write. *Abraham Lincoln* won the Caldecott Medal in 1940. Look for all the d'Aulaire books (though some are out of print), but begin with these American history favorites:

- ♥ *Leif the Lucky*
- ♥ *Columbus*
- ♥ *Pocahontas*
- ♥ *Benjamin Franklin*
- ♥ *George Washington*
- ♥ *The Star Spangled Banner*
- ♥ *Abraham Lincoln*
- ♥ *Buffalo Bill*

Genevieve Foster

Biography-based history series, 1940–1960. Elementary through Junior High.

Frustrated by her children's complaint that history was boring, Genevieve Foster set out to turn that grumble on its ear and ended up writing an outstanding series of history books. Foster weaves in all sorts of stories and anecdotes to make famous historical characters and the events of their times come alive for children. With a deft, energetic writing style, she chronicles the advances in literature, science, philosophy, and music in countries all over the world during the life of each title character. Highly recommended by numerous historians and lovers of literature, this wonderful series sets a grand stage for the study of specific time periods. Her titles include:

- ♥ *Augustus Caesar's World*
- ♥ *The World of Columbus and Sons*
- ♥ *The World of Captain John Smith*
- ♥ *The World of William Penn*
- ♥ *George Washington's World*
- ♥ *Abraham Lincoln's World*

Jean Fritz

Histories and biographies, 1960–2000. Elementary through Junior High.

The child of missionary parents in China, Jean Fritz grew up yearning to know the culture and history of her native America. A skilled novelist, she turned her combined passions for writing and history into a series of meticulously researched but hugely enjoyable children's history tales. Her books include obscure, hilarious facts about American heroes and are standard fare for historical education in the elementary and junior high years. For enjoyable history, you can't get better than her "question series" for children. Her other series of biographies for older children is slightly more serious, but still fascinating. These are a matchless resource for teaching history to children.

Question Series (for ages 6–12):
- ♥ *And Then What Happened, Paul Revere?*
- ♥ *Can't You Make Them Behave, King George?*
- ♥ *What's the Big Idea, Ben Franklin?*
- ♥ *Where Do You Think You're Going, Christopher Columbus?*
- ♥ *Where Was Patrick Henry on the 29th of May?*
- ♥ *Who's That Stepping on Plymouth Rock?*
- ♥ *Why Don't You Get a Horse, Sam Adams?*
- ♥ *Will You Sign Here, John Hancock?*
- ♥ *You Want Women to Vote, Lizzie Stanton?*

Junior High/High School Biographies:
- ♥ *Bully for You, Teddy Roosevelt!*
- ♥ *The Great Little Madison*
- ♥ *Harriet Beecher Stowe and the Beecher Preachers*
- ♥ *Make Way for Sam Houston*
- ♥ *Stonewall*
- ♥ *Traitor: The Case of Benedict Arnold*

Cheryl Harness

Illustrated histories, 1990 to Present. Elementary.

With a love of history and a skill for illustration in the tradition of Jessie Wilcox Smith and Howard Pyle, Harness has created a series of historical picture books that are as entertaining as any fictional tale, yet they impart an astonishing amount of historical detail and biographical information. Her lush, bright illustrations painstakingly picture the trappings of each time period, and she tells the stories of little pilgrims, young presidents, or creative inventors with insight and humor. Most of her stories center on great figures or times in American history. Her books are too numerous to list in full, so be sure to search out as many titles as you can. These are some of our favorites:

- ♥ *The Amazing Impossible Erie Canal*
- ♥ *They're Off! The Pony Express*
- ♥ *Three Young Pilgrims*
- ♥ *Young John Quincy*

♥ *Young Teddy Roosevelt*

G. A. Henty

Historical fiction series, 1869–1908. Junior High through High School.

G. A. Henty was an Englishman who turned his own adventuresome life and love of history into a series of fascinating novels that even today are lauded for their historical accuracy. With a keen eye for detail, he created riveting plots around major historical events and brought a distinctly Christian flavor to his tales through his hearty portrayal of virtue and honor in his characters. Though most of his heroes are boys, these are stories for all children. It has been said that if you read every Henty novel on England, you would have a complete history of the British Isles. With over 120 books to his credit, Henty continues to be widely read and his books readily available due to the enthusiasm they have inspired in publishers and young readers. A complete list is available in the appendix.

If You... Series

1960 to Present. Elementary.

This series of books, written and illustrated by various authors, gives a fascinating look into the realities of different periods in history. With detailed research, the authors answer practical questions for young readers such as what people ate, how they lived, and how they celebrated. A fascinating, fact-filled supplement to the teaching of history, this series has many titles:

- ♥ *If You Grew Up with Abraham Lincoln* by Ann McGovern
- ♥ *If You Grew Up with George Washington* by Ruth Belov Gross
- ♥ *If You Lived 100 Years Ago* by Ann McGovern
- ♥ *If You Lived at the Time of Martin Luther King* by Ellen Levine
- ♥ *If You Lived at the Time of the American Revolution* by Kay Moore
- ♥ *If You Lived at the Time of the Civil War* by Kay Moore
- ♥ *If You Lived in Colonial Times* by Ann McGovern
- ♥ *If You Lived in Williamsburg in Colonial Days* by Barbara Brenner
- ♥ *If You Lived in the Days of the Knights* by Ann McGovern
- ♥ *If You Lived When There Was Slavery in America* by Anne Kamma
- ♥ *If You Lived with the Sioux Indians* by Ann McGovern
- ♥ *If You Lived with the Iroquois* by Ellen Levine
- ♥ *If You Lived with the Hopi* by Anne Kamma
- ♥ *If You Lived with the Indians of the Northwest Coast* by Anne Kamma
- ♥ *If You Lived with the Cherokee* by Peter and Connie Roop

- ♥ *If You Sailed on the Mayflower in 1620*
  by Ann McGovern
- ♥ *If You Traveled on the Underground Railroad*
  by Ellen Levine
- ♥ *If You Traveled West in a Covered Wagon* by Ellen Levine
- ♥ *If You Were at the First Thanksgiving* by Anne Kamma
- ♥ *If You Were There When They Signed the Constitution*
  by Elizabeth Levy
- ♥ *If Your Name Was Changed at Ellis Island*
  by Ellen Levine

Landmark History Series

1950–1970. Upper Elementary through Junior High.

With a strong conviction that historical books for children should be of the highest quality, Bennett Cerf, the founder of Random House (one of the largest publishing companies in the world) recruited top-notch authors of his day to write about specific people and periods in American history. His brilliant idea led to the publication of over a hundred historical books between 1950 and 1970. The Landmark books epitomize the difference between history textbooks and historical literature: They were written by excellent, proven writers—often novelists—who had a personal, specific interest in the people and times of which they wrote. This matchless series provides insight into almost every historical period. Though many of the books are out of print (still widely available through used-bookstores), quite a few have been republished in paperback editions in the past few years and are readily available. A list of more than 150 Landmark titles appears in an appendix of this book.

David Macaulay

Architectural series, 1973 to Present. Elementary through Junior High.

Artist and architect David Macaulay has created a colorful and enlightening series of books based on the inner workings and detailed aspects of historic structures. From the Egyptian pyramids to a Gothic cathedral to a medieval castle, his careful, colorful drawings illuminate the process of their construction, the origins of the materials used, and the impact they made on the world around them. A great glimpse into history from an architectural perspective, his titles include:

- ♥ *Castle*
- ♥ *Cathedral: The Story of Its Construction*
- ♥ *City: A Story of Roman Planning and Construction*
- ♥ *Mill*
- ♥ *Mosque*
- ♥ *Pyramid*
- ♥ *Ship*
- ♥ *Underground*

Betsy and Giulio Maestro

The American Story Series, 1987–2000. Elementary.

With Betsy as writer and Giulio as artist, this husband-wife team has created a colorful series of books outlining the history of America. With clear explanations of events such as the writing of the Constitution or the turmoil of the French and Indian War, they bring insight, engaging illustration, and a simple presentation of America's history to their readers. The series includes:

- ♥ *The Discovery of the Americas: From Prehistory Through the Age of Columbus*
- ♥ *Exploration and Conquest: The Americas after Columbus 1500–1620*
- ♥ *The New Americans: Colonial Times 1620–1689*
- ♥ *The Struggle for a Continent: The French and Indian Wars 1689–1783*
- ♥ *Liberty or Death: The American Revolution 1763–1783*
- ♥ *A More Perfect Union: The Story of Our Constitution*

"Meet" Biography Series

1960s. Elementary.

A simply told series of biographies for younger children, these short, illustrated readers are a great way to introduce children to famous historical leaders. Focusing on the life and times of each historical figure, they offer a simple, but

informative biography for children in their first years of reading. Though many of the original titles in this series are now out of print (you can find them in used book stores), the five listed below have recently been republished:
- ♥ *Meet Abraham Lincoln* by Barbara Cary
- ♥ *Meet Christopher Columbus* by James T. de Kay
- ♥ *Meet George Washington* by Joan Heilbroner
- ♥ *Meet Martin Luther King, Jr.* by James T. de Kay
- ♥ *Meet Thomas Jefferson* by Marvin Barrett

Diane Stanley

Biographies, 1986–2000. Family.

A medical artist who suddenly discovered her true love in illustrating children's books, Diane Stanley has invested her series of beautifully illustrated biographies with her passion for art, her wide travels, and her zeal for history. These books were staples of my historical education, engaging my mind with historical anecdotes, insights, and detail as good as that of any novel, while captivating my imagination with colorful, humorous illustrations. These are matchless companions to the study of many different historical periods. Several of her books were written with Peter Vennema. Titles include:
- ♥ *Bard of Avon: The Story of William Shakespeare*
- ♥ *Charles Dickens: The Man Who Had Great Expectations*
- ♥ *Cleopatra*
- ♥ *Good Queen Bess: The Story of Elizabeth I of England*

♥ *Joan of Arc*
♥ *The Last Princess: The Story of Princess Ka'iulani
   of Hawaii*
♥ *Leonardo da Vinci*
♥ *Michelangelo*
♥ *Peter the Great*
♥ *Saladin: Noble Prince of Islam*
♥ *Shaka: King of the Zulus*

10
Spiritual Reading for Children

God be thanked for books!
They are the voices of the distant and
the dead, and make us heirs of the spiritual life of past ages.

~ W. E. Channing

Amidst the clink of spoons deep in cereal bowls and the thumping of small childish feet each morning, there always came a space of quiet at the breakfast table. However restless we children might be, we knew that stillness was required for the ten minutes of my dad's devotional reading. We often forgot to be restive, though, as we were quickly engrossed in the stories of missionaries and Christian heroes with which my dad was filling our morning-fresh minds. To our surprise, we were often quieter at the end (or noisily opinionated, depending on personality), stung to thought by the stories of faith we had heard.

This unusual childish thoughtfulness usually continued after breakfast as my mom drew us close on the couch almost every day to read aloud a chapter out of Catherine Vos's *The Child's Story Bible*. I still remember those stories; the battle scenes, love epics, and faith quests of the Bible danced to life in the simple, engaging narrative of that Bible storybook. At chapter's close, my mom would thump the book shut and explain the stories to us, illuminating the heart choices and spiritual bravery of the great Bible heroes. She would pray with us, telling us that we were going to be just like the people whose stories we had read.

To this day, I remember those times. The Scripture my mom read aloud, the hero tales my dad found for us, and the biographies of Christian missionaries and visionaries with which my mom stocked my reading basket still fund what C. S. Lewis would call my spiritual imagination. From my littlest girlhood, this immersion in a world of spiritually powerful stories began my day. The daily readings formed a foundation of thought and a frame through which I looked at every part of my existence.

In a culture where only four percent of adults hold a biblical worldview (according to research by the Barna Group[18]), there is a rising panic to figure out how to pass a living faith on to children. As an adult who not only accepts but also passionately embraces the lively Christian faith of my parents, I can say with certainty that it's not as mysterious a thing as you might think. Despite the abundant debate about which books or programs to use, passing on the faith can be relatively simple.

All it takes is a daily commitment to exposing children to the Bible and the lives of its heroes. Children also need the real stories of their parents' faith in conjunction with the truth of God's Word. When day after day they are also hemmed in by great stories describing the grace of God, the courage of His people, and the reality of His Spirit in the world, faith is gradually passed on through a natural, enjoyable process.

I am sure that finding deep, insightful things to say every single morning wasn't easy for my parents. Part of their wisdom dwelt in the fact that they used every resource available to them. They were always on a search for books that illumined the lives of heroes, brought Scripture to life, and helped us kids to understand truth in a clearer way. They coupled their collections of great hero tales and biographies with their own faith to make the kingdom of God come alive to us.

One of the first great biographies I encountered in my youth was the story of Brother Andrew, the young Dutch boy who grew up to smuggle thousands of Bibles into Communist Europe. The courage he showed and his incredible devotion to Scripture left an indelible image on my mind, illustrating the excitement of loving God so deeply and serving His people so willingly. The book was also a downright thrilling story.

The *Hero Tales* series, another collection I loved, formed our family devotionals for quite a while. The short stories of Christian heroes accompanied by Scripture succinctly and powerfully brought home lessons in character quality and faith, as well as the importance of living well for God.

As you have probably gathered by now, I think that story has a God-given power to model and inspire by the way it brings elusive concepts to vivid life. Spiritual and biblical stories are no exception. Real, artfully told stories of missionaries, speakers, and leaders vividly illustrate what serving God looks like.

Thus, I decided to include a full chapter on books that are specifically faith oriented—biographies, devotionals, study guides, and children's Bibles. These books will aid you as parents in daily gifting your children with stories of faith, deep spiritual truth, and a vividly portrayed love for Christ.

Kay Arthur

Discover 4 Yourself Inductive Bible Studies for Kids, 1990s to Present. Elementary through Junior High.

Using the same great tools and step-by-step instruction that distinguish her *Precept upon Precept* Bible studies for adults, Kay Arthur has created a line of studies just for kids. These books are tools that will teach your children how to approach Scripture and help them to gain deep insight through word study, cross-referencing, and personal application. They make great gifts for children just beginning to have their own devotionals.

Joyce Vollmer Brown

Courageous Christians, 2000. Family.

This book offers sixty short biographies that walk kids through a fascinating hall of faith. Each fast-paced, inspiring story is accompanied by carefully chosen Scripture, making this book perfect for family devotions or read-aloud.

Ron and Rebekah Coriell

A Child's Book of Character Building (Books One and Two), 1981. Young Child through Elementary.

These simple studies use clear and engaging stories from the Bible and everyday life to plainly illustrate godly character to children. Each chapter focuses on a single biblical character quality and includes concise definitions of each quality and supporting scripture. These books provide training in the basic Christian exercise of character and Scripture application.

Meryl Doney

How the Bible Came to Us, 1985. Elementary through Junior High.

With short articles, mini-chapters, and a plethora of photographs, illustrations, and charts, this informative book gives a quick history of how the Bible came into being.

Covering translation, printing, origins, and more, it provides a framework on which to build an understanding of the Bible's fascinating history.

Mabel Hale

Beautiful Girlhood, 1922. Elementary through Junior High.

With a cup of tea and a candle, my mom read one chapter of this book aloud to me each week for a year when I was ten. Exploring basic, timeless topics of gracious womanhood, beauty, and solid character, this inspirational collection of essays written for girls almost a hundred years ago remains relevant today. Short, persuasive chapters make this an easy mother-daughter read-aloud and a great tool for introducing specific concepts of Christian womanhood.

Angela Elwell Hunt

The Tale of Three Trees, 1989. Family.

On a high mountain grow three great trees, all dreaming of what they will become—a gilded treasure chest, a proud ship, or simply the tallest tree in the world. Their wishes are fulfilled in strange and unexpected ways as they each play a pivotal part in the life of Christ. Simple, deeply colored paintings complement this creatively retold gospel folktale.

Dave and Neta Jackson

Trailblazer series, 1991 to Present. Elementary through Junior High.

With the desire to bring Christian history alive to kids, the Jacksons have written a riveting series of fictional tales based on true events in the lives of great Christian missionaries and leaders. Each action-packed, virtue-driven story features a teen protagonist in a series of adventures that illumines the life and times of Christian leaders. The books also include a short biography at the back and a page at the front outlining what is fact and what is fiction. A complete list of titles is provided in the appendix of this book. You can also find descriptions at www.trailblazerbooks.com.

Hero Tales (four volumes), 1996. Family.

Each volume of this series has fifteen chapters, each focusing on a famous Christian missionary or leader. Each chapter includes a short biography and three short, dramatized (but true) stories that highlight a specific character quality. Engagingly written, these stories are perfect for family devotionals as they bring Christian history to light while bringing out the strong themes of virtue, character, and courage displayed in each leader's life.

Lamplighter Publishing

Rare Collector Series, 1990s to Present. Family.

"Inspiring literature that models unwavering character motivates us to adopt a similar moral code as we emulate the characters that have been etched into our awakened conscience." That quote on the Lamplighter website aptly captures the force of this elegantly bound series of great biographies, allegories, and family stories. Mark Hamby established Lamplighter Publishing to provide families with spiritually invigorating literature.

Drawing from the wealth of Victorian moral stories, biographies, and allegories written in the past century, Lamplighter selects and republishes stories that are well-written and communicate God's reality, truth, and goodness in a compelling way. Each book features characters that are dramatic and loveable. One of my friends claims *The Basket of Flowers* as her favorite book. In it, Mary, the daughter of the King's gardener, learns the principles of godliness through the flowers in her father's garden. Another friend's favorite is *Sir Knight of the Splendid Way*, an allegory that pictures the heart's journey to heaven through the story of a brave young knight who must journey to the City of the Great King. Perfect for read-aloud or personal reading for perceptive older children, these stories are a splendid mix of story and strong moral inspiration. The books themselves are quite beautiful and make gifts that will be passed down and treasured. A few favorite titles:

♥ *The Basket of Flowers* by Christoph von Schmid
♥ *The Hidden Hand* by E. D. E. N. Southworth
♥ *Ishmael* by E. D. E. N. Southworth
♥ *Sir Knight of the Splendid Way* by W. E. Cule
♥ *Teddy's Button* by Amy LeFeuvre
♥ *Titus: A Comrade of the Cross* by Florence M. Kingsley

Max Lucado

Wemmicks Collection, 1997–2006. Young Child through Elementary.

The Wemmicks, a community of small wooden people, constantly rate each other by appearance and skill, giving stars to the prettiest and grey dots to the dullest. With a heavy heart and many grey dots, Punchinello makes his way to the house of his maker to discover who he was truly meant to be. Each book is a simple but artfully told story that reflects themes of identity in Christ, grace, calling, and unconditional love. Whimsically illustrated, this series creates a humorous storybook world that brings human foibles and need to light. Really fun for reading aloud, the series includes:

♥ *Best of All*
♥ *If Only I Had a Green Nose*
♥ *Punchinello and the Most Marvelous Gift*
♥ *You Are Special*
♥ *Your Special Gift*

Other Spiritual Picture Books:
- ❤ *All You Ever Need*
- ❤ *Because I Love You*
- ❤ *Coming Home*
- ❤ *Just the Way You Are*

Robert Boyd Munger

My Heart, Christ's Home: Retold for Children, 1992. Young Children.

A classic spiritual work for adults, Munger's imaginative picturing of Christ coming to the house of his heart is here retold and illustrated for children. Imagining what Christ might find within him, Munger pictures each room of the house as representing an area of life: desires in the dining room, meeting Christ daily in the living room, cleaning out the secrets in the darkest closet. An engaging but surprisingly poignant story, this is a great tool for discussing spiritual issues with children.

Marian M. Schoolland

Leading Little Ones to God, 1962. Young Child.

With simple prayers, hymns, and short stories, this book gently introduces young children to basic tenets of Christian belief from sin and salvation to prayer and the nature of God.

Made up of several parts with titles such as "God Is Very Great," each section has five to eight short chapters. A great spiritual tool for parents.

Patricia St. John

A Young Person's Guide to Knowing God, 2001. Elementary through Junior High.

With her characteristic flair for weaving intriguing, spiritually poignant stories, Patricia St. John put together this collection of stories, prayers, and guided questions to introduce young people to the God she loved. St. John uses tales ranging from her childhood in Switzerland to her days as a missionary in Morocco to instruct and inspire. Her voice is compassionate but confident. As an author, she is a spiritual mentor to her young readers, making this an excellent study tool for an older child. Shaw Books published a version of this book as *Stories to Share: A Family Treasury of Faith* in 1997, and though it is out of print, I highly recommend it if you can find a used copy.

J. E. White

Tiger and Tom and Other Stories for Boys, 1877. Elementary through Junior High.

This collection of short virtue stories for boys has remained popular and in print for years because of its adventurous take on morality tales. This fun collection for boys to read on their own ranges from travel stories to orphan dramas to mountain adventures and conveys a basic picture of strong, manly character while also entertaining restless boys.

The King's Daughter and Other Stories for Girls, 1877. Elementary through Junior High.

This girlish companion to *Tiger and Tom* mixes true tales of virtuous women and princesses with short, fictional stories of noble-hearted young women in a variety of adventures and places. Entertaining but pithy, these stories repeatedly present and affirm the values of virtue, faith, purity, and joy.

Catherine F. Vos

The Child's Story Bible, 1935. Young Child through Junior High.

Driven by her passion for Scripture and her desire to present the living story of the Bible to her children, Vos took every historical and narrative passage in the Bible and wove it into a scripturally faithful but child-friendly storybook. It includes 110 Old Testament chapters and 92 New Testament stories. My mom read this to us every day as part of our devotions. A family classic.

Brandon and Mindy Withrow

History Lives series, 2006–2009. Elementary.

With a deep desire to expose children to the colorful epic of Christian history and faith, this husband-wife team set out to write a collection of gripping tales for kids that captured the drama of the sinners and saints who shaped the church. Each book focuses on a different time period in church history. The series includes:

- ♥ *Peril and Peace: Chronicles of the Ancient Church*
- ♥ *Monks and Mystics: Chronicles of the Medieval Church*
- ♥ *Courage and Conviction: Chronicles of the Reformation Church*
- ♥ *Hearts and Hands: Chronicles of the Awakening Church*
- ♥ *Rescue and Redeem: Chronicles of the Modern Church*

YWAM (Youth with a Mission)

Christian Heroes: Then & Now series, 1990s. Elementary.

A vibrant missionary community with bases around the world, YWAM Publishing began with tracts and a prayer diary and soon progressed to dynamic biographies of great missionaries and leaders. These books are simply written so that they are accessible to children, yet they also poignantly capture the faith and passion that sent mission-minded men and women to the ends of the earth to share the gospel. In-depth unit studies are now available to accompany many of the biographies. You can find a complete list of their titles at www.ywampublishing.com. A few of the many titles include:

- ❤ *Adoniram Judson: Bound for Burma*
- ❤ *Amy Carmichael: Rescuer of Precious Gems*
- ❤ *Eric Liddell: Something Greater Than Gold*
- ❤ *George Müller: The Guardian of Bristol's Orphans*
- ❤ *Hudson Taylor: Deep in the Heart of China*
- ❤ *Mary Slessor: Forward into Calabar*
- ❤ *William Carey: Obliged to Go*

11
Poetry

Poetry is the language in which man explores his own amazement.
~ Christopher Fry

Autumn had come to our bit of Tennessee yard, jewelling the trees and stripping away the green of summer grass. Pale sunlight filtered in through the small square of my garret room window, followed by the chill, swift rush of a harvest wind. I was curled on my bed with my eight-year-old fingers wrapped tightly around a pen and a notebook resting on my knees. At the wind gust, I lifted my small, hot face and closed my eyes. The next instant found my eyes un-squinched and my fingers tripping over themselves in their eagerness to catch the words that finally fell upon my waiting brain:

> The wind fills the sky
> It blows swift and strong
> It blows night and day

O wind, sing your song!
Sing it always!

It was my first attempt at poetry. I felt, with a sense of pink-cheeked pride, that I had joined the ranks of the writers I was just beginning to encounter who considered the world a song. I loved these people who experienced the drip and drop of hours and days as a cadence, who found a poem waiting in the details of mundane hours. I may have been small, but I was already in love with the starlit imagination of Robert Louis Stevenson's *A Child's Garden of Verses*, Christina Rossetti's *Who Has Seen the Wind?* and the high drama of "The Highwayman" (which all starry-eyed girls know is recited by Anne in the movie version of *Anne of Green Gables*).

Poetry was weaving its rhythmic magic in my life.

To introduce young children to poetry is to set a rhythm to their play, a lovely cadence to their discovery of the smallest bits of everyday life. Poetry is the lens through which we find the miraculous in the mundane. It is also the word-woven net in which great writers have caught the whispers of mystery, nobility, and transcendence that invade even the most ordinary of lives. The earlier children are brought into this world, the earlier they enter into a marvelous awareness of cadence in reality, of beauty lurking in normal corners, of delight to be culled from average days.

It began early in my home. Once a week my mom would pile the lot of us on the couch and open a big book of poetry. We began with a gem of a book called *A Child's Treasury of*

Poems, which combined the most beloved verse and ditties for children with classic scenes of art.

From there we progressed to larger tomes, beginning with my mom's childhood favorite, *Best Loved Poems of the American People*. She would spend whole mornings reading us epic story poems, passionate odes to nature, or contemplations of mystic souls. We soon began our foray into the more challenging realm of memorization. Every Clarkson child was required to memorize Rudyard Kipling's "If." Inspired by *Anne of Green Gables*, I decided to memorize "The Highwayman." Once I saw *Sense and Sensibility*, I was intent upon memorizing the Shakespearean sonnet so beloved by Marianne:

> Let me not to the marriage of true minds
> Admit impediments . . .

By the time I reached my high school years, I was familiar enough with the basic canon of classic poetry to journey on in that land by myself. My appetite whetted by the simpler rhymes of my childhood, I found a feast of word and thought waiting in such classic poets as Wordsworth, Frost, Auden, and Herbert.

In those famed poets, I discovered a shared experience of love, of need, of grief. They expressed the as-yet inarticulate thoughts inhabiting my growing soul and wakened me to the reality of my deepest human musings. To read poetry was to stoop to the ground and observe the intricacy of nature, to lift my face to the sky and contemplate the realities of life. Poetry taught me to consider the happenstances of my life as somehow sacred, worth the investment of my thought, my wonder, and my care. Poetry preserves wonder and restores imagination.

We lose so much in our modern culture by our unfamiliarity with the classic poets. Pop music has in large part replaced our appetite for poetry. But catchy words are no substitute for well-worded wonder, nor do they provide that space of mind in which we encounter the hushed depths of contemplation.

A child raised in an atmosphere of lyrical thought will bear a soul sensitized to beauty, to the intricacy of the daily, and to the grandeur of the best human thoughts. The books in this chapter are full of whimsy and lyricism. There are epic poems chronicling the exploits of grand souls, poems pondering unfathomable questions, ditties of delight in nature, odes to creation, and fanciful views of daily life. But they all weave together in a rainbow of dark and bright that surrounds the mind in a constant wonder. In the end, poetry helps to set in motion a barely heard song. When that song is begun in the earliest years of childhood, it grows stronger with the passing years.

Illustration

Especially for younger children, illustrations can be a great way to pique interest in the poetic world. Many of the books recommended below have beautiful illustrations. If your children are unfamiliar with poetry, use these first as a means of introduction.

Memorization

Memorizing great poems can be a delightful challenge and mental exercise for your children. Several of the books below are compilations of poetry specifically chosen for memorization. John Hollander's *Committed to Memory* is my favorite.

Mark Daniel (editor)

A Child's Treasury of Poems, 1986. Young Child through Elementary.

This lovely book was my first exposure to poetry. It's full of nature verses, traditional ditties, and story poems chosen especially to intrigue young children. The text is accompanied by a breathtaking collection of art reproductions—garden scenes, portraits of children, landscapes—all beautiful, innocent, and deeply engaging. Though out of print, this is an idyllic book that I highly recommend owning if you can find it.

Hazel Felleman (editor)

Best Loved Poems of the American People, 1936. Family.

This is one of the best anthologies of purely enjoyable poems. My mom grew up with an older version and passed it down to her kids. Felleman chose great poetry from every imaginable genre and era according to the delight each poem inspired through generations. While not an academic collection, it includes many classics and is a basic title for any poetry library.

John Hollander (editor)

Committed to Memory: 100 Best Poems to Memorize, 1996. Junior High/Family.

A poet and literary critic himself, Hollander has selected what he considers some of the loveliest and most easily memorized poems from the world's favorites. Divided into sections titled "Sonnets," "Songs," "Counsels," "Tales," and "Meditations" this collection offers an intriguing introduction to memorizing and enjoying classic poems.

Leslie Pockell (editor)

The 100 Best Poems of All Time, 2001. Junior High/Family.

This comparatively slim volume is an excellent introduction to good poetry. A great tool for exposing an older child to some of the basic classics, this is also easy to peruse and presents a collection of poetic gems for memorization.

Jack Prelutsky

Something Big Has Been Here, 1990. Young Child through Elementary.

Beloved for his zany, inventive poems for kids, Prelutsky has written a collection of poems that will tickle the funny bones and poetic interest of young children. With wacky illustrations and simple verse, this volume of poetry for children may be silly, but it's downright fun and will whet kid's appetites for more serious poetry later on. My brothers especially loved this book. Read aloud and laugh.

Michael Rosen (editor)

Classic Poetry: An Illustrated Collection, 1998. Junior High/Family.

This illustrated collection of classic poems is one of my favorite books for introducing children to poetry. It prints classic poems in chronological order (beginning with Shakespeare) and pairs them with a portrait of the poet, a short biography, and marvelous illustrations specially suited to the mood and story of the poem. A glossary explains poetic terms and styles.

Alvin Schwartz (editor)

And the Green Grass Grew All Around: Folk Poetry from Everyone, 1992. Family.

This amusingly illustrated collection of folk poetry provides a fun, light-hearted contrast to the more serious classic poems. Full of everyday ditties and workaday lyrics, this book celebrates the rhythms and songs of generations of folk poetry. Colorful, funny illustrations accompany the text.

Sterling Publishing Company

Poetry for Young People series, 1990 to Present. Elementary through Junior High.

This illustrated collection is an indispensable tool for exposing children to the great poets. Each slim picture book is titled after a famous poet and features his or her best child-friendly works. An illustrator was specially chosen to capture the mood and emotion of each respective poet. From Robert Frost's pastoral poetry, with its breezy watercolor illustrations of farms and fields, to the bright jungle illustrations that accompany the poetry of Rudyard Kipling, these books are visually inviting and easily approachable by a curious child. A full list is available at the publisher's website: www.sterlingpublishing.com. Some of the best titles include:

♥ *William Blake*, edited by John Maynard

♥ *Robert Browning*, edited by Eileen Gillooly

♥ *Samuel Taylor Coleridge*, edited by James Engell

♥ *Emily Dickinson*, edited by Frances Schoonmaker Bolin

♥ *Robert Frost*, edited by Gary D. Schmidt

♥ *Langston Hughes*, edited by David Roessel & Arnold Rampersad

♥ *Rudyard Kipling*, edited by Eileen Gillooly

♥ *Henry Wadsworth Longfellow*, edited by Frances Schoonmaker

♥ *Edna St. Vincent Millay*, edited by Frances Schoonmaker

♥ *Carl Sandburg*, edited by Frances Schoonmaker Bolin

♥ *Robert Louis Stevenson*, edited by Frances Schoonmaker

♥ *Walt Whitman*, edited by Jonathan Levin

♥ *William Wordsworth*, edited by Dr. Alan Liu

♥ *William Butler Yeats*, edited by Jonathan Allison

Robert Louis Stevenson

A Child's Garden of Verses, 1885. Young Child through Elementary.

This lovely collection of Golden Age novelist Robert Louis Stevenson's lyrical verse is a classic of childhood. Marked by their dreamy imaginations of adventure, outdoor exploration, and childhood whimsy, these poems have remained beloved since their publication over a hundred years ago. They make a fun family read-aloud and are simple enough to capture the reading attention of a young child. There are countless versions with a variety illustrators, but one of my favorites is the edition illustrated by famed artist Tasha Tudor. Her old-fashioned drawings perfectly complement the poems.

Louis Untermeyer (editor and contributing poet)

The Golden Books Family Treasury of Poetry, 1971. Family.

Originally titled *The Golden Book of Poems for the Very Young*, this family poetry collection is probably my favorite childhood anthology. With sections focusing on nature poems, story poems, legends, old ditties, and more, this book covers a wonderful range of thoughtful, dramatic, and beautiful poems for children. Joan Walsh Anglund's intricate, whimsical illustrations in bright colors or pen and ink perfectly complement the poems. I would take this book down to my room and pore over it for hours of solitary delight, but it is also an ideal read-aloud.

12
Music, Art, and Nature

A man should hear a little music, read a little poetry,
and see a fine picture every day of his life,
in order that worldly cares may not obliterate the sense
of the beautiful which God has implanted in the human soul.

~ Johann Wolfgang von Goethe

While the subjects in this chapter are not specifically literary, I strongly believe that they are great shapers of story and are in turn shaped by great stories. The worlds of music, art, and literature have always been inextricably intertwined, each funding the thought and influence of the others. As part of discovering the great world of story, it can be fascinating to trace the music and art that accompanied the creation of literary masterpieces. As to nature, it is the art of God. I hope that this chapter will supplement the souls and education of your kids, providing you with solid resources and books in every subject of study. Enjoy!

Classical Music

I play the notes as they are written,
but it is God who makes the music.

~ J. S. Bach

The whir of wheels on the highway had settled over my friend's car as she traveled home from a summertime journey with her husband and two little ones. With a sleepy quiet invading the car, she reached out and switched on some classical music, assuming the children in the back were asleep. The aching strains of a violin sang out from the classical station, and she had just closed her eyes to enjoy it when there was a stirring behind her.

"That's Vivaldi, Mama," piped up the shrill, sweet voice of her four-year-old golden-haired little princess. "He's my favorite."

"I like Bach best," mumbled her sleepy six-year-old brother.

My friend's husband nearly drove off the road in astonishment. How in the world, he inquired, did his very young children know the names and recognize the music of two such great composers? With a glint of delighted smugness in her eye, my friend explained that she and the kids had been listening to the Classical Kids audio series and reading picture books about the lives of the composers.

The children had naturally picked up on the music, quickly choosing their favorites.

Just like my friend's children, I whetted my musical appetite on radio dramas of the lives of the great composers and on colorful, entertaining picture books describing their fascinating lives. The books were so entertaining and the music so sprightly and beautiful that it would be hard not to be interested. Yet knowledge of classical music is not common in our modern culture. In a pop-music age, people barely have exposure to the classical composers and often perceive classical music in the same way they perceive great art—as a rarefied, intellectual subject for a select few. But music is music, and classical music is simply the historic collection of the most inspired melodies and music the world has known.

No child should grow up entirely without classical music. To ignore classical music is to disregard one of the greatest artistic forces in the world. Furthermore, an increasing body of research suggests that classical music literally heightens activity and reasoning ability in the brain, creating unique connections by simple listening.[19] Listening to music and taking music lessons appear to lead to greater success in other areas of study and development.[20] It is also fascinating to consider the universal nature of music; many anthropologists believe that there isn't a single culture in the world without some form of music. To expose children to the great music of the ages is to acquaint them with the thoughts of people's souls throughout the centuries. Music is an ongoing, universal language.

I am deeply thankful that my parents ushered me into the worldwide, continuing conversation of music. They discovered a way to expose me to its history and scope through the medium of stories—of the composers, their music, and of the gifted people who played them. With the resources in this chapter, you can easily shepherd your children into a world of melody, deep thought, and soaring emotion. Before long, you too will have a car populated with budding young music critics eager to share their favorite composer.

Classical Music Collections

There are numerous great collections of classical music. The website www.arkivmusic.com has extensive collections, reviews, and suggestions for the best CDs of classical music.

The NPR Guide to Building a Classical CD Collection: The 350 Essential Works is a great guide to the best classical music around. Highly recommended and acclaimed, this book will take you through the plethora of classical pieces, recommending lesser-known works by famous composers as well as the great classics. This is an excellent guide for a parent or older child interested in really delving into the world of classical music.

Anna Harwell Celenza

Composer series, 2000–2006. Elementary.

"If my books can make classical music more accessible to kids, that would be a dream come true." With that passion, Celenza set out to write a series of books that introduces children not just to great musicians but also to their greatest works. Her stories focus on the fascinating dramas leading up to the creation of specific classical masterpieces such as Beethoven's *Eroica* Symphony, or Haydn's Symphony no. 45, and she brings both a storyteller's insight and a musician's passion to her books. With bright, playful illustrations, these books take children straight into the fascinating world of the great composers. From the courts of kings to garret studios, Celenza illuminates the intricate stories behind some of the greatest musical creations. Her books include:

- ♥ *The Farewell Symphony* (Haydn)
- ♥ *The Heroic Symphony* (Beethoven)
- ♥ *Bach's Goldberg Variations*
- ♥ *Gershwin's Rhapsody in Blue*
- ♥ *Pictures at an Exhibition* (Russian Artists and Musicians)

Julie Downing

Mozart Tonight, 1991. Young Child.

Opening night has finally come for Mozart's amazing new opera, *Don Giovanni*, and all Prague has adorned itself for the grand first performance. In this sumptuously illustrated picture book, Downing recreates the splendor and pomp of Mozart's time, sketching a brief, child-oriented biography of his remarkable life.

Susan Hammond (producer)

Classical Kids audio series, 1990–1999. Family.

To this day, I can hear a strain of classical music and identify it. This ability is due in large part to the hours of my childhood spent listening to this marvelous collection of audio dramas. Each title presents the life of a great classical musician through his adventurous encounters with children. From the mysterious orphan Katerina in Vivaldi's Venice to the frustrated Christoph whose mother is landlady to a deaf and eccentric Beethoven, these are colorful, entertaining stories laced with the true histories of the great composers. Each drama is woven through with the actual music of the composer, making an instant, memorable connection between music and story in children's minds. I can't recommend these excellent, entertaining dramas highly enough.

The series includes:
- ♥ *Beethoven Lives Upstairs*
- ♥ *Hallelujah Handel*
- ♥ *Mozart's Magic Fantasy*
- ♥ *Mozart's Magnificent Voyage*
- ♥ *Mr. Bach Comes to Call*
- ♥ *Song of the Unicorn*
- ♥ *Tchaikovsky Discovers America*
- ♥ *Vivaldi's Ring of Mystery*

Patrick Kavanaugh

Spiritual Lives of the Great Composers, 1996. Junior High / Family.

A composer, conductor, and deeply committed Christian, Kavanaugh brought a love of music and a vast knowledge of its history to his quest to discover what spiritual faith drove the lives of the great classical composers. He presents his findings in this collection of twenty short biographies that expose the Christian belief and deeply held (though not always well-known) spirituality of some of the world's best-loved composers. Each chapter includes a suggested listening list of the composer's best music. A great educational resource, especially for older kids.

Lloyd Moss

Zin! Zin! Zin! A Violin, 1995. Caldecott Honor Book. Young Child.

    Zany pictures, crazy musicians, and delightfully rhymed couplets make this jaunty children's book a joyful introduction to the musical world of the symphony. With pictures and poems featuring specific sets of musical instruments and locating their spot within the whole, this fast-paced read-aloud introduces children to the world of the symphony. This book is all-out fun.

Ann Rachlin

Famous Children series, 1992–1994. Elementary.

    With playful illustrations and simple, biographical text, these short picture-book biographies delve into the childhoods of famous musicians. Easy to read and filled with historically accurate yet whimsical illustrations, they manage to pack in a lot of biographical detail. These books are worded in such a way that children will remember the stories of how the great musicians got their start, even in childhood. The series includes:

- ❤ *Bach*
- ❤ *Beethoven*
- ❤ *Brahms*
- ❤ *Chopin*

- ♥ *Hayden*
- ♥ *Mozart*
- ♥ *Schubert*
- ♥ *Schumann*
- ♥ *Tchaikovsky*

Jane Stuart Smith and Betty Carlson

The Gift of Music, 1987. High School/Family.

Highly recommended by well-known Christian philosopher Francis Schaeffer, this book is a faith-affirming resource for families or older children. Tracing the history and development of classical music, Smith and Carlson focus on the worldviews of the composers whose creations shaped and were shaped by the ideas of their time. With discernment and skill, they explain how deeply the Christian faith and belief of some great composers drove their music, while equally exploring how the lack of faith informed the music of others. Part musical history, part philosophy, this is an excellent resource for a student of classical music.

Barrie Carson Turner

Living Music series, 1996. Family.

These informative books for parents and their children offer a wealth of information on some of the most common instruments of classical music. Each book describes the origin and history of its instrument, outlining its construction, its place within a symphony or grouping of other instruments, and the technique required to play it. Filled with photographs, the books also include biographies of the great classical composers who wrote music specifically for the featured instrument. Each book is accompanied by a CD of the composers' songs. A great educational resource, the series includes:

ೞ *The Living Clarinet*
ೞ *The Living Flute*
ೞ *The Living Piano*
ೞ *The Living Violin*

Mike Venezia

Getting to Know the World's Greatest Composers series, 1994–1999. Young Child.

With humor and a good dose of silliness, Venezia presents the lives of the great composers to children in a strange but entertaining mixture of cartoons and musical history. Each book focuses on the life of a single artist and provides simple, encyclopedic facts and interesting anecdotes illustrated through amusing cartoon conversations and larger illustrations of the composers' lives. There are fourteen titles in the series featuring musicians from Bach to the Beatles. A complete list can be found at www.mikevenezia.com.

Art

Art is contemplation.

~ Auguste Rodin

I was probably five or six when first I saw his small, solemn face. It was full and rounded, the face of a young child with dark, thoughtful eyes and tiny, pursed lips. Dolled up in a jacket of crimson velvet embroidered with gold, he was obviously born to luxury, his fair head capped in red velvet with a sweeping white plume. Small as he was, there was straightness to his gaze and an unfathomable solemnity in his steady look. One chubby little hand was lifted in a gesture of command far beyond his years, while the other clutched a golden scepter. His name, I was to find out later, was Edward. At the time his portrait was made, he was the future king of England and his artist, Hans Holbein, seemed to have caught a glimpse of the grandeur into which he would soon grow.

I saw him countless other times as I grew up, his small, solemn face staring up at me from the cover of *Come Look with Me,* a lovely volume that we used often in my home to study classic art. Almost twenty more years would pass before I saw his real portrait face to face in the Denver Museum of Art. My startled delight in finding the real masterpiece hanging before me was akin to that of finding an old, near-forgotten friend.

303

Therein lies the delight of a good book of art.

Through the glossy pages of an art book, you can befriend the masterpieces of history. The deepest visions and thoughts of the master painters—their epic subjects or artistic contemplations—can become a daily dose of mystery in the confines of your own life and home. Future kings and mythical heroes can companion your hours, exquisite landscapes or scenes of childhood deepen the beauty of your own day. The creativity of generations can invade your world from the humble pages of the book you prop on your table.

I'm always amazed to find how academic many people perceive the study of art to be. There seems to be an unspoken consensus that the study of classic art is for the hopelessly intellectual, certainly not for the average young family. Many moms I have spoken with consider art a daunting area of study, or else they find it frivolous—an extracurricular activity to be pursued only when there is nothing else to be learned. Especially in the last few decades of rising media and entertainment, great art has taken on a musty, rarefied air and a sense of being beyond the grasp of the average curious adult, not to mention children.

On the contrary, art is simply the marvelous, many-splendored record of a thousand different people attempting to record the beauty, the grief, the breadth, and the depth of life as it stirred their souls. Art is a pictorial tour through the deepest emotions that have plagued and blessed humanity through the centuries.

Children need to be exposed to great art. Art can introduce children to the color and drama of other cultures and of past times. Art pictures spiritual belief; it embodies faith, exposing us moderns to the sacred realities of past generations. Art stirs imagination, expanding our inner picture of reality. Art is history. Art is contemplation (to quote the artist Rodin). Art is challenge. Art is an education in what it means to be human.

This education is available to you and your children through the medium of books. Some wonderful series written in the past few years introduce the lives and works of the great artists through fun, captivating stories. Stores are full of oversized, affordable books of great art through the centuries. Many contemporary artists are becoming passionate about opening up the world of great art to kids; and that passion has come out in book series, dramatized retellings of artist's lives, and creative plots made to introduce children to the drama, beauty, and ancient history of art.

Your children can grow up familiar with artistic excellence and with the subtle depth of contemplation that invades the great masterpieces. We have the unparalleled opportunity in our time to be surrounded by masters of creativity and thought simply through the presence of a few, well-chosen art books. A world of beauty is just waiting for your discovery.

Variety

Try to collect a wide variety of art books so that your children are familiar with the many different schools of art.

Barnes and Noble has a collection of art books focusing on different periods in artistic history, as well as books focusing only on a single, individual artist. The great changes in art history often parallel upheavals in the history of philosophy, politics, and faith. It can be a great companion to the study of how ideas affect every area of human endeavor.

Discernment

Classic art depicts an endless realm of reality and imagination; it sometimes includes nudity, battle scenes, or mythological epics. While each family has its own standard for what is acceptable, be aware of what paintings are included in any given book of art or museum exhibit you choose to visit, especially general art collections not specifically designed for children.

Worldview

Because we live in a postmodern[21] society that largely rejects the idea of art having an objective truth or meaning, many of the resources available, even for children, espouse this view. I believe that the books below will greatly widen and deepen the minds of children, exposing them to the beauty of the world's greatest artists. However, I recommend that parents be involved in this process, using a watchful eye to explain theories of art that don't fit a Christian worldview.

Laurence Anholt

Anholt's Artists Books for Children, 1994–2009. Elementary.

Based loosely on the real-life encounters of great artists with children, these whimsical picture books are children's biographies of famous artists while also being compelling stories in and of themselves. With protagonists such as Marie, the little ballerina who modeled for Degas, or Camille, whose family befriended the troubled painter Van Gogh, each book chronicles how the artists' encounters with the children inspired and softened them in their creativity. This is a great read-aloud series that will introduce children to the lives and lesser-known stories of great artists. The series includes:

♥ *Camille and the Sunflowers: A Story About Vincent van Gogh*
♥ *Cezanne and the Apple Boy*
♥ *Degas and the Little Dancer*
♥ *Leonardo and the Flying Boy*
♥ *The Magical Garden of Claude Monet*
♥ *Matisse, the King of Color*
♥ *Picasso and the Girl with a Ponytail*

Christina Björk

Linnea in Monet's Garden, 1987. Young Child through Elementary.

Linnea is a little European girl whose dream comes true when she travels to Paris to walk in the footsteps of the famous painter Monet with her elderly friend Mr. Bloom. Fresh and fun, this is a creative exploration of the life and times of Monet, the foremost Impressionist painter. The text is interspersed with colorful, exuberant watercolor paintings of Linnea exploring Paris and Monet's home in Giverny, black-and-white photos of Monet and his family, and reproductions of his masterpieces. This book has a delightful European tang and will make you want to sit in the garden with baguettes, apples, and a pleasantly blank canvas. Companions to this book include *Linnea's Almanac* and *Linnea's Windowsill Garden*.

Gladys Blizzard

Come Look with Me series, 1990–1993. Young Child through Elementary.

An art teacher and curator of art education at a university museum, Blizzard based these books on the times she spent exposing her grandchildren to art. Each glossy, oversized book includes twelve pieces of art within a specific category. Each double-page spread includes a big, bright reproduction of a masterpiece on one side with text opposite. Simple, pointed questions help children to analyze each painting, while a brief biography or evaluation of the artist's medium gives historical insight. These books expose children in a memorable way to some of the world's greatest masterpieces, while the questions and insights help children to own their experience of great art. Highly recommended.

♥ *Come Look with Me: Animals in Art*

♥ *Come Look with Me: Enjoying Art with Children*

♥ *Come Look with Me: Exploring Landscape Art with Children*

♥ *Come Look with Me: World Of Play*

Come Look with Me titles by other authors::

♥ *Come Look with Me: American Indian Art* by Stephanie Salomon and Charles Davey

♥ *Come Look with Me: Art in Early America* by Randy Osofsky

♥ *Come Look with Me: The Artist at Work* by R. Sarah Richardson

♥ *Come Look with Me: Asian Art* by Kimberly Lane

♥ *Come Look with Me: Discovering African-American Art for Children* by James Haywood Rolling, Jr.

♥ *Come Look with Me: Exploring Modern Art* by Jessica Noelani Wright

♥ *Come Look with Me: Women in Art* by Jennifer Tarr Coyne

Colleen Carroll

How Artists See series, 1996–2008. Family.

Selecting sixteen pieces of great art for each book, Carroll explores how artists perceive such everyday realities as work, family, and play, and she brings the world of art to the level of a curious child. With a picture-book feel and simple, engaging text aimed at young readers, this series guides children into an awareness of the world's masterpieces, opens their eyes to what it means to see the world artistically, questions them about creativity, and provides them with sketches of the lives and times of the artists. Each book includes a list of museums where the art may be seen and an age-appropriate reading list. The series has many titles, including:

- ❤ *How Artists See Animals*
- ❤ *How Artists See Cities*
- ❤ *How Artists See Families*
- ❤ *How Artists See Heroes*
- ❤ *How Artists See Home*
- ❤ *How Artists See People*
- ❤ *How Artists See Work*

Tony Hart

Famous Children series, 1994. Young Child.

With playful illustrations and childlike text, these short picture-book biographies delve into the childhoods of famous

artists. Simple, fun, and easy to read, they still manage to pack in a great deal of biographical detail worded so that children will remember the stories of how the great artists got their start, even in childhood. This series includes:
- ♥ *Leonardo da Vinci*
- ♥ *Michelangelo*
- ♥ *Picasso*
- ♥ *Toulouse-Lautrec*

MaryAnn Kohl and Kim Solga

Discovering Great Artists: Hands-On Art for Children in the Styles of the Great Masters, 1997. Young Child through Elementary.

A simple but great resource for teaching the history of art as well as getting kids involved in art-making themselves, this book covers five periods in art history. Selecting great works of artists from each era, it offers a black-and-white sketch of each masterpiece accompanied by a short biography of the painter and a hands-on craft to get kids creating in the same style as the master.

James Mayhew

Katie series, 1989–2005. Elementary.

   With incorrigible curiosity and a love of fun, Katie visits an art museum with her grandmother and stumbles right into the paintings. From sharing lunch with Monet's son Jean to laughing with Gauguin's dancing Breton girls, Katie romps through the lively scenes of some of the world's best art, learning to love their beauty all the while. These fun, entertaining books are a wonderful introduction to art. Set in the context of a funny story seen through the eyes of a little girl, each book in the series focuses on a specific painter or genre. The series includes:

   ♥ *Katie and the Mona Lisa*
   ♥ *Katie and the Spanish Princess*
   ♥ *Katie and the Sunflowers*
   ♥ *Katie Meets the Impressionists*
   ♥ *Katie's Picture Show*
   ♥ *Katie's Sunday Afternoon*

Mike Venezia

Getting to Know the World's Greatest Artists series, 1988–2008. Young Child through Elementary.

   With humor and a bit of silliness, Venezia presents the lives of the great artists to children in a strange but entertaining mixture of cartoons and reproductions of great art. Each book focuses on the life of a single artist and provides simple, encyclopedic facts and interesting anecdotes illustrated through amusing cartoon conversations and larger illustrations of the artists' lives. There are forty-eight titles available; you can find a complete listing at www.mikevenezia.com.

Nature

In nature's infinite book of secrecy
A little I can read. . . .

~ William Shakespeare

Late-summer light was thick over the lush green of my backyard as my best friend and I snuck through the grass, wicker baskets in hand. A mere fifteen minutes later, we were creeping back, baskets loaded. With spy-worthy stealth, we darted to my room and made quick work of dismantling my dresser top and bookshelves. We artistically arranged piles of leaves, a collection of rocks, a jar with fireflies, several pieces of twig and branch, and one golden butterfly.

Beside each of them, we set a snippet of paper on which we had painstakingly copied a description from one of the many books that littered my floor. When all was in order, we allowed ourselves a giggle and called my mom in to be the first patron of our official nature and science "museum." With appropriate enthusiasm, she toured the exhibits and turned to me with a slightly quizzical look, wondering where I had gotten the idea.

From infancy I have been a self-described hater of math and not usually inclined to science, but my mom should have known why I was suddenly curious about the natural drama in my backyard. We had been reading, you see. She had plied me with books about the outdoors and picture books about naturalists. Field guides to butterflies, rocks, and reptiles were stacked in our library, and I had been exploring them, gradually gaining a hunger to venture out and find the creatures I had seen in their pages.

In the chapter on historical fiction, I mentioned that I was unaware of the process of education at work in me while reading books I enjoyed; it was the same with much of my nature study. Though I read the books during "school hours," I decided to pursue the ideas they presented simply because I found it all so interesting. True learning is like that: It sparks and stirs intrigues so that the natural outgrowth is a desire for more knowledge. Science and nature can sometimes be seen as complicated subjects to teach, but as with all learning, I believe these subjects to be within the realm of easy learning if great books and the freedom of exploration accompany them.

A large part of education is simple, eye-opening exposure to the realities in the world around us. Good nature books with vivid illustrations show children what is lurking in the nearby and unexplored realms of meadow and pond, spurring them to go and seek. With such discoveries to be made, making a museum provides a fun afternoon. Catching and identifying butterflies, making a rock collection, and roaming the fields are all natural outgrowths of children being exposed to the hidden splendor of the natural world. Books introduce these possibilities.

Children need exposure to God's vast creation. They are so surrounded in this time by electronics, concrete, and indoor environments that it can be hard to get them out into wilder spaces. Yet God states over and over in the Bible that one of the primary ways that He is known is through His creation. (See Psalm 19:1–6, for example.) Meadows, mountains, wind, and animals all speak of His character, revealing the essence of who He is in His power, beauty, and wildness. An education in nature and science isn't just about test scores or college prep; it is about exposure to the artwork of God made visible in His world.

Whether your child is a born scientist or a house-loving soul resistant to the vagaries of nature, the books listed here will kindle an interest in the natural world. Whether your children go on to be scientists or artists, they all should have a life-giving exposure to creation that is necessary to any well-rounded soul. These books will set the stage for much more complex studies in chemistry, biology, and earth sciences in the high school years, making a necessary subject of study a fascinating delight as well.

At a friend's house a couple of years ago, I ambled into the library and picked up a book. So captivating was the writing that it took me a few minutes to realize I was engrossed in a tome on particle physics. The magic of books was working again. It will for your kids as well.

Worldview

Though the majority of the books listed for this section are written from a generally Christian worldview, there are several by secular authors as well. Science and nature are tricky subjects when it comes to worldview. While I am always aware of the beliefs and values being communicated through any book and am careful to recommend only what I find to be soul-building, there are some nature books so beautifully written and presented that they are worth the effort involved in explaining secular viewpoints to children.

I have included such books as the Magic School Bus series because although they are written from a secular worldview, the fun and scientific interest they wake in children is worth parents taking the time to screen for and/or explain evolutionary concepts. I have listed a caution next to any book not written from a specifically Christian worldview, but I feel that all of these books will contribute overall to a healthy enjoyment and knowledge of God's world.

Literariness

I have chosen to focus primarily on literary nature books in this chapter. By literary, I mean books that creatively teach about the natural world through story, illustration, or biography. I have, however, included a few specifically informational books as well as a list of great field guides and nature study books by well-known naturalist societies and authors.

Field Guides and Science Series

A sturdy field guide is indispensable for a budding scientist. I toted around an Audubon butterfly guide for several years of butterfly hunting in my childhood; because of it, I still remember the names of many of my insect finds to this day. Many nature and science societies have produced field guides and nature books specifically for children. These are not all written from a specifically Christian worldview, but they are, nonetheless, excellent field guides. A few of the classics are listed below.

Apologia's Young Explorer Series

This is an elementary science curriculum with a whole-books feel and approach as well as being solidly Christian in values. Jeannie Fulbright, a mom with a passion for making science approachable and enjoyable for kids, wrote each of these engaging guides. Using the immersion approach of each book covering a single scientific topic, the series gives kids a chance to dig deeply into each subject studied. With colorful illustrations and a read-aloud-friendly text, these are an excellent basis for elementary science study. Highly recommended. Titles include:

- ♥ *Exploring Creation with Astronomy*
- ♥ *Exploring Creation with Botany*
- ♥ *Exploring Creation with Zoology 1: Flying Creatures of the Fifth Day*
- ♥ *Exploring Creation with Zoology 2: Swimming Creatures of the Fifth Day*
- ♥ *Exploring Creation with Zoology 3: Land Animals of the Sixth Day*
- ♥ *Exploring Creation with Human Anatomy and Physiology*

National Audubon Society's First Field Guides

With glossy pictures and simple text, the Audubon society presents its beautiful field guides in a modified form for children. With hundreds of species covered in each book, these bright, engaging volumes help children to identify the strange creatures in their own backyard.

Dover Science Books for Children

Specializing in educational books, Dover Publishing has an extensive list of scientific books for children. With topics in chemistry, biology, physics, and other scientific disciplines, these books provide detailed instruction in nature and science studies.

Peterson Field Guides for Young Naturalists and Peterson First Guides

Long considered as setting the standard in field guides, the Peterson series has numerous titles covering everything from birds and butterflies to plants and rocks. In the two series for younger readers, the authors combine color photographs and line drawings with detailed explanations and facts, making the natural world immediately identifiable and familiar to young explorers. Take these with you on a nature walk and see what your kids find.

Nature and Science Magazines

One of the great resources my parents used to teach us nature and science was good magazines designed especially for children. The following were our favorites:

Nature Friend

This family-run monthly nature journal is written from a strong Christian perspective and is great for young kids. With varied articles on subjects such as snowflakes, black bears, or other creatures, the magazine also features nature drawing and photography. You can subscribe at www.NatureFriendMagazine.com.

KIDS Discover

This magazine provides detailed insights into all sorts of scientific subjects, but it is not solely science oriented; it also explores history, cultures, countries, etc. Supplementing amusing stories of history with facts, photos, anecdotes, and cartoons, this magazine will provide your kids with education in areas you might never have thought of. Go to www.KidsDiscover.com for more information.

Jeanne Bendick

Science books and biographies, 1960s. Elementary through Junior High.

"If I were a fairy godmother, my gift to every child would be curiosity." With that wish infusing her work, Jeanne Bendick wrote a series of books for children focusing on scientific history and discovery. Known for her ability to simply explain complex ideas and to present scientific history as fascinating and full of fun, Bendick brings science and scientific history to colorful, amusing life. Her books include:

- ♥ *Along Came Galileo*
- ♥ *Archimedes and the Door to Science*
- ♥ *Galen and the Gateway to Medicine*
- ♥ *Mathematics Illustrated Dictionary*
- ♥ *The Mystery of the Periodic Table*

Christian Liberty Press

Christian Liberty Nature Readers, 1980s. Elementary.

These simple readers pair beautiful, realistic illustrations of the natural world with text that simply explains facts about nature and its creatures. Each numbered book is geared in vocabulary and depth to the corresponding grade level and includes vocabulary lists as well as questions dispersed throughout the nature stories and facts to prompt narration and discussion. A basic series to supplement a child's study of nature.

Henry Cole

I Took a Walk, 1998. Young Child.

Resplendent with detailed acrylic illustrations, this picture book guides young children through a variety of natural habitats—woods, meadows, streams, and ponds—alerting them to the diverse animals, insects, and plants abiding within each area. Die-cut flaps include an "I spy" list of creatures and plants for which a child can search in each habitat. A great book for showing young children how to be observant in nature.

Also written and illustrated by Cole:
- ♥ *Jack's Garden*
- ♥ *On the Way to the Beach*

Joanna Cole

The Magic School Bus series, 1986–1996. Elementary.

When the eccentric teacher Miss Frizzle comes on the scene, her students never know where they might end up—on Jupiter, on a ride through the bloodstream, or even inside the earth. This brilliant series of picture books exposes children to a wide variety of scientific knowledge through zany, imaginative field trips on a magical bus. With humorous illustrations and a plethora of scientific facts showing up in the characters' conversations and as side notes, these books impart a surprising amount of scientific insight while also being the hysterical sort of story that your kids won't want to put down.

Caution: While most of the science in these books is true and fascinating, the writer definitely comes from a secular slant. She accepts evolutionary theory as fact, which might need some explaining for younger or less-discerning children.

There are many titles in the series and quite a few have been added in the past few years since the books were turned into a popular kids' TV program. I still like the earliest titles the best, each written by Joanna Cole and illustrated by Bruce Degan:

♥ *The Magic School Bus and the Electric Field Trip*
♥ *The Magic School Bus at the Waterworks*
♥ *The Magic School Bus Inside a Beehive*
♥ *The Magic School Bus Inside a Hurricane*
♥ *The Magic School Bus Inside the Human Body*
♥ *The Magic School Bus Inside the Earth*
♥ *The Magic School Bus Lost in the Solar System*
♥ *The Magic School Bus on the Ocean Floor*

Anna Botsford Comstock

Handbook of Nature Study, 1911. Family.

Considered by many to be the mother of nature study, Comstock was one of the first women professors at Cornell University as well as a gifted nature artist. Passionate about the study of nature, she wrote this guide as a handbook for teachers in preparing nature study lessons for their young students. The first section focuses on the methods and means of good nature study and instruction, and the rest of the book is a marvelous guide to the natural world, covering just about every living thing except humans. Short chapters and stories make this easily accessible to children wanting to look up a specific item, but its comprehensive length (around 800 pages) makes it an excellent planning and teaching tool for parents. It really has no equal and is as relevant today as when it was published a hundred years ago.

Jacqueline Davies

The Boy Who Drew Birds: A Story of John James Audubon, 2004. Young Child through Elementary.

With beautiful watercolor illustrations, photographs of birds and plants, maps, and pages from a nature journal, this lovely picture book is a short biography of John James Audubon, one of America's best-known naturalists. Describing the influential time he spent roaming the fields near his father's farm in Pennsylvania, this story captivatingly illustrates how Audubon came to study, draw, and trace the migration of his beloved birds. This beautiful book about a man who passionately loved nature will likely inspire lively outdoor curiosity in young readers.

Ric Ergenbright

The Art of God, 1999. Family.

Acclaimed landscape photographer Rick Ergenbright collected some of his most stunningly beautiful photographs for a collection of pictures that showcase the "art of God." Focusing on what we can know of the character of God through just through His physical creation, Ergenbright has compiled a set of photos that demonstrate God's beauty, power, and mystery. With insightful, spiritual contemplations accompanying the pictures, this makes a great family devotional or oversized coffee-table book.

Holling C. Holling

Paddle-to-the-Sea, 1941. Caldecott Honor Book. Elementary through Junior High.

An artist and naturalist, Holling devoted much of his talent to creating children's books illustrated with fascinating pictures that illumine science, nature, and geography along with his stories. *Paddle-to-the-Sea* tells about the journey of a hand-carved canoe launched in the headwaters of the Great Lakes as it journeys to the sea. This expedition ushers the little canoe, and young readers, into a fascinating exploration of tides, seasons, currents, wild creatures and their habitats, and the history of the waters it travels. Holling's pictures are brightly colored and full of detail.

Minn of the Mississippi, 1951. Newbery Honor Book.
Elementary through Junior High.

This colorful story is told through the eyes of Minn, a clever snapping turtle who makes her home in the muddy Mississippi River. The reader journeys through the hot, fascinating world of life on the river with its diverse creatures, its explorers and riverboat captains, and its legendary floods. This is a fascinating historical and scientific look at one of America's natural treasures.

Also written and illustrated by Holling:
- ♥ *Pagoo*
- ♥ *Seabird*
- ♥ *Tree in the Trail*

Clare Walker Leslie

Keeping a Nature Journal: Discover a Whole New Way of Seeing the World Around You, 1998. Elementary through Junior High.

Written by a long-time nature journaler, this book introduces readers to the wonder-inspiring habit of journaling their encounters with nature. With chapters focusing on getting started, exploring the outdoors, drawing technique, and learning to be observant, this book skillfully teaches its reader how to see nature, sketch it, write about it, and create a record of outdoor experience. It includes many illustrated sample pages from the author's own journal and encourages wonder in nature and creativity in recording what is seen. An excellent tool for a thoughtful child ready to delve deeper into God's creation, this would also be a great way to get a family started in nature studies together.

Caution: While this book is not written from a specifically Christian viewpoint, there is little in it that I feel would be objectionable. However, there are a few paragraphs of a vague earth-centered spirituality that might be offensive to some.

Thomas Locker

Sky Tree: Seeing Science through Art, 1995. Elementary.

With his flair for enriching childhood education through his art-filled books, Locker presents a series of paintings of a single tree through the changing seasons. Whether picturing the crimson fire of its autumn foliage or the wink of starlight through its bare winter branches, Locker's stunning paintings illustrate the gradual changes of the tree and the earth around it. A few simple questions on each page guide children into considering the scientific and artistic points of the painting. While it is definitely more on the contemplative than informative side, I love this book (and the following Locker titles) for the way they kindle a child's wonder at the beauty of nature.

Other nature/art books written and illustrated by Locker include:

❤ *Cloud Dance*
❤ *Mountain Dance*
❤ *Water Dance*

Henry Morris

Men of Science, Men of God, 1982. Junior High.

One of the most difficult challenges that Christians face in entering scientific fields today is the common assumption that God and science are mutually exclusive. This collection of 101 biographies of great scientists demonstrates the deeply held Christian faith of many of the world's foremost scientists. A great read-aloud and discussion book for families, this will also encourage children to embrace their faith as they encounter the incredible universe God created.

New Leaf Publishing

Nature photography books, 2000–2003. Family.

The Wonder of It All: The Creation Account According to the Book of Job is a breathtakingly beautiful book that has permanent residence on the coffee table in our home. Few books inspire such wild awe in God's creation as this photographic journey through God's scriptural conversation with Job. Author, editor, and photographer Steve Terrill has filled this book with insights from creation scientists and carefully chosen quotes to illuminate these stunning photographs of mountains, rivers, animals, valleys, and oceans. This book will inspire readers to a deeper study of and awe at God's creation.

How Majestic Is Thy Name: Delighting in the Grandeur of God, the next book in the series, is written by Steve Halliday with photography by Steve Terrill. This is a breathtaking photographic tour through the wonders of creation, supplemented by poignant passages from Scripture and incredible scientific facts.

The Hand That Paints the Sky: Delighting in the Creator's Canvas (also by Halliday) completes the set with a collection of sky photography that is artfully blended with watercolor painting to create sunsets and sunrises of almost surreal beauty. With an introduction by Joni Eareckson Tada and a special message from musician Cindy Morgan, this is a lovely end to a matchless series. These books provide endless awe, entertainment, and motivation to young readers in exploring God's creation.

Lawrence O. Richards

It Couldn't Just Happen: Fascinating Facts About God's World, 1987. Junior High.

Filled with fascinating facts and written in simple, engaging language, this faith-based book by a Christian author sets out to answer children's questions about the origins of the universe. With chapters focusing on such subjects as the origins of the planets, the beginning of life, and the "record of the rocks," this book explains point by point in short, easily readable sections why evolution can't explain the existence of our fascinating world. A strong apologetic for kids that affirms faith in a creative, all-powerful God, this book also offers a wide and varied body of scientific knowledge.

Ernest Thompson Seton

Wild Animals I Have Known, 1898. Junior High/Family.

A gifted artist and skilled storyteller, Seton was one of the founders of the Boy Scouts of America. When a group of boys repeatedly vandalized his home, Seton countered by inviting them home for the weekend and captivating them with his adventurous stories of wild animals. *Wild Animals I Have*

Known is just such a set of his tales that are both scientifically accurate and yet romantic in their depiction of such wild characters as the crow Silverspot, the wolf Old Lobo, and Bingo the hound. This is a wonderful read-aloud series for a family that provides a thrilling story while outlining the lives, habitats, and habits of wild creatures. The text is complemented by dozens of black-and-white illustrations by the author.

Albert Payson Terhune

Lad: A Dog, 1919. Elementary through Junior High.

Some of the best-loved dog stories of all time, these tales about Lad, a heroic and beautiful collie, capture the affection and joy that exists between a good dog and his master. Originally published as magazine stories, the chapters are short, making for easy reading that will thrill the heart of any dog lover.

Epilogue

In the shadows of a late-night kitchen, with the hum of a refrigerator muffling our whispers, I was finally able to sit down with one of my dearest book friends and talk books. A short visit on a conference weekend had made it almost impossible to snatch any time, but we grabbed at the late-night hour, perching at her kitchen countertop with mugs of herbal tea and a stack of old books between us. We had become instant kindred spirits a couple of years earlier when we discovered our shared wonder in the world of children's stories, and it was with the air of conspiring treasure-hunters that we inspected her latest finds.

One by one, she handed over the gems she had culled from dusty shops and library sales as I skimmed the time-tanned pages, exclaiming at the lively stories and quaint illustrations of the rare books. When the pile had dwindled and our muffled laughter had hushed, she picked up the last book, a slim, worn little volume with a jet-black cover and placed it in my hands. I glanced up, surprised. I knew this book. It was an old favorite, a rare volume I loved to peruse when I visited her house.

"I want you to have this."

I was startled. This was no casual gift—it was a book we both knew to be rare, one I had searched for in numerous bookshops without success. The memoir of a family in the fifties raised in the topsy-turvy delight of literature, the little book embodied the life my friend was trying to impart to her own children. It was precious to her, and I knew it. I glanced up to make sure I had understood, ready to protest, but I was met by the steady light of my friend's eyes and her knowing smile.

"I want *you* to have this now. I know you'll love it every bit as much as me, and besides, you can pass it on when you're ready."

I hugged the book (yes, you get a little crazy when you become a book lover) and smiled back at my friend because I knew that what she was giving me wasn't just a costly old book. It was her offering of the treasure that had brought her own love of literature to life. In giving it to me, she put her own deep love of story into my hands, trusting that I would take it and be kindled even further in turn.

That's exactly what I hope *this* book has done for you. I hope you leave the reading of this volume feeling that we have pored over these stories together at the kitchen table, by the fire, or in a threadbare corner of your favorite couch. I hope that somehow in that sharing of stories, you have caught the thrill that is the beginning of a lifelong love of literature. It's my turn now to pass into your capable and interested hands the slim, battered volume that is the deep love of reading, in the hope that your own heart will be sparked to begin an adventurous journey into the great books of the world.

By doing this, we are all creating a real life story. I want to encourage you, as you live this life of books out in your home and with your children, to make the story your own. I have given you lists of my old favorite books and suggestions for how you might enjoy or pursue reading day to day. But ultimately, you will create your own rich habits of reading. You will discover new books that I have never heard of and craft your own legacy of the written word. My friend passed on her precious book knowing that it would spur me in similar ways but also different ways than it did her.

She didn't pass on a reading list; she passed on a reading life—and that is what I want to pass on to you.

So here you are. The little book is now in your hands. Imagine me giving you just such a smile as my friend gave me; imagine the same excited eyes and my assurance that I know you'll love these stories just as much as I have, that you will find the same kindled heart in the company of great stories. Bring your own heart and love and creativity to reading and collecting stories. Enjoy this rare tale that is a life marked by reading.

Oh, and when you're ready, pass it on.

Appendix I
Caldecott Medalists

The Caldecott Medal, named in honor of nineteenth-century English illustrator Randolph Caldecott, is awarded by the American Library Association to the artist of the year's most distinguished American picture book for children.

2009 – *The House in the Night,* illustrated by Beth Krommes, written by Susan Marie Swanson

2008 – *The Invention of Hugo Cabret* by Brian Selznick

2007 – *Flotsam* by David Wiesner

2006 – *The Hello, Goodbye Window,* illustrated by Chris Raschka, written by Norton Juster

2005 – *Kitten's First Full Moon* by Kevin Henkes

2004 – *The Man Who Walked Between the Towers* by Mordicai Gerstein

2003 – *My Friend Rabbit* by Eric Rohmann

2002 – *The Three Pigs* by David Wiesner

2001 – *So You Want to Be President?* illustrated by David Small, written by Judith St. George

2000 – *Joseph Had a Little Overcoat* by Simms Taback

1999 – *Snowflake Bentley,* illustrated by Mary Azarian, written by Jacqueline Briggs Martin

1998 – *Rapunzel* by Paul O. Zelinsky

1997 – *Golem* by David Wisniewski

1996 – *Officer Buckle and Gloria* by Peggy Rathmann

1995 – *Smoky Night*, illustrated by David Diaz, written by Eve Bunting

1994 – *Grandfather's Journey* by Allen Say

1993 – *Mirette on the High Wire* by Emily Arnold McCully

1992 – *Tuesday* by David Wiesner

1991 – *Black and White* by David Macaulay

1990 – *Lon Po Po: A Red-Riding Hood Story from China* by Ed Young

1989 – *Song and Dance Man*, illustrated by Stephen Gammell, written by Karen Ackerman

1988 – *Owl Moon*, illustrated by John Schoenherr, written by Jane Yolen

1987 – *Hey, Al*, illustrated by Richard Egielski, written by Arthur Yorinks

1986 – *The Polar Express* by Chris Van Allsburg

1985 – *Saint George and the Dragon*, illustrated by Trina Schart Hyman, retold by Margaret Hodges

1984 – *The Glorious Flight: Across the Channel with Louis Bleriot* by Alice & Martin Provenson

1983 – *Shadow*, translated and illustrated by Marcia Brown; original text in French by Blaise Cendrars

1982 – *Jumanji* by Chris Van Allsburg

1981 – *Fables* by Arnold Lobel

1980 – *Ox-Cart Man*, illustrated by Barbara Cooney, written by Donald Hall

1979 – *The Girl Who Loved Wild Horses* by Paul Goble

1978 – *Noah's Ark* by Peter Spier

1977 – *Ashanti to Zulu: African Traditions*, illustrated by Leo & Diane Dillon, written by Margaret Musgrove

1976 – *Why Mosquitoes Buzz in People's Ears*, illustrated by Leo & Diane Dillon, retold by Verna Aardema

1975 – *Arrow to the Sun* by Gerald McDermott

1974 – *Duffy and the Devil*, illustrated by Margot Zemach, retold by Harve Zemach

1973 – *The Funny Little Woman*, illustrated by Blair Lent, retold by Arlene Mosel

1972 – *One Fine Day*, retold and illustrated by Nonny Hogrogian

1971 – *A Story A Story*, retold and illustrated by Gail E. Haley

1970 – *Sylvester and the Magic Pebble* by William Steig

1969 – *The Fool of the World and the Flying Ship*, illustrated by Uri Shulevitz, retold by Arthur Ransome

1968 – *Drummer Hoff*, illustrated by Ed Emberley, adapted by Barbara Emberley

1967 – *Sam, Bangs & Moonshine* by Evaline Ness

1966 – *Always Room for One More*, illustrated by Nonny Hogrogian, written by Sorche Nic Leodhas (Leclaire Alger)

1965 – *May I Bring a Friend?* illustrated by Beni Montresor, written by Beatrice Schenk de Regniers

1964 – *Where the Wild Things Are* by Maurice Sendak

1963 – *The Snowy Day* by Ezra Jack Keats

1962 – *Once a Mouse*, retold and illustrated by Marcia Brown

1961 – *Baboushka and the Three Kings*, illustrated by Nicolas Sidjakov, written by Ruth Robbins

1960 – *Nine Days to Christmas*, illustrated by Marie Hall Ets, written by Marie Hall Ets and Aurora Labastida

1959 – *Chanticleer and the Fox*, by Barbara Cooney

1958 – *Time of Wonder* by Robert McCloskey

1957 – *A Tree Is Nice*, illustrated by Marc Simont, written by Janice Udry

1956 – *Frog Went A-Courtin'*, illustrated by Feodor Rojankovsky, retold by John Langstaff

1955 – *Cinderella, or the Little Glass Slipper*, by Marcia Brown, translated from Charles Perrault

1954 – *Madeline's Rescue* by Ludwig Bemelmans

1953 – *The Biggest Bear* by Lynd Ward

1952 – *Finders Keepers*, illustrated by Nicolas (Nicholas Mordvinoff), written by Will (William Lipkind)

1951 – *The Egg Tree* by Katherine Milhous

1950 – *Song of the Swallows* by Leo Politi

1949 – *The Big Snow* by Berta & Elmer Hader

1948 – *White Snow, Bright Snow*, illustrated by Roger Duvoisin, written by Alvin Tresselt

1947 – *The Little Island*, illustrated by Leonard Weisgard, written by Golden MacDonald (Margaret Wise Brown)

1946 – *The Rooster Crows* by Maud & Miska Petersham

1945 – *Prayer for a Child,* illustrated by Elizabeth Orton Jones, written by Rachel Field

1944 – *Many Moons,* illustrated by Louis Slobodkin, written by James Thurber

1943 – *The Little House* by Virginia Lee Burton

1942 – *Make Way for Ducklings* by Robert McCloskey

1941 – *They Were Strong and Good* by Robert Lawson

1940 – *Abraham Lincoln* by Ingri & Edgar Parin d'Aulaire

1939 – *Mei Li* by Thomas Handforth

1938 – *Animals of the Bible: A Picture Book,* illustrated by Dorothy P. Lathrop

Appendix II
Newbery Medalists

The Newbery Medal, named for eighteenth-century British bookseller John Newbery, is awarded by the American Library Association to the author of the year's most distinguished contribution to American literature for children.

2009 – *The Graveyard Book* by Neil Gaiman
2008 – *Good Masters! Sweet Ladies! Voices from a Medieval Village* by Laura Amy Schlitz
2007 – *The Higher Power of Lucky* by Susan Patron
2006 – *Criss Cross* by Lynne Rae Perkins
2005 – *Kira-Kira* by Cynthia Kadohata
2004 – *The Tale of Despereaux* by Kate DiCamillo
2003 – *Crispin: The Cross of Lead* by Avi
2002 – *A Single Shard* by Linda Sue Park
2001 – *A Year Down Yonder* by Richard Peck
2000 – *Bud, Not Buddy* by Christopher Paul Curtis
1999 – *Holes* by Louis Sachar
1998 – *Out of the Dust* by Karen Hesse
1997 – *The View from Saturday* by E. L. Konigsburg
1996 – *The Midwife's Apprentice* by Karen Cushman
1995 – *Walk Two Moons* by Sharon Creech
1994 – *The Giver* by Lois Lowry

1993 – *Missing May* by Cynthia Rylant

1992 – *Shiloh* by Phyllis Reynolds Naylor

1991 – *Maniac Magee* by Jerry Spinelli

1990 – *Number the Stars* by Lois Lowry

1989 – *Joyful Noise: Poems for Two Voices* by Paul Fleischman

1988 – *Lincoln: A Photobiography* by Russell Freedman

1987 – *The Whipping Boy* by Sid Fleischman

1986 – *Sarah, Plain and Tall* by Patricia MacLachlan

1985 – *The Hero and the Crown* by Robin McKinley

1984 – *Dear Mr. Henshaw* by Beverly Cleary

1983 – *Dicey's Song* by Cynthia Voigt

1982 – *A Visit to William Blake's Inn: Poems for Innocent and Experienced Travelers* by Nancy Willard

1981 – *Jacob Have I Loved* by Katherine Paterson

1980 – *A Gathering of Days: A New England Girl's Journal, 1830–1832* by Joan W. Blos

1979 – *The Westing Game* by Ellen Raskin

1978 – *Bridge to Terabithia* by Katherine Paterson

1977 – *Roll of Thunder, Hear My Cry* by Mildred D. Taylor

1976 – *The Grey King* by Susan Cooper

1975 – *M. C. Higgins, the Great* by Virginia Hamilton

1974 – *The Slave Dancer* by Paula Fox

1973 – *Julie of the Wolves* by Jean Craighead George

1972 – *Mrs. Frisby and the Rats of NIMH* by Robert C. O'Brien

1971 – *Summer of the Swans* by Betsy Byars

1970 – *Sounder* by William H. Armstrong

1969 – *The High King* by Lloyd Alexander

1968 – *From the Mixed-Up Files of Mrs. Basil E. Frankweiler*
    by E. L. Konigsburg

1967 – *Up a Road Slowly* by Irene Hunt

1966 – *I, Juan de Pareja* by Elizabeth Borton de Treviño

1965 – *Shadow of a Bull* by Maia Wojciechowska

1964 – *It's Like This, Cat* by Emily Neville

1963 – *A Wrinkle in Time* by Madeleine L'Engle

1962 – *The Bronze Bow* by Elizabeth George Speare

1961 – *Island of the Blue Dolphins* by Scott O'Dell

1960 – *Onion John* by Joseph Krumgold

1959 – *The Witch of Blackbird Pond* by Elizabeth George
    Speare

1958 – *Rifles for Watie* by Harold Keith

1957 – *Miracles on Maple Hill* by Virginia Sorensen

1956 – *Carry On, Mr. Bowditch* by Jean Lee Latham

1955 – *The Wheel on the School* by Meindert DeJong

1954 – *. . . And Now Miguel* by Joseph Krumgold

1953 – *Secret of the Andes* by Ann Nolan Clark

1952 – *Ginger Pye* by Eleanor Estes

1951 – *Amos Fortune, Free Man* by Elizabeth Yates

1950 – *The Door in the Wall* by Marguerite de Angeli

1949 – *King of the Wind* by Marguerite Henry

1948 – *The Twenty-One Balloons* by William Pène du Bois

1947 – *Miss Hickory* by Carolyn Sherwin Bailey

1946 – *Strawberry Girl* by Lois Lenski

1945 – *Rabbit Hill* by Robert Lawson

1944 – *Johnny Tremain* by Esther Forbes

1943 – *Adam of the Road* by Elizabeth Janet Gray

1942 – *The Matchlock Gun* by Walter Edmonds

1941 – *Call It Courage* by Armstrong Sperry

1940 – *Daniel Boone* by James Daugherty

1939 – *Thimble Summer* by Elizabeth Enright

1938 – *The White Stag* by Kate Seredy

1937 – *Roller Skates* by Ruth Sawyer

1936 – *Caddie Woodlawn* by Carol Ryrie Brink

1935 – *Dobry* by Monica Shannon

1934 – *Invincible Louisa: The Story of the Author of* Little Women by Cornelia Meigs

1933 – *Young Fu of the Upper Yangtze* by Elizabeth Lewis

1932 – *Waterless Mountain* by Laura Adams Armer

1931 – *The Cat Who Went to Heaven* by Elizabeth Coatsworth

1930 – *Hitty, Her First Hundred Years* by Rachel Field

1929 – *The Trumpeter of Krakow* by Eric P. Kelly

1928 – *Gay Neck, the Story of a Pigeon* by Dhan Gopal Mukerji

1927 – *Smoky, the Cowhorse* by Will James

1926 – *Shen of the Sea* by Arthur Bowie Chrisman

1925 – *Tales from Silver Lands* by Charles Finger

1924 – *The Dark Frigate* by Charles Hawes

1923 – *The Voyages of Doctor Dolittle* by Hugh Lofting

1922 – *The Story of Mankind* by Hendrik Willem van Loon

Appendix III
Historical Fiction by G. A. Henty

G. A. Henty was known as the Prince of Storytellers and the Boy's Own Historian. He often wrote by pacing back and forth in his study and dictating stories as fast as his secretary could record them. Henty's boy heroes are diligent, courageous, intelligent and dedicated to their country and cause even in the face of great peril. One of the rare criticisms Henty faced in his day was that his heroes were "too Christian." Though recognized by historians for their accuracy, Mr. Henty's stories are filled with daring and adventure and free of the drudgery often associated with the study of history.

All But Lost, Volumes I, II and III (1869)

At Aboukir and Acre: A Story of Napoleon's Invasion of Egypt (1899)

At Agincourt: A Tale of the White Hoods of Paris (1897)

At the Point of the Bayonet: A Tale of the Mahratta War (1902)

Beric the Briton: A Story of the Roman Invasion (1893)

Bonnie Prince Charlie: A Tale of Fontenoy and Culloden (1888)

Both Sides the Border: A Tale of Hotspur and Glendower (1899)

The Bravest of the Brave, or, With Peterborough in Spain (1887)

By Conduct and Courage: A Story of Nelson's Days (1905)

By England's Aid: The Freeing of the Netherlands, 1585–1604 (1891)

By Pike and Dyke: A Tale of the Rise of the Dutch Republic (1890)

By Right of Conquest: With Cortez in Mexico (1891)

By Sheer Pluck: A Tale of the Ashanti War (1884)

Captain Bayley's Heir: A Tale of the Gold Fields of California (1889)

The Cat of Bubastes: A Tale of Ancient Egypt (1889)

A Chapter of Adventures: Through the Bombardment of Alexandria (a.k.a. *The Young Midshipman*) (1891)

Colonel Thorndyke's Secret (a.k.a. *The Brahmin's Treasure*) (1898)

Condemned as a Nihilist: A Story of Escape from Siberia (1893)

The Cornet of Horse: A Tale of Marlborough's Wars (1881)

The Curse of Carne's Hold: A Tale of Adventure (1889)

The Dash for Khartoum: A Tale of the Nile Expedition (1892)

Dorothy's Double: The Story of a Great Deception (1894)

The Dragon and the Raven: The Days of King Alfred (1886)

Facing Death: The Hero of the Vaughan Pit — A Tale of the Coal Mines (1882)

A Final Reckoning: A Tale of Bush Life in Australia (1887)

For Name and Fame: Through Afghan Passes (1886)

For the Temple: A Tale of the Fall of Jerusalem (1888)

Friends Though Divided: A Tale of the Civil War (1883)
Gabriel Allen, M.P. (1888)
Held Fast for England: A Tale of the Siege of Gibraltar (1892)
A Hidden Foe (1891)
A Highland Chief (from *In Freedom's Cause*) (1906)
In Freedom's Cause: A Story of Wallace and Bruce (1885)
In Greek Waters: A Story of the Grecian War of Independence (1821–1827) (1893)
In the Hands of the Cave Dwellers (1900)
In the Heart of the Rockies: A Story of Adventure in Colorado (1895)
In the Irish Brigade: A Tale of War in Flanders and Spain (1901)
In the Reign of Terror: The Adventures of a Westminster Boy (1888)
In Times of Peril: A Tale of India (1881)
Jack Archer: A Tale of the Crimea (1883)
A Jacobite Exile, Being the Adventures of a Young Englishman in the Service of Charles XII of Sweden (1894)
John Hawke's Fortune: A Story of Monmouth's Rebellion (1901)
A Knight of the White Cross: A Tale of the Siege of Rhodes (1896)
The Lion of St. Mark: A Story of Venice in the Fourteenth Century (1889)
The Lion of the North: A Tale of the Times of Gustavus Adolphus (1886)
The Lost Heir (1899)

Maori and Settler: A Tale of the New Zealand War (1891)

A March on London, Being a Story of Wat Tyler's Insurrection
    (1898)

The March to Coomassie (1874)

No Surrender! A Tale of the Rising in La Vendée (1900)

One of the 28th: A Tale of Waterloo (1890)

On the Irrawaddy: A Story of the First Burmese War (1897)

Orange and Green: A Tale of the Boyne and Limerick (1888)

Out on the Pampas: The Young Settlers (1871)

Out With Garibaldi: A Story of the Liberation of Italy (1901)

The Plague Ship

The Queen's Cup: A Novel (1897)

Redskin and Cowboy: A Tale of the Western Plains (1892)

*Redskins and Colonists, or, a Boy's Adventures in the Early
    Days of Virginia* (1908)

*A Roving Commission, or, Through the Black Insurrection at
    Hayti* (1900)

Rujub, the Juggler (1893)

A Search for a Secret (1867)

St. Bartholomew's Eve: A Tale of the Huguenot Wars (1895)

Saint George For England: A Tale of Cressy and Poitiers
    (1885)

Sturdy and Strong: How George Andrews Made His Way
    (1888)

*Through Russian Snows: A Story of Napoleon's Retreat from
    Moscow* (1896)

Through the Fray: A Tale of the Luddite Riots (1886)

Through the Sikh War: A Tale of the Conquest of the Punjab (1894)

Through Three Campaigns: A Story of Chitral, Tirah, and Ashantee (1904)

The Tiger of Mysore: A Story of the War with Tippoo Saib (1896)

To Herat and Cabul: A Story of the First Afghan War (1902)

The Treasure of the Incas: A Tale of Adventure in Peru (1903)

True to the Old Flag: A Tale of the American War of Independence (1885)

Under Drake's Flag: A Tale of the Spanish Main (1883)

Under Wellington's Command (1899)

When London Burned: A Story of Restoration Times and the Great Fire (1898)

Winning His Spurs: A Tale of the Crusades (1882)

With Buller in Natal: A Born Leader (1901)

With Clive in India: The Beginnings of an Empire (1884)

With Cochrane the Dauntless: A Tale of the Exploits of Lord Cochrane in South American Waters (1897)

With Frederick the Great: A Tale of the Seven Years' War (1898)

With Kitchener in the Soudan: A Story of Atbara and Omdurman (1903)

With Lee in Virginia: A Story of the American Civil War (1890)

With Moore at Corunna (1898)

With Roberts to Pretoria: A Tale of the South African War (1902)

With the Allies to Pekin: A Story of the Relief of the Legations
(1903)
With the British Legion: A Story of the Carlist Wars (1902)
With Wolfe in Canada: The Winning of a Continent (1887)
Woman of the Commune: A Tale of Two Sieges of Paris (1895)
Won by the Sword: A Story of the Thirty Years' War (1900)
Wulf the Saxon: A Story of the Norman Conquest (1895)
The Young Buglers: A Tale of the Peninsular War (1880)
The Young Carthaginian: A Story of the Times of Hannibal
(1887)
The Young Colonists: A Tale of the Zulu and Boer Wars (1885)
The Young Franc-Tireurs, and Their Adventures in the
Franco-Prussian War (1872)

Appendix IV
Landmark History Books

Each book in the Landmark series, which was first published by Random House more than fifty years ago, brings to life a historical event or life of a historical figure. Among the notable authors who contributed to the Landmark series: Poet laureate Robert Penn Warren, Nobel and Pulitzer Prize winner Pearl S. Buck, and Supreme Court Justice William O. Douglas. These books are rich, rewarding reading, capable of inspiring not only a love for good books but also an understanding and appreciation of history. Many of these titles are now out of print but are worth seeking out online and at used book stores.

Abe Lincoln: Log Cabin to White House by Sterling North
The Adventures and Discoveries of Marco Polo by Richard J. Walsh
The Adventures of Ulysses by Gerald Gottlieb
The Alaska Gold Rush by May McNeer
Alexander Hamilton and Aaron Burr by Anna & Russell Crouse
Alexander the Great by John Gunther
The American Revolution by Bruce Bliven, Jr.

Americans into Orbit: The Story of Project Mercury by Gene
  Gurney
America's First World War: General Pershing and the Yanks
  by Henry Castor
Andrew Carnegie and the Age of Steel by Katherine B.
  Shippen
Balboa: Swordsman and Conquistador by Felix Riesenberg
The Barbary Pirates by C. S. Forester
The Battle for Iwo Jima by Robert Leckie
The Battle for the Atlantic by Jay Williams
The Battle of Britain by Quentin Reynolds
The Battle of the Bulge by John Toland
Ben Franklin of Old Philadelphia by Margaret Cousins
Ben-Gurion and the Birth of Israel by Joan Comay
Betsy Ross and the Flag by Jane Mayer
Buffalo Bill's Great Wild West Show by Walter Havighurst
The Building of the First Transcontinental Railroad by Adele
  Nathan
The California Gold Rush by May McNeer
Captain Cook Explores the South Seas by Armstrong Sperry
Captain Cortes Conquers Mexico by William Johnson
Catherine the Great by Katherine Scherman
Chief of the Cossacks by Harold Lamb
Clara Barton: Founder of the American Red Cross by Helen
  Boylston
Cleopatra of Egypt by Leonora Hornblow
Clipper Ship Days by John Jennings
Combat Nurses of World War II by Wyatt Blassingame

The Coming of the Mormons by Jim Kjelgaard
The Commandos of World War II by Hodding Carter
Commodore Perry and the Opening of Japan by Ferdinand Kuhn
The Conquest of the North and South Poles by Russell Owen
The Copper Kings of Montana by Marian T. Place
The Crusades by Anthony West
Custer's Last Stand by Quentin Reynolds
Daniel Boone and the Opening of the Wilderness by John Mason Brown
Davy Crockett by Stewart H. Holbrook
Disaster at Johnstown: The Great Flood by Hildegarde Dolson
The Doctors Who Conquered Yellow Fever by Ralph Nading Hill
Dolley Madison by Jane Mayer
Dwight D. Eisenhower by Malcolm Moos
The Early Days of Automobiles by Elizabeth Janeway
The Erie Canal by Samuel Hopkins Adams
Ethan Allen and the Green Mountain Boys by Slater Brown
Evangeline and the Acadians by Robert Tallant
The Exploits of Xenophon by Geoffrey Household
The Explorations of Père Marquette by Jim Kjelgaard
Exploring the Himalaya by William O. Douglas
The F.B.I. by Quentin Reynolds
The Fall of Constantinople by Bernadine Kielty
Famous Pirates of the New World by A. B. C. Whipple

Ferdinand Magellan: Master Mariner by Seymour Gates
    Pond
The First Men in the World by Anne Terry White
The First Overland Mail by Robert Pinkerton
The First Transatlantic Cable by Adele Nathan
Flat Tops by Edmund Castillo
The Flight and Adventures of Charles II by Charles Norman
Florence Nightingale by Ruth Fox Hume
The Flying Aces of World War I by Gene Gurney
The Flying Tigers by John Toland
The French Foreign Legion by Wyatt Blassingame
From Casablanca to Berlin by Bruce Bliven, Jr.
From Pearl Harbor to Okinawa by Bruce Bliven Jr.
Garibaldi: Father of Modern Italy by Marcia Davenport
General Brock and Niagara Falls by Samuel Hopkins
    Adams
Genghis Khan and the Mongol Horde by Harold Lamb
George Washington Carver by Anne Terry White
George Washington: Frontier Colonel by Sterling North
Geronimo: Wolf of the Warpath by Ralph Moody
Gettysburg by MacKinlay Kantor
The Golden Age of Railroads by Stewart H. Holbrook
Great American Fighter Pilots of World War II by Robert D.
    Loomis
Great Men of Medicine by Ruth Fox Hume
Guadalcanal Diary by Richard Tregaskis
Hawaii: Gem of the Pacific by Oscar Lewis

Hero of Trafalgar: The Story of Lord Nelson by A. B. C. Whipple

Heroines of the Early West by Nancy Wilson Ross

Hudson's Bay Company by Richard Morenus

Jesus of Nazareth by Harry Emerson Fosdick

Joan of Arc by Nancy Wilson Ross

John F. Kennedy and PT 109 by Richard Tregaskis

John James Audubon by Margaret & John Kieran

John Paul Jones: Fighting Sailor by Armstrong Sperry

Julius Caesar by John Gunther

King Arthur and His Knights by Mabel Louise Robinson

Kit Carson and the Wild Frontier by Ralph Moody

The Landing of the Pilgrims by James Daugherty

Lawrence of Arabia by Alistair MacLean

Lee and Grant at Appomattox by MacKinlay Kantor

Leonardo da Vinci by Emily Hahn

The Lewis and Clark Expedition by Richard L. Neuberger

The Life of Saint Patrick by Quentin Reynolds

The Life of Saint Paul by Harry Emerson Fosdick

Lincoln and Douglas: The Years of Decision by Regina Z. Kelly

The Louisiana Purchase by Robert Tallant

The Magna Charta by James Daugherty

The Man Who Changed China: The Story of Sun Yat-sen by Pearl S. Buck

Marie Antoinette by Bernadine Kielty

The Marquis de Lafayette: Bright Sword for Freedom by Hodding Carter

Martin Luther by Harry Emerson Fosdick
Mary, Queen of Scots by Emily Hahn
Medal of Honor Heroes by Colonel Red Reeder
Medical Corps Heroes of World War II by Wyatt
     Blassingame
Midway: Battle for the Pacific by Edmund L. Castillo
The Mississippi Bubble by Thomas B. Costain
Mr. Bell Invents the Telephone by Katherine B. Shippen
The Monitor and the Merrimac by Fletcher Pratt
The Mysterious Voyage of Captain Kidd by A. B. C. Whipple
Napoleon and the Battle of Waterloo by Frances Winwar
Old Ironsides: The Fighting Constitution by Harry Hansen
Our Independence and the Constitution by Dorothy Canfield
     Fisher
The Panama Canal by Bob Considine
Paul Revere and the Minute Men by Dorothy Canfield
     Fisher
Peter Stuyvesant of Old New York by Anna & Russell
     Crouse
The Pharaohs of Ancient Egypt by Elizabeth Payne
The Pirate Lafitte and the Battle of New Orleans by Robert
     Tallant
Pocahontas and Captain John Smith by Marie Lawson
The Pony Express by Samuel Hopkins Adams
Prehistoric America by Anne Terry White
Queen Elizabeth and the Spanish Armada by Frances
     Winwar
Queen Victoria by Noel Streatfeild

Remember the Alamo! by Robert Penn Warren
The Rise and Fall of Adolf Hitler by William L. Shirer
Robert E. Lee and the Road of Honor by Hodding Carter
Robert Fulton and the Steamboat by Ralph Nading Hill
Rogers' Rangers and the French and Indian War by Bradford
    Smith
The Royal Canadian Mounted Police by Richard L.
    Neuberger
Sam Houston: The Tallest Texan by William Johnson
The Santa Fe Trail by Samuel Hopkins Adams
The Seabees of World War II by Edmund Castillo
Sequoyah: Leader of the Cherokees by Alice Marriott
Simon Bolivar: The Great Liberator by Arnold Whitridge
The Sinking of the Bismarck by William L. Shirer
The Slave Who Freed Haiti: The Story of Toussaint L'ouverture
    by Katherine Scherman
Stonewall Jackson by Jonathan Daniels
The Story of Albert Schweitzer by Anita Daniel
The Story of Atomic Energy by Laura Fermi
The Story of Australia by A. Grove Day
The Story of D-Day: June 6, 1944 by Bruce Bliven Jr.
The Story of Oklahoma by Lon Tinkle
The Story of San Francisco by Charlotte Jackson
The Story of Scotland Yard by Laurence Thompson
The Story of Submarines by George Weller
The Story of the Air Force by Robert Loomis
The Story of the Naval Academy by Felix Riesenberg, Jr.
The Story of the Paratroops by George Weller

The Story of the Secret Service by Ferdinand Kuhn
The Story of the Thirteen Colonies by Clifford Lindsey
    Alderman
The Story of the U.S. Coast Guard by Eugene Rachlis
The Story of the U.S. Marines by George Hunt
The Story of Thomas Alva Edison by Margaret Cousins
The Swamp Fox of the Revolution by Stewart H. Holbrook
Teddy Roosevelt and the Rough Riders by Henry Castor
The Texas Rangers by Will Henry
Thirty Seconds Over Tokyo by Ted Lawson & Bob
    Considine
Thomas Jefferson: Father of Democracy by Vincent Sheean
Tippecanoe and Tyler, Too! by Stanley Young
To California by Covered Wagon by George R. Stewart
Trappers and Traders of the Far West by James Daugherty
The United Nations in War and Peace by T. R. Fehrenback
The U.S. Border Patrol by Clement Hellyer
The U.S. Frogmen of World War II by Wyatt Blassingame
Up the Trail from Texas by J. Frank Dobie
The Vikings by Elizabeth Janeway
The Voyages of Christopher Columbus by Armstrong Sperry
The Voyages of Henry Hudson by Eugene Rachlis
Walk in Space: The Story of Project Gemini by Gene Gurney
Walter Raleigh by Henrietta Buckmaster
War Chief of the Seminoles by May McNeer
The War in Korea: 1950–1953 by Robert Leckie
The West Point Story by Colonel Red Reeder & Nardi
    Reeder Campion

Wild Bill Hickok Tames the West by Stewart H. Holbrook
Will Shakespeare and the Globe Theater by Anne Terry White
William Penn: Quaker Hero by Hildegarde Dolson
William the Conqueror by Thomas B. Costain
Winston Churchill by Quentin Reynolds
The Winter at Valley Forge by F. Van Wyck Mason
The Witchcraft of Salem Village by Shirley Jackson
Women of Courage by Dorothy Nathan
The World's Greatest Showman: The Life of P. T. Barnum by J.
   Bryan III
The Wright Brothers by Quentin Reynolds
Wyatt Earp: U.S. Marshal by Stewart H. Holbrook
Young Mark Twain and the Mississippi by Harnett T. Kane

Appendix V
The Trailblazer Series

Dave and Neta Jackson's award-winning Trailblazer books are action-packed historical novels based on the lives of true heroes of the Christian faith. Each book portrays a significant period in a hero or heroine's life and ministry as seen through the eyes of a young protagonist. Each book includes a brief biographical overview of the hero's life.

1. *Kidnapped by River Rats* (William & Catherine Booth)
2. *The Queen's Smuggler* (William Tyndale)
3. *Spy for the Night Riders* (Martin Luther)
4. *The Hidden Jewel* (Amy Carmichael)
5. *Escape from the Slave Traders* (David Livingstone)
6. *The Chimney Sweep's Ransom* (John Wesley)
7. *The Bandit of Ashley Downs* (George Müller)
8. *Imprisoned in the Golden City* (Adoniram & Ann Judson)
9. *Shanghaied to China* (Hudson Taylor)
10. *Listen for the Whippoorwill* (Harriet Tubman)
11. *Attack in the Rye Grass* (Marcus & Narcissa Whitman)
12. *Trial by Poison* (Mary Slessor)
13. *Flight of the Fugitives* (Gladys Aylward)
14. *The Betrayer's Fortune* (Menno Simons)
15. *Abandoned on the Wild Frontier* (Peter Cartwright)

16. *Danger on the Flying Trapeze* (Dwight L. Moody)
17. *The Runaway's Revenge* (John Newton)
18. *The Thieves of Tyburn Square* (Elizabeth Fry)
19. *Quest for the Lost Prince* (Samuel Morris)
20. *The Warrior's Challenge* (David Zeisberger)
21. *The Drummer Boy's Battle* (Florence Nightingale)
22. *Traitor in the Tower* (John Bunyan)
23. *Defeat of the Ghost Riders* (Mary McLeod Bethune)
24. *The Fate of the Yellow Woodbee* (Nate Saint)
25. *The Gold Miners' Rescue* (Sheldon Jackson)
26. *The Mayflower Secret* (William Bradford)
27. *Assassins in the Cathedral* (Festo Kivengere)
28. *Mask of the Wolf Boy* (Jonathan & Rosalind Goforth)
29. *Race for the Record* (Joy Ridderhof)
30. *Ambushed in Jaguar Swamp* (Barbrooke Grubb)
31. *The Forty-Acre Swindle* (George Washington Carver)
32. *Hostage on the Nighthawk* (William Penn)
33. *Journey to the End of the Earth* (William Seymour)
34. *Drawn by a China Moon* (Lottie Moon)
35. *Sinking the Dayspring* (John G. Paton)
36. *Roundup of the Street Rovers* (Charles Loring Brace)
37. *Risking the Forbidden Game* (Maude Cary)
38. *Blinded by the Shining Path* (Rómulo Sauñe)
39. *Exiled to the Red River* (Chief Spokane Garry)
40. *Caught in the Rebel Camp* (Frederick Douglass)

Appendix VI
A Few of My Favorite Things

Favorite Read-Alouds for the Whole Family
The Chronicles of Narnia by C. S. Lewis
Freckles by Gene Stratton Porter
The Gold Thread by Norman Macleod
James Herriot's Treasury for Children by James Herriot
Just David by Eleanor H. Porter
Little Men by Louisa May Alcott
The Railway Children by E. Nesbit
The Secret Garden by Frances Hodgson Burnett
Treasures of the Snow by Patricia St. John

Favorites for Girls
All-of-a-Kind-Family by Sydney Taylor
Anne of Green Gables series by Lucy Maud Montgomery
Calico Captive by Elizabeth George Speare
Ellen by E. M. Almedingen
Heidi by Johanna Spyri
A Little Princess by Frances Hodgson Burnett
The Little White Horse by Elizabeth Goudge
Little Women by Louisa May Alcott
Rebecca of Sunnybrook Farm by Kate Douglas Wiggin

The Secret Garden by Frances Hodgson Burnett

Favorites for Boys

The Black Arrow by Robert Louis Stevenson
Kidnapped by Robert Louis Stevenson
The Little Britches series by Ralph Moody
Little Lord Fauntleroy by Frances Hodgson Burnett
Little Men by Louisa May Alcott
The Merry Adventures of Robin Hood by Howard Pyle
Rascal by Sterling North
The Redwall series by Brian Jacques
The Story of King Arthur and His Knights by Howard Pyle
The Adventures of Tom Sawyer by Mark Twain

My Favorite Audiobooks

Cheaper by the Dozen by Frank B. Gilbreth and Ernestine
    Gilbreth Cary (read by Dana Ivey)
Rainbow Valley by Lucy Maud Montgomery (read by
    Nadia May)
The Story of the Treasure Seekers by E. Nesbit (read by
    Johanna Ward)
Holes by Louis Sachar (read by Kerry Beyer)
The Chronicles of Narnia by C. S. Lewis (Focus on the
    Family Radio Theatre)
Little Lord Fauntleroy by Frances Hodgson Burnett (read
    by Johanna Ward)
The Secret Garden by Frances Hodgson Burnett (Focus on
    the Family Radio Theatre)

Notes

1. Vigen Guroian, *Tending the Heart of Virtue: How Classic Stories Wake a Child's Moral Imagination* (New York: Oxford University Press, 1998), 1–5.

2. Keith Stanovich and Anne E. Cunningham, "What Reading Does for the Mind," *American Educator* 22 (Spring/Summer 1998).

3. Keith E. Stanovich, *Progress in Understanding Reading: Scientific Foundations and New Frontiers* (New York: Guilford Press, 2000), 151–52.

4. Children, Youth, and Family Consortium, "Childhood Literacy: Early Efforts Yield Lifelong Results," http://www.cyfc.umn.edu/publications/seeds/series2v1/earlyefforts.html (accessed October 16, 2009).

5. Madeleine L'Engle, *A Circle of Quiet* (New York: Farrar, Straus and Giroux, 1972), 149.

6. National Endowment for the Arts, *Reading at Risk: A Study of Literary Reading in America* (July 2004) 4–7. A free copy of this report may be requested at www.arts.gov.

7. Ibid., 2–7.

8. National Endowment for the Arts, *To Read or Not to Read: A Question of National Importance* (November 2007), 5–6. A free copy of this report may be requested at www.arts.gov.

9. Ibid., 9–10, 13, 15.

10. Ibid., 5.

11. American Heart Association, "Many Teens Spend 30 Hours a Week On 'Screen Time' During High School," March 14, 2008, http://americanheart.mediaroom.com/index.php?s=43&item=363 (accessed October 28, 2009).

12. CNN.com, "TV viewing at 'all-time high,' Nielsen says," February

24, 2009, http://www.cnn.com/2009/SHOWBIZ/TV/02/24/us.video.nielsen (accessed October 28, 2009).

13. Herbert E. Krugman, "Brain Wave Measures of Media Involvement," *Journal of Advertising Research* 11.1 (1971): 3–9.

14. Wes Moore, "Television: Opiate of the Masses," *Journal of Cognitive Liberties* 2.2 (2001), 59–66.

15. Sebastian Wren, "Topics in Early Reading Coherence: Understanding the Brain and Reading," 2001, http://www.sedl.org/reading/topics/brainreading.html (accessed September 7, 2009).

16. Kaiser Family Foundation, *Generation M: Media in the Lives of 8–18-Year-Olds, Executive Summary* (March 2005), 6.

17. Charlotte Mason, *A Philosophy of Education* (Wheaton, IL: Tyndale, 1989), 339. Originally published in 1925.

18. The Barna Group, "Barna Survey Examines Changes in Worldview Among Christians over the Past 13 Years," March 6, 2009, http://www.barna.org/barna-update/article/21-transformation/252-barna-survey-examines-changes-in-worldview-among-christians-over-the-past-13-years (accessed September 30, 2009).

19. Laurence O'Donnell, "Music and the Brain," *Brain and Mind: Electronic Magazine on Neuroscience* 15 (July–September 2002), http://www.cerebromente.org.br/n15/mente/musica.html (accessed September 7, 2009).

20. American Music Conference, "Research Briefs: Did You Know?," http://www.amc-music.com/research_briefs.htm (accessed September 7, 2009).

21. A postmodern worldview is based on the belief that there is no objective reality or absolute truth. Postmodernists see human experience as subjective. In this view, reality changes according to how each person experiences it, making it impossible to use defining statements about what is universally true or real for all people. For a more in-depth explanation, check out Dr. David Noebel's book *Understanding the Times* (Manitou Springs, CO: Summit Press, 2006).

Index of Authors and Illustrators

Index of Titles

Z